ABALOS + SENTKIEWICZ

NUEVO PRIMITIVISMO/ NEW PRIMITIVISM

"The 'present' cannot support the cultures of Europe, or even the archaic or primitive civilizations; it must instead explore the pre- and post-historic mind; it must go into the places where remote futures meet remote pasts."

Robert Smithson
A Sedimentation of the Mind: Earth Projects

NEW PRIMITIVISM
ABALOS + SENTKIEWICZ

First edition, 2020
ISBN 978-607-9489-59-5
© Arquine, SA de CV
Ámsterdam 163 A
Colonia Hipódromo, 06100
Ciudad de México
arquine.com

Authors
Iñaki Ábalos, Renata Sentkiewicz, José de Andrés Moncayo

Texts
©Iñaki Ábalos, Renata Sentkiewicz

Photography
José Hevia, except: Jesús Rocandio (pp. 150-157 and 337); Zhang Yong (pp. 102–117, 180–187, 254-259, and 310-323); Fincas Cortesín (pp. 24–25 and 28–29).

Concept and initial layout
Iñaki Ábalos, José de Andrés Moncayo

AS+ Coordinator
José de Andrés Moncayo

Arquine

Director
Miquel Adrià

Editorial Director
Brenda Soto

Editorial Assistance
Valeria Fuentes

Design
David Kimura + Gabriela Varela

Translation
Fionn Petch, Quentin Pope

ABALOS + SENTKIEWICZ

NUEVO PRIMITIVISMO/ NEW PRIMITIVISM

Arquine

Contents

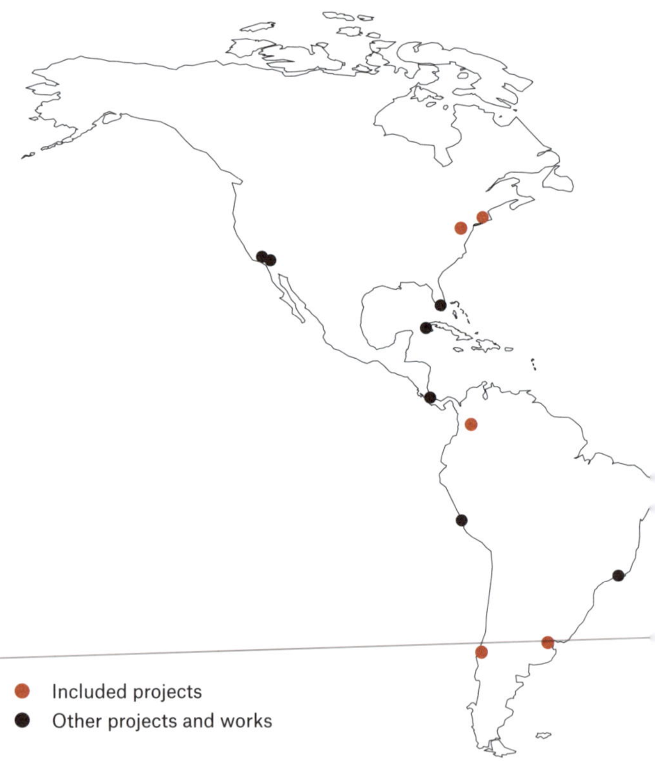

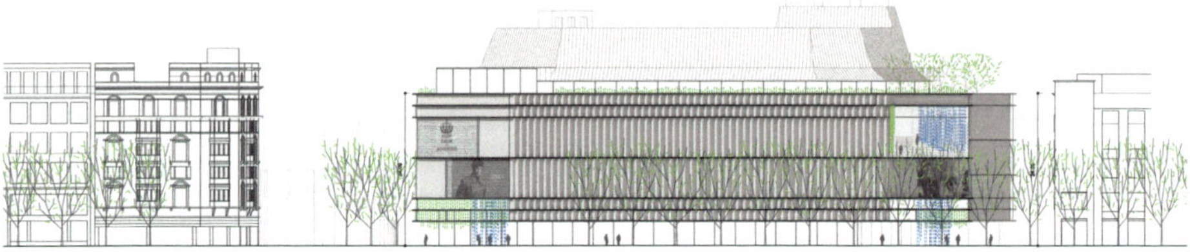

向明中学
XiangMing Middle School
N0.1 RuiJin Road
卜令公寓
BuLing Apartment
瑞
金
路
淮 海 中 路
Middle HuaiHai Road
N
1 5 10m

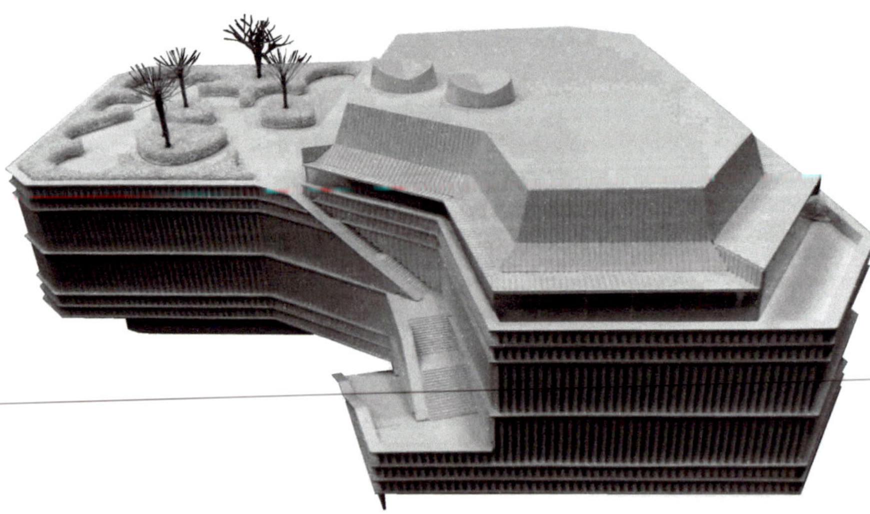

Longfeng Mall. French Concession, Shanghai, China. 2014–

A small, Near-Zero Emissions shopping mall over a metro station under construction. The development respects the magnificent nearby Art Deco building, by architect László Hudec (a powerful influence on the city of Shanghai, and particularly on this neighbourhood). This project therefore presents a unique opportunity to display technical and compositional resources to envisage more ambitious approaches to these shopping centres in the city's most upscale area. This mall coexists in harmony with Hudec's building without sacrificing its unique and attractive appearance. Plants filter the air and create shade, waterwalls condense humidity to temper the atmosphere and solar chimneys give the project's interiors the feel of a garden in the springtime; these criteria helped combine aesthetic appeal with passive technologies to give users a special experience.

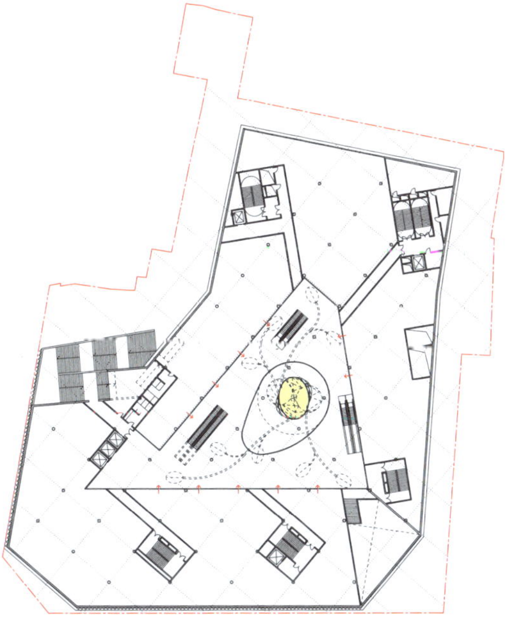

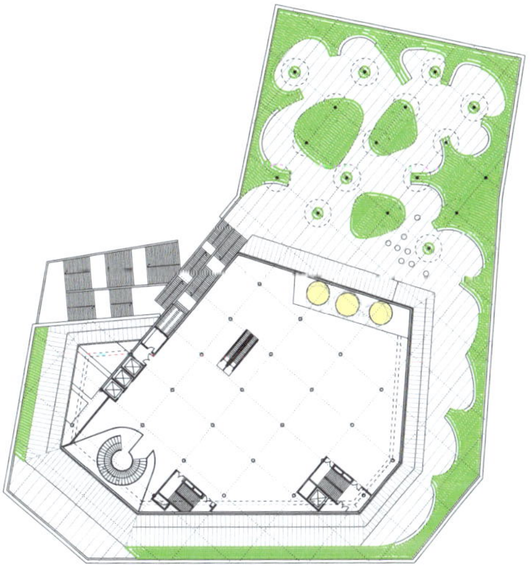

Initial conceptual scheme

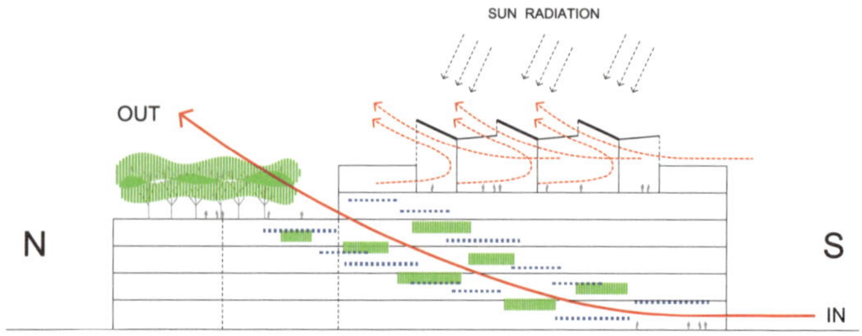

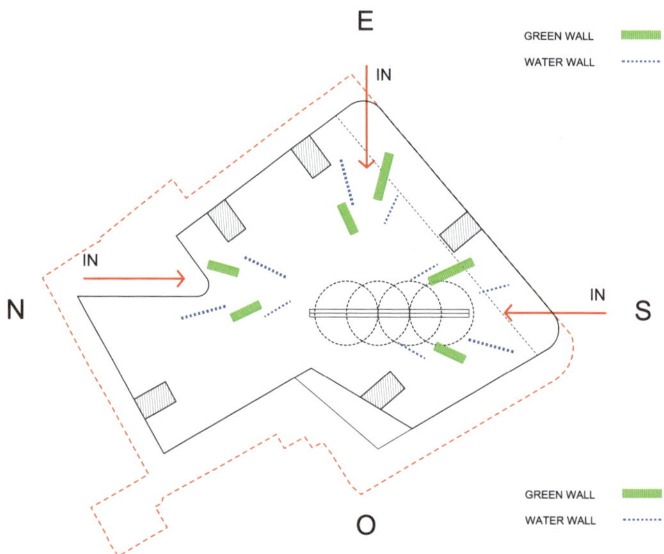

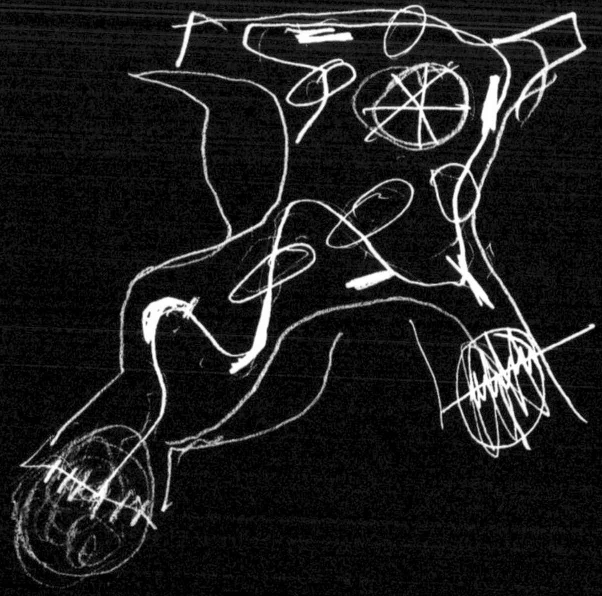

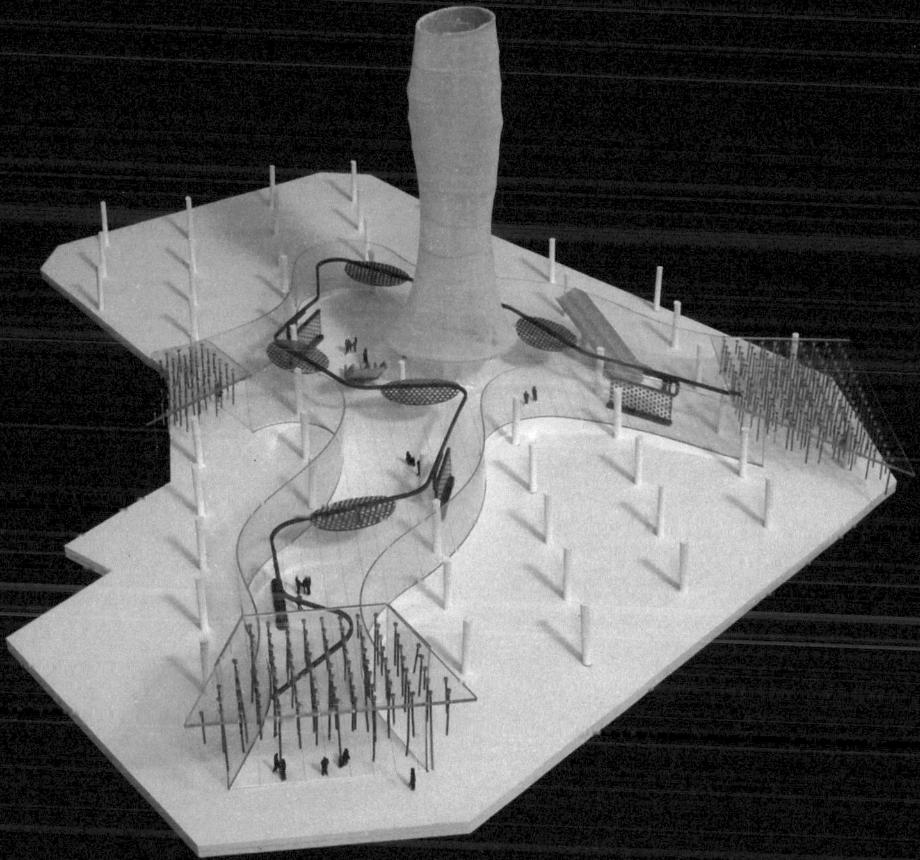

Thermally active elements

Lantern/central ventilation

- Channels buoyancy of convective flows from the street.
- Increased comfort.
- Entry of natural and artificial light.

Hanging Gardens

- Filtration of urban polluted air.
- Decreased Perceived Temperature (PT).

Waterwalls

- Condense humidity.
- Directs air flows.
- Increase human comfort.

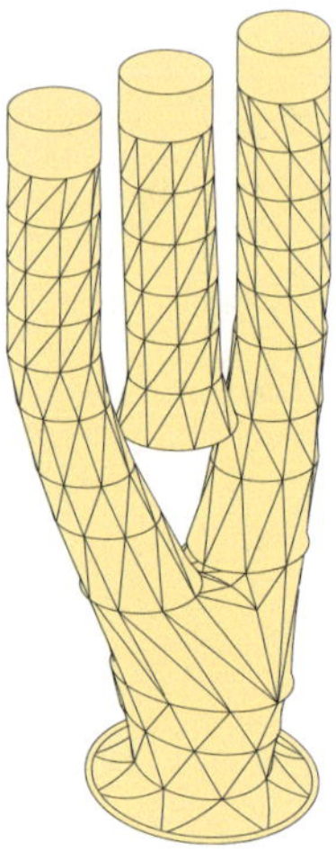

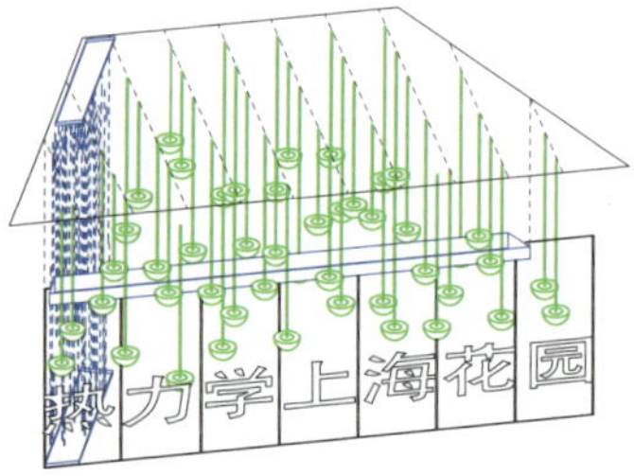

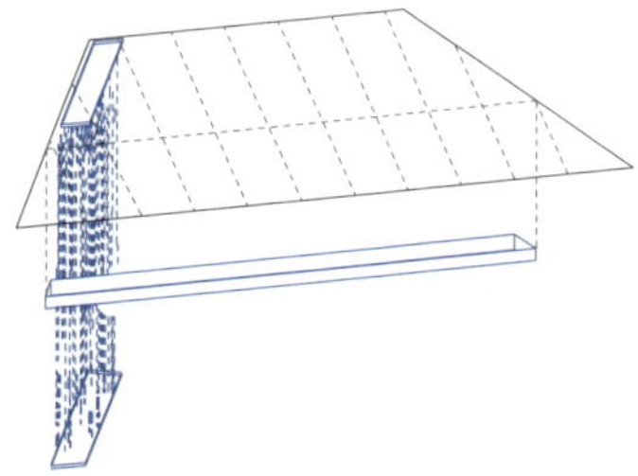

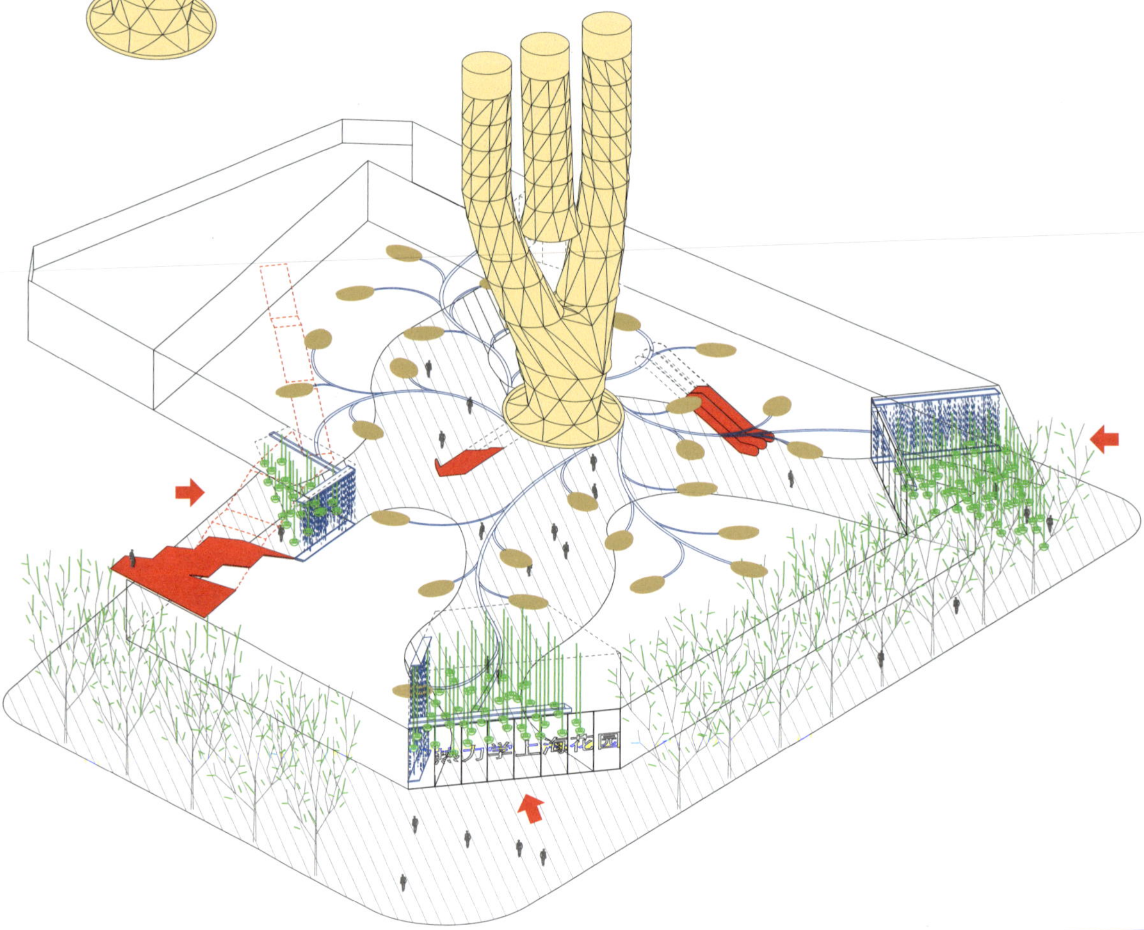

KEEP
CALM
AND
ADVERTISE
热力学上海花园

Villa with Two Patios. Casares, Málaga, Spain. 2014-2018

With its sea views and the African coast in the distance, this villa features a layout typical of Mediterranean architecture: everything revolves around a large, central hall and connects two courtyards (one at the front, the other to the rear), positioned to take advantage of the direction of the sunlight and prevailing breezes, as well as sea views. Surrounded by large terraces ideally suited to outdoor living, the house's design takes full advantage of the sloping terrain. Various ancillary constructions complete the residential programme. The house is built entirely of reinforced white concrete. The landscaping complements and articulates the different exteriors to create open-air living areas.

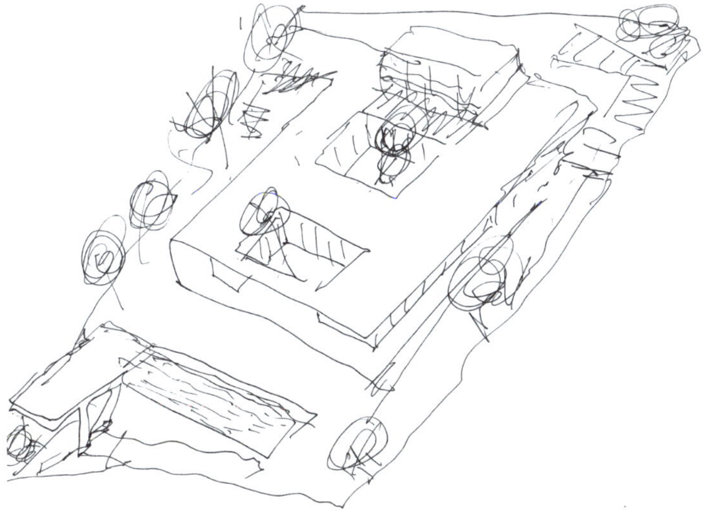

0 1 2 5m

Cultural and Leisure Centre. Azuqueca de Henares, Guadalajara, Spain. 2007-2011

In Azuqueca, Madrid's "dry port" known as a "photovoltaic city" due to the widespread use of its warehouses as photovoltaic surfaces, we proposed a new building with an interior formed by a series of rooms replicating the layout of Mora House (2000), so that diverse needy social groups can enjoy a privileged space within the community. The Cultural and Leisure Centre is designed as a contemporary variation on the traditional social club, with a series of halls and rooms slightly jumbled together and always giving priority to recreational activities, reading, games, conversations and dancing. It consists of a low-slung, south-facing pavilion—which provides a visual backdrop for the plot of land intended to be made into a park, opposite the city council's offices—and a vertical volume housing the Centre's offices, storerooms and other installations. The project's layout, construction systems, installations, ventilation, exterior protection and landscaping have been studied to create a specific atmosphere and as a zero-emissions building, based on the Castilian *meseta*'s characteristic typology of connected spaces and alternating courtyards, together with the use of green roofs and geothermal technologies as the main energy source.

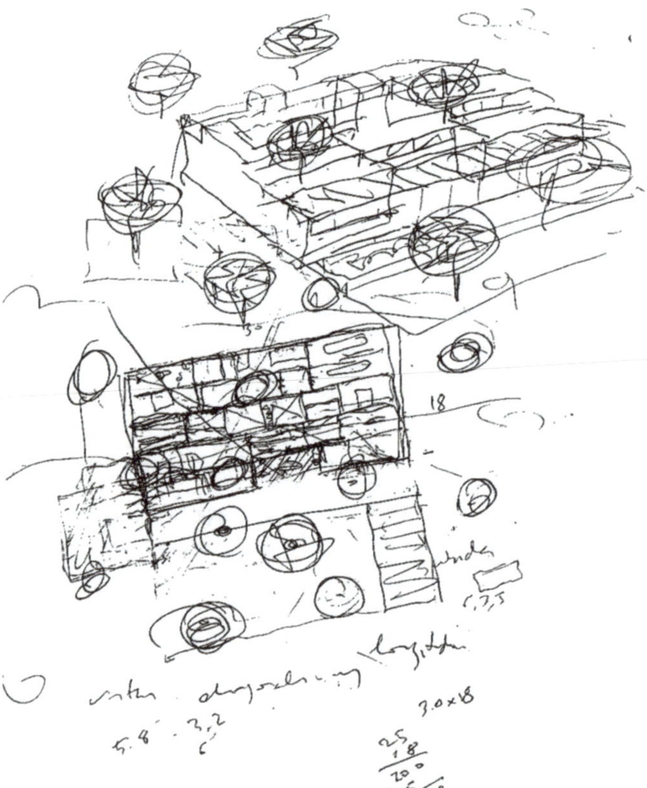

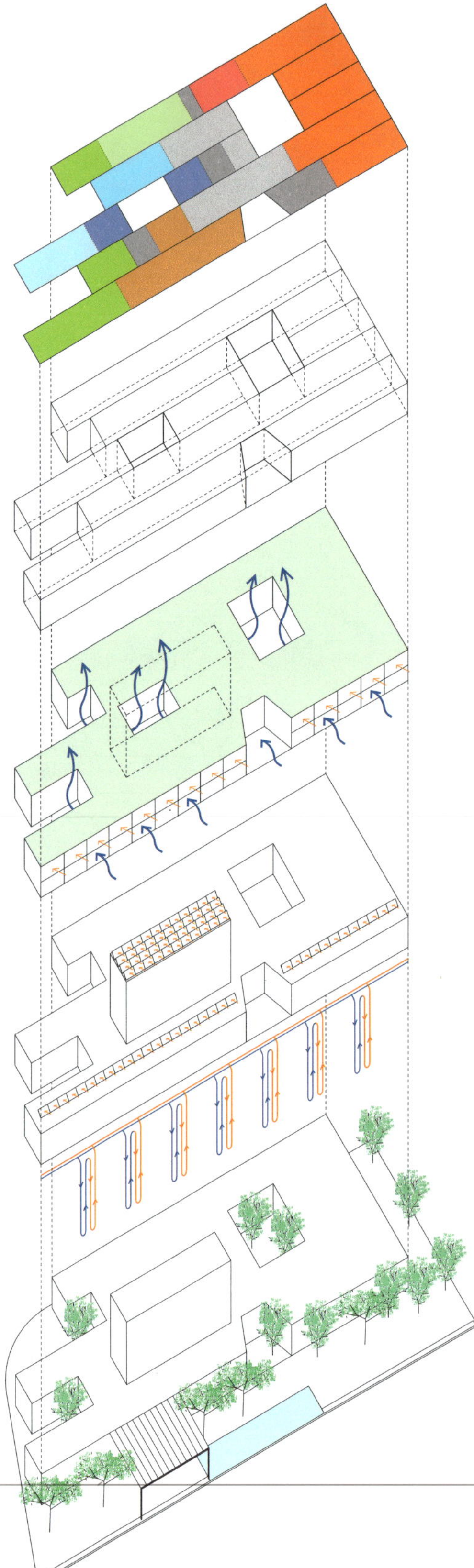

Social

Leisure programme for older adults in industrial city with high levels of unemployment and early retirement.

- Gym and rehabilitation
- Games
- Library and periodicals
- Internet
- Television
- Cafeteria
- Multipurpose room
- Services
- Lobby and corridors

Typology

Echoes traditional building types in the Castilla La Mancha region: five-bay country houses with interstitial courtyards.

Architecture

Passive measures

Green roof
Natural ventilation
South-facing solar collector in winter

Active measures

Geothermal
Photovoltaic

Landscaping

Adiabatic cooling (water pad).
Strategically located deciduous and non-deciduous tree plantations.
Awnings.

SALA DE JUEGOS/ AJEDREZ ETC.
GIMNASIO - REHABILITACIÓN
BOTIQUÍN
Cuarto limpieza
SALA 1
SALA DE PRENSA Y BIBLIOTECA
VESTÍBULO
PATIO
SALA DE TELEVISIÓN
INTERNET
INTERNET
ASEOS
VESTÍBULO
SALÓN MULTIUSOS
SALA DE BILLAR
ASEOS
disp. Cafetería
Basuras
Comunic.
VESTÍBULO
SALA DE JUEGOS
CAFETERÍA
conserje
RECEPCIÓN
Basuras
Cuarto limpieza
ACCESO SALÓN MULTIUSOS
TOLDO
focos iluminación solar
fuentes
lamina de agua
baculos
arbusto
arbusto
baculos
0 1 5 10 m

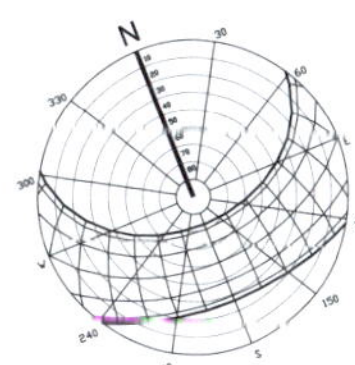
N

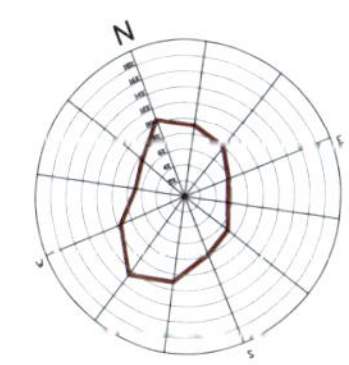
N

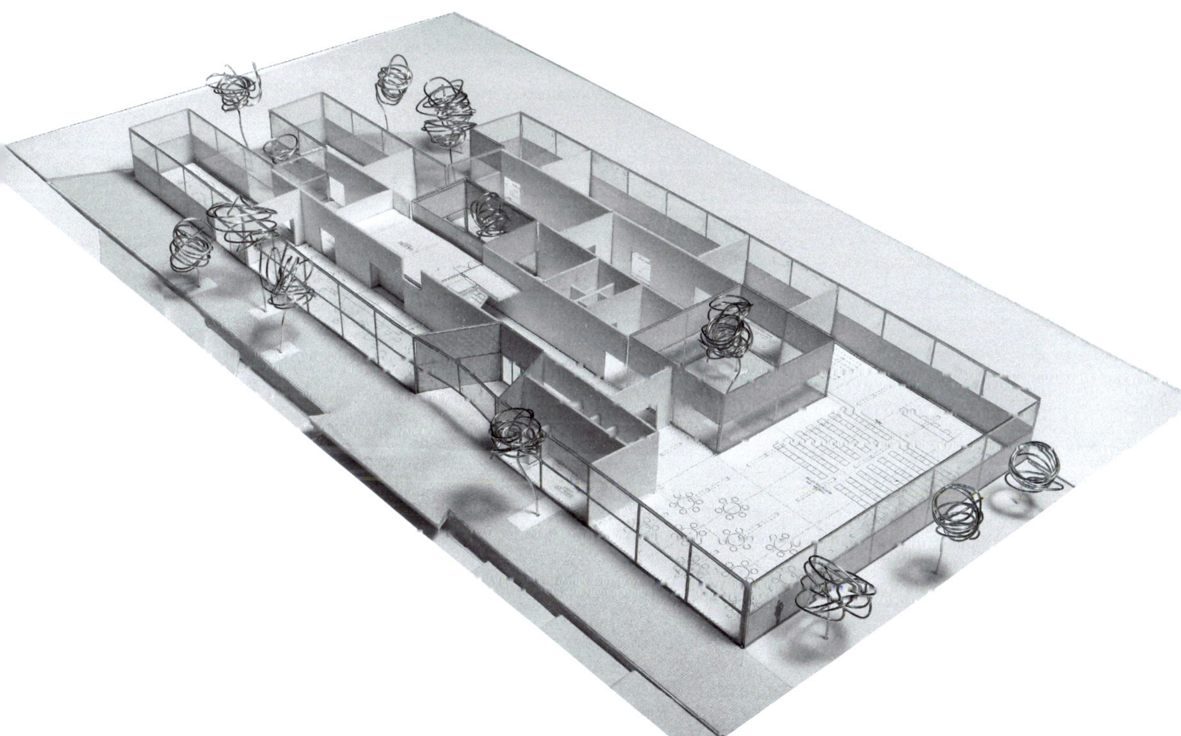

Energy concept

The building has been designed according to the European Near-Zero Energy Buildings (NZEB) standards through the optimization of the thermal envelope from the perspective of lighting / radiation / insulation, and the application of renewable energy sources, both for the air conditioning and electricity supply.

Passive measures: thermal envelope

An envelope has been designed with a high degree of thermal insulation and a distribution of openings and solid areas that optimize natural lighting without having a negative impact on the need for cooling, thanks to the brise-soleils and the quality of glazing used (1.1 W/m²K). The outdoor landscaping passively regulates temperatures in the summer and winter months. The green roof ensures a high level of thermal insulation in winter and, due to the adiabatic cooling (caused by the evaporation of a sheet of water), a reduction in the energy gain through transmission by means of the roof and the lowering of refrigeration loads.

Active measures

Air conditioning provided by a geothermal heat pump (for heating and cooling) offers an optimum performance for the building's load profile, anticipating operating coefficients greater than four. Electricity use is compensated by the generation of 7 kWh from 40 m² of monocrystalline photovoltaic roof panels.

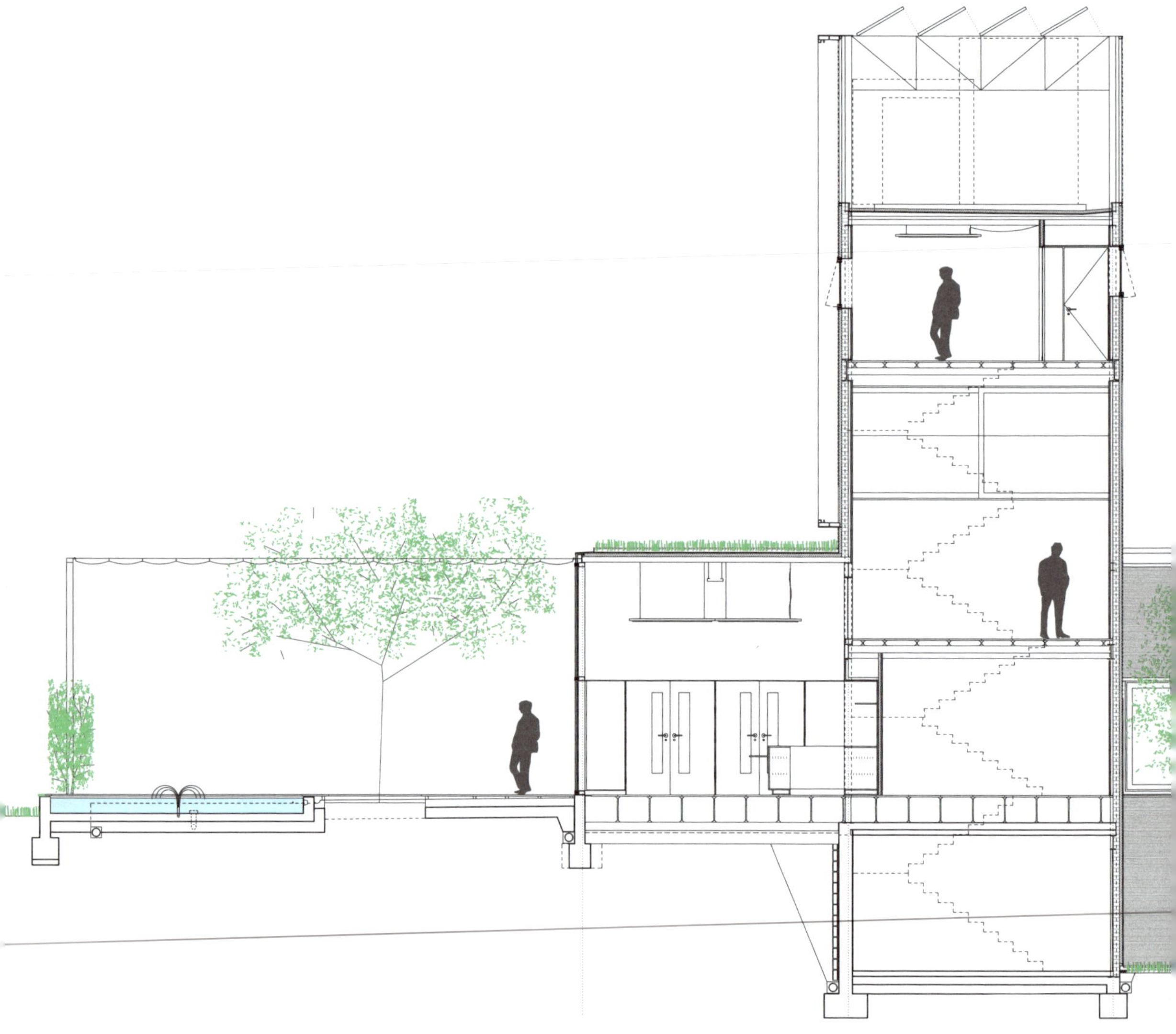

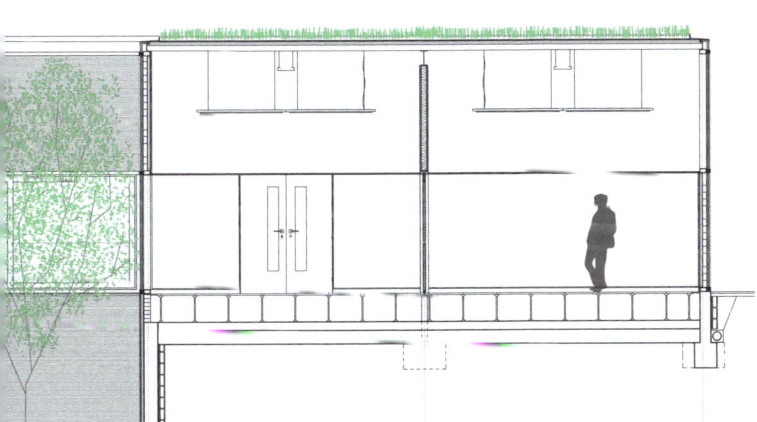
0 0.5 1 2 m

Four Energy Observatories. Island of La Palma, Canary Islands, Spain. 2006-2007

An observatory is somewhere that uses different technologies to interface with nature, translating the primary and direct experience of perception into actual knowledge. We are particularly interested in this concept of the observatory as a typology in which technical aspects, nature and architecture interact to intensify the dialogue between man and the world. The island of La Palma is a unique product of a series of volcanic eruptions (its volcanoes are still active) that have produced a high-relief terrain. Described by Alexander von Humboldt as a fortress that rises up in the middle of the ocean, is has one of the highest average altitudes among islands in the world. This topography, as well as its location in relation to the north-easterly trade winds, gives the island a special connection to water. This meteorological relationship deter-

mines markedly different climates and levels of rainfall in the northern and eastern zones compared to the southern and western sides of the island. This project seeks to provide both local residents and visitors to the island of La Palma with the tools they need to take a fresh look at the island and experience nature in all its intensity. This goal is connected to a further two objectives that round off the design proposal. One is to give this intervention a definitive aspect, as unique interventions created in connection to the island's landscape. In other words, this aims to set it apart from the many arbitrary and disjointed proposals which are ultimately harmful and destructive to the exceptional landscape of the island as a whole.

I. Air Observatory
28°45'17.18"N / 17°53'25.13"W

II. Solar Observatory
28°39'47.94"N / 17°56'33.12"W

IV. Water Observatory
28°41'03.42"N / 17°45'46.74"W

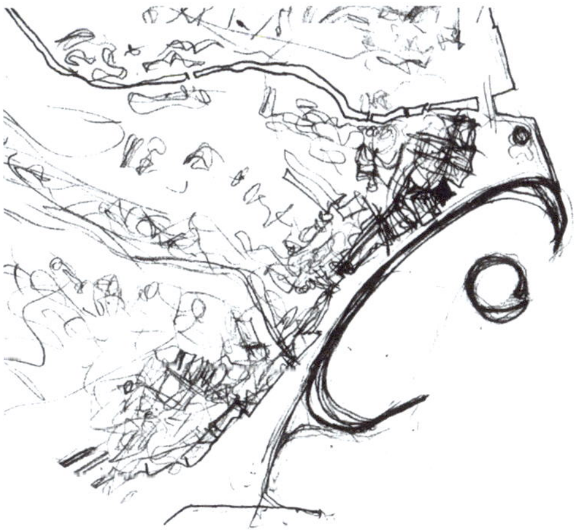

III. Earth Observatory
28°27'35.74"N / 17°51'15.02"W

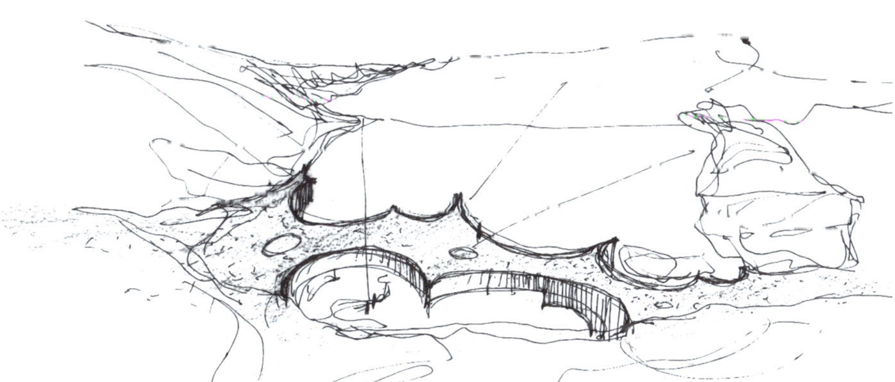

I. Air Observatory. Roque de los Muchachos

To the north, the Roque de los Muchachos observatory uses La Palma's unique air quality for observational astronomy in order to make observing the cosmos and astrophysics more understandable, as something that can be experienced. It also reveals its unique topographical and ecological surroundings: an observation point looking over the Caldera de Taburiente National Park and the nearby islands, and a strategic point in the network of paths covering the north of the island.

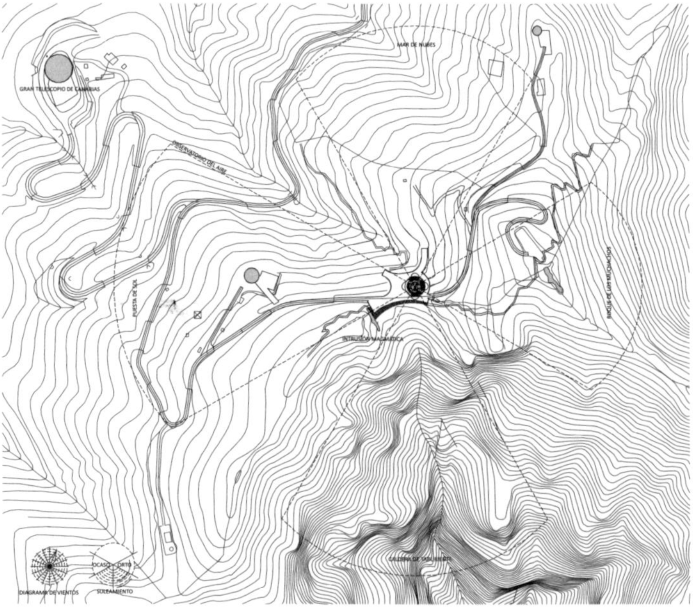

II. Solar Observatory. El Time Viewpoint

To the west, a Solar (or Fire) Observatory is planned as somewhere dedicated to the setting sun and to the subtropical landscape as the "remembered paradise", as Lévi-Strauss defined the west in his book *Tristes Tropiques*. Located in the area of El Time, with views over the Caldera de Taburiente, the fertile Aridane valley, the Tazacorte banana plantations, the sea and the island of El Hierro, its installations will include a long wished-for school of hotel administration.

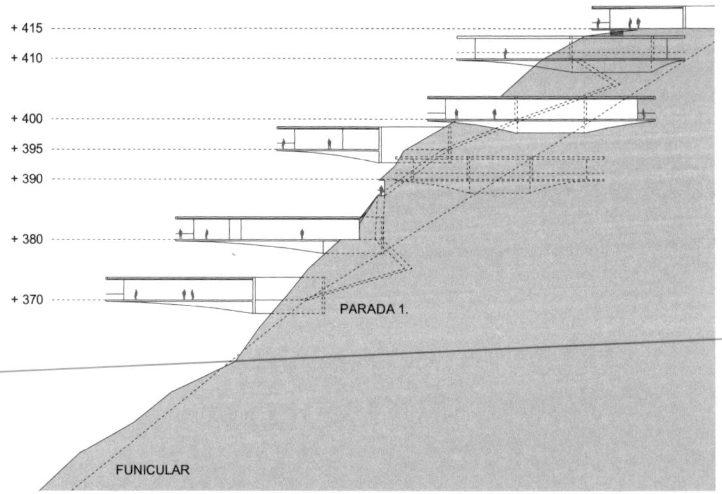

III. Earth Observatory. Fuencaliente

To the south, between the San Antonio volcano, the lighthouse and the salt plains of Fuencaliente, using the recently discovered Fuente Santa, we plan to create an Earth Observatory that can explain how the island formed (a process still underway) and to convey the movement of the archipelago's tectonic plates and geomorphological make-up, as well as an introduction to geological time and the principles of contemporary volcanology.

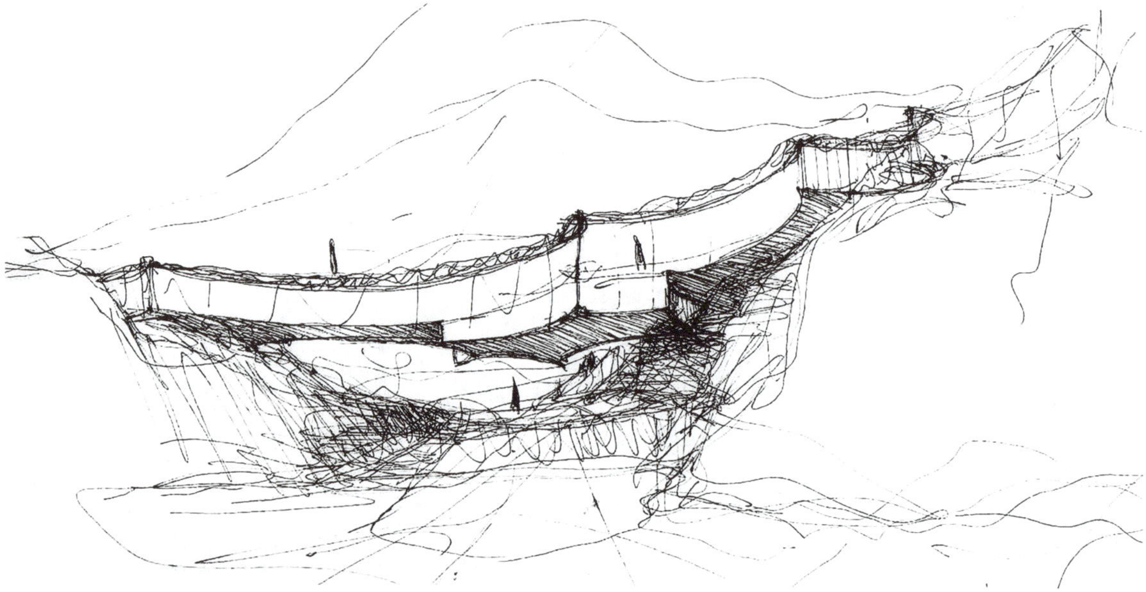

IV. Water Observatory. Santa Cruz

To the east, a Water Observatory is planned with the creation of an artificial island that connects meteorology with hydraulic and port engineering. It is a record of material culture associated with the water, as well as an immediate, physical experience of the historical links to navigation and water brought to the island by trade winds, the fundamental reason for its pioneering classification as a biosphere reserve.

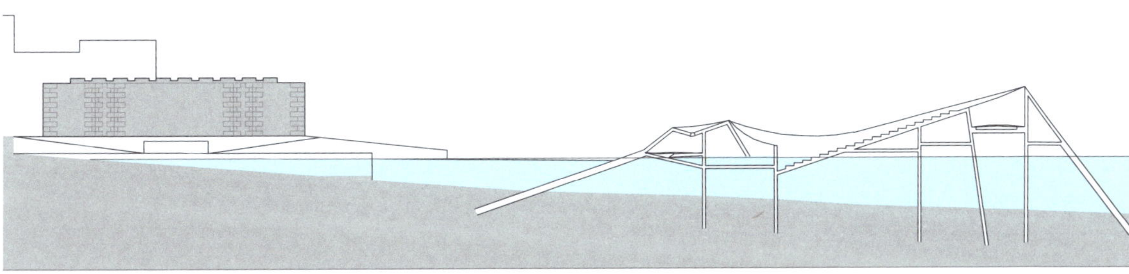

Biobío Regional Theatre. Concepción, Chile. 2011

This building had to provide a spatial response to an ambivalent location that is both uniquely beautiful yet physically cut off from urban life. It also needed to transform an essentially introverted programme into an opportunity to catalyse public life and social interaction. The solution was to create an "experiential place" that connects culture to the geographical surroundings; to make the roofs accessible by giving them a certain movement that can intensify the relation with the landscape and multiply the centre's activities by encouraging spontaneous creativity. This stratified, undulating geometry also creates a polysemic interpretation that can refer equally to the world of drama, the aquatic landscape (as an observation deck), and to the dark universe of seismic activity.

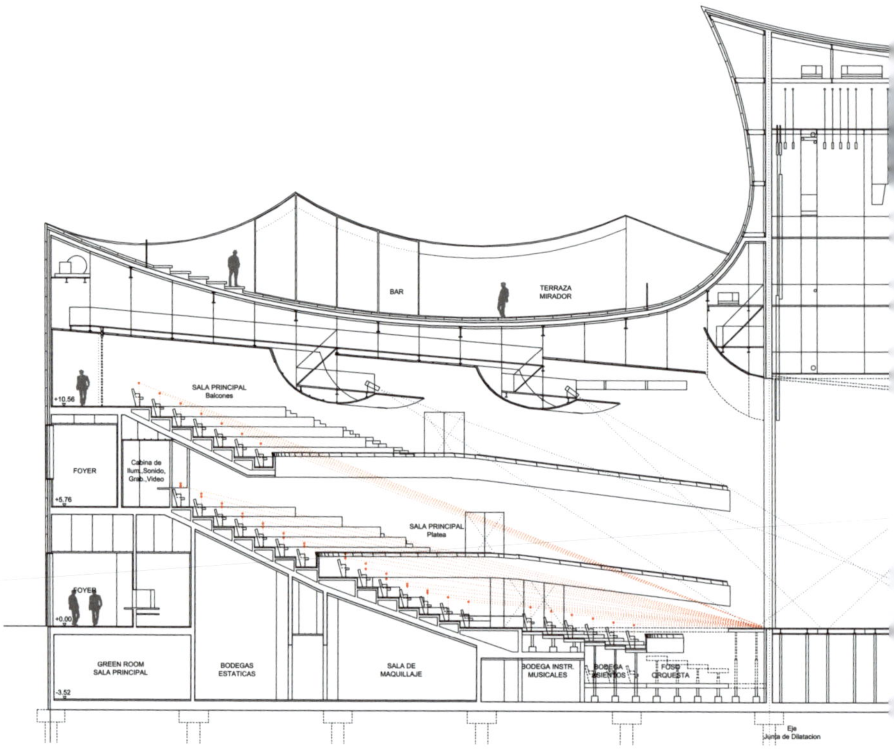

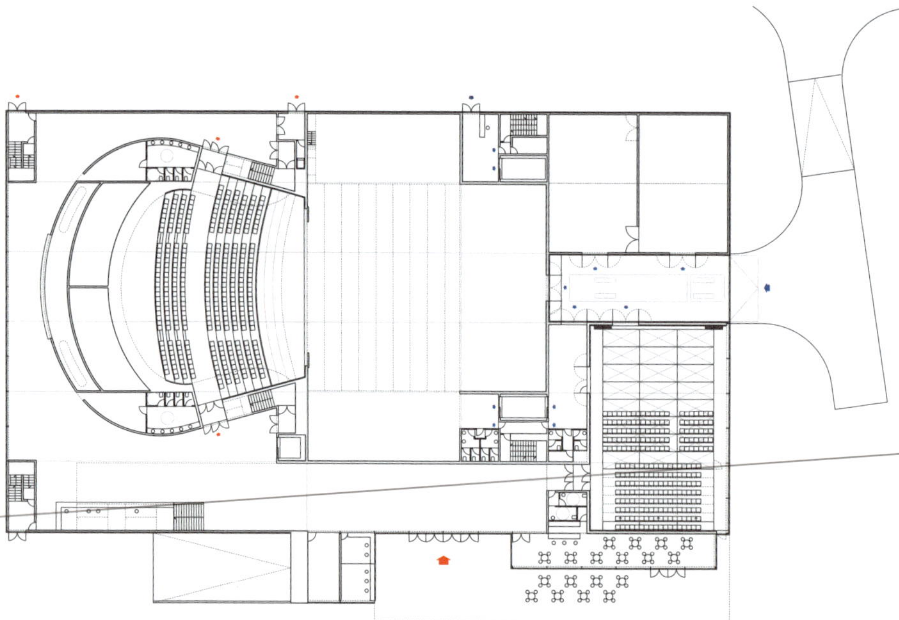

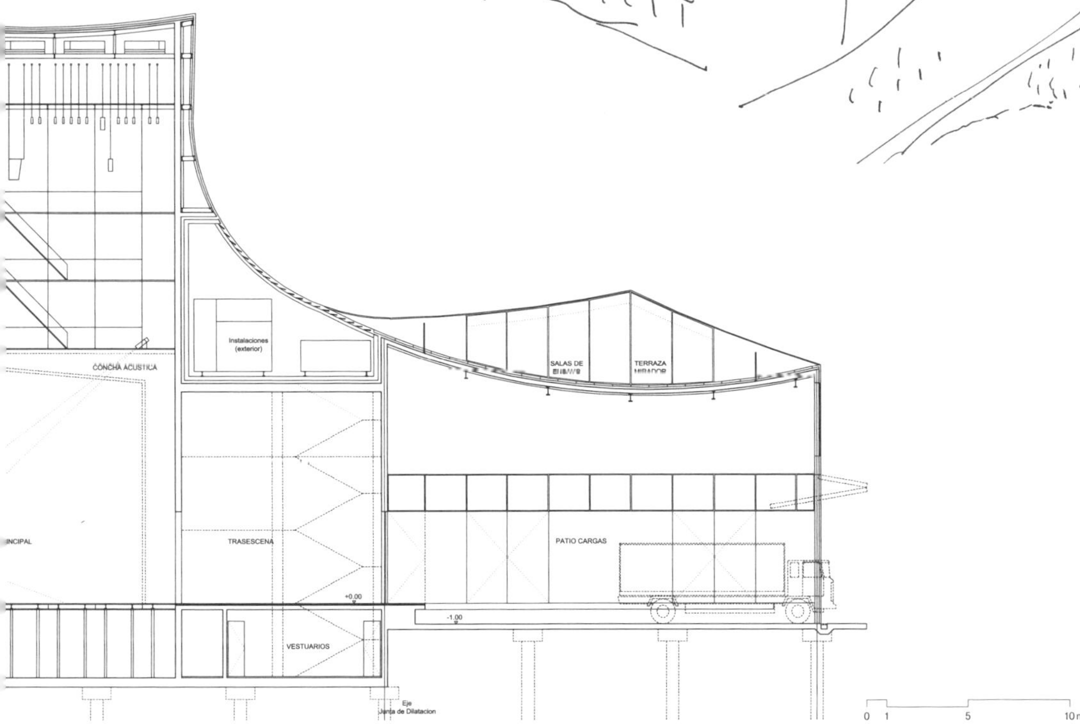

CONCHA ACUSTICA
Instalaciones
(exterior)
SALAS DE
TERRAZA
INCIPAL
TRASESCENA
PATIO CARGAS
+0.00
-1.00
VESTUARIOS
Eje
Junta de Dilatacion
0 1 5 10m

Multigenerational Centre and Start-Up Incubator. Seoul, South Korea. 2017

This programme includes somewhere for different generations to come together and acquire new learning, as well as a variety of social and cultural services. This complexity makes it possible to connect the proposed design not only to residential vernacular typologies, as well as a long tradition of mixed-used Western monasteries, a relationship that almost literally corresponds to contemporary programmatic needs, and which helps us forge a direct link between the city of the past and the challenges facing the city today. With these key references, we create a high-rise, mixed-use prototype

consisting of a series of spaces connected at their perimeter through stairs on the façade leading to the upper levels that house the communal parts of the programme, the most socially and culturally important of which is the Jimjilbang, a Korean sauna that is the heart of the country's public life. Inside, a series of programmes seeks to strike a balance to become a Net Zero Energy Building, and is crowned by a rooftop observatory with views across the skyline of Seoul. The prototype has a characteristic structural envelope that meets the need for a parametric balance between structural loads, energy gains and losses by orientation and the particular lighting needs for each interior programme, culminating in a membrane that intrinsically expresses the architectural balance between tectonic and thermodynamic requirements.

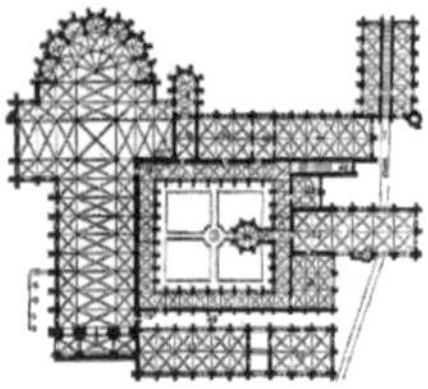

Monastery

Daecheong

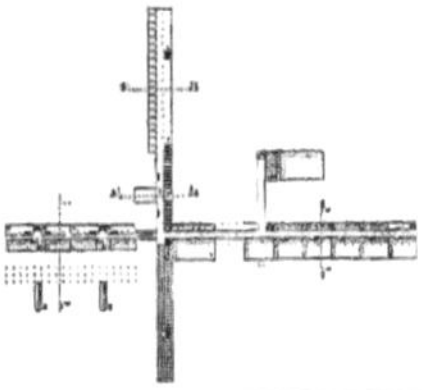

Commune

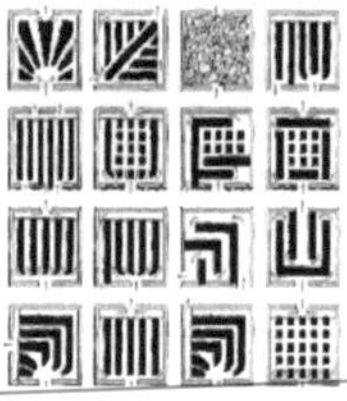

Ondol patterns

Cloister

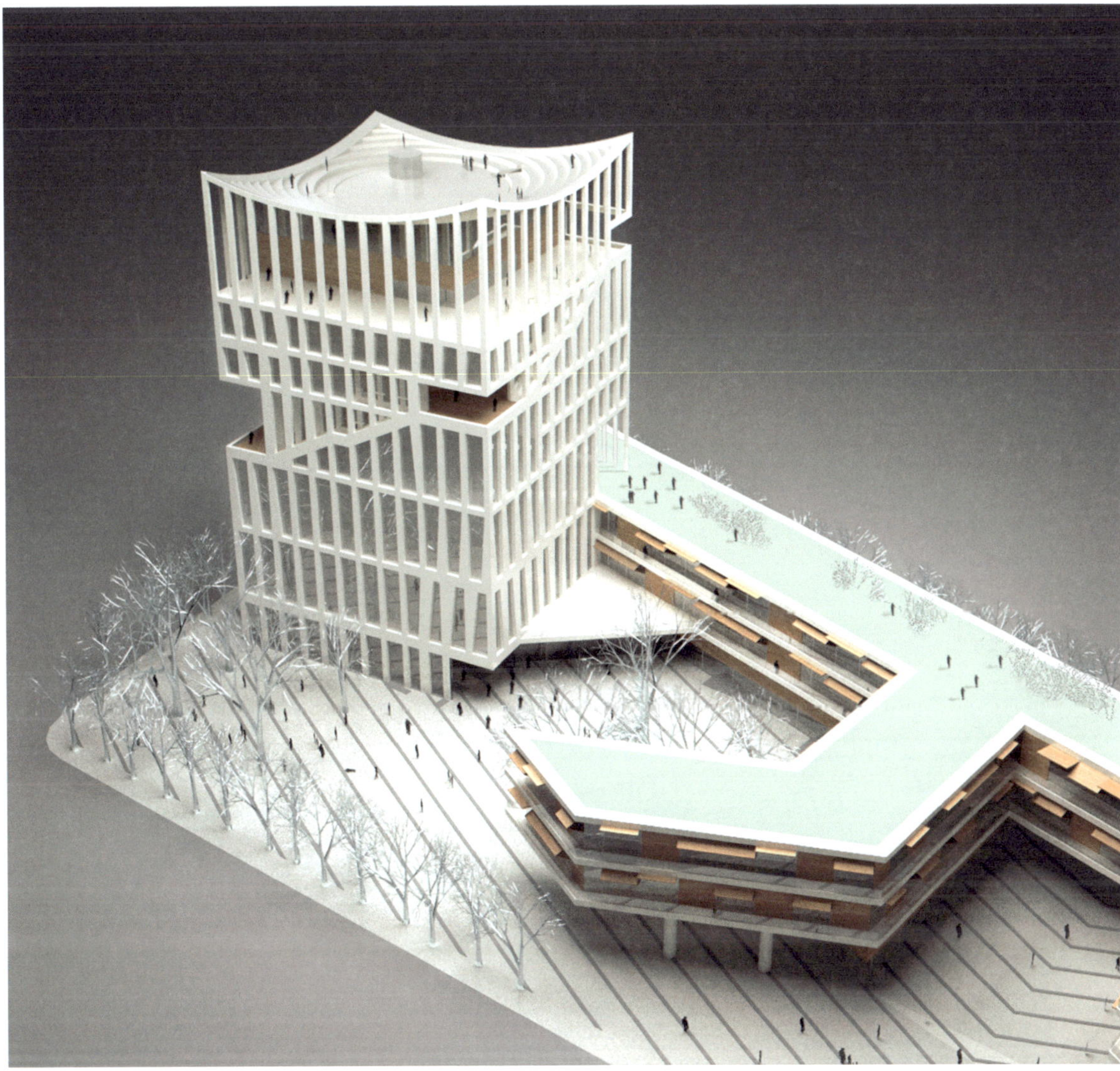

Door patterns

Chapel

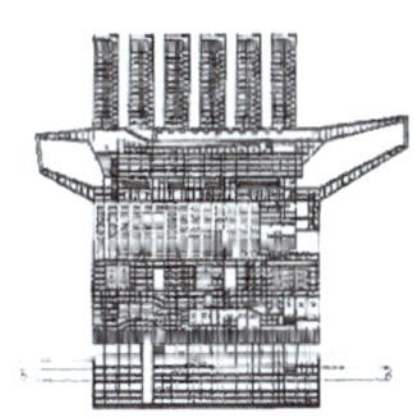

Mixed-use

Roofs

AS+ prototype

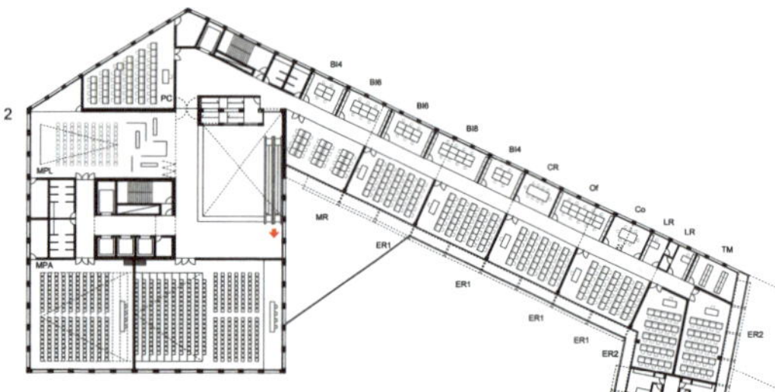

TOTAL AREA : 2607M2

COMMON AREA : MPA. MULTI-PURPOSE AUDITORIUM 250+310M2;
50+ CAMPUS : MPL. MULTI-PURPOSE LOBBY 223M2; PC. PC EDUCATION ROOM 120M2;
BI. 50+ BUSINESS INCUBATOR 283M2; EZ. EDUCATION ZONE 732M2;
DWELLINGS : H. HOUSEHOLDS 22 X 48M2

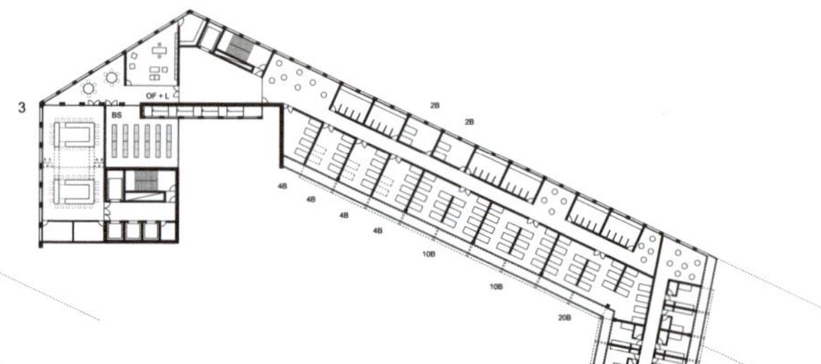

TOTAL AREA : 2013 M2

50+ CAMPUS : TZ. TRAINING ZONE 650M2; OF. OFFICE 255M2; BS. BOOK STORAGE 88M2;
L. LOUNGE 30M2;
DWELLINGS : H. HOUSEHOLDS 26 X 48M2;

TOTAL AREA : 3346 M2

START-UP: SPR. SIMPLE PRODUCTION ROOM 193M2; DL. DEVICE LAB 200M2; TL. TESTING LAB 90M2; PPR. PRECISION PROCESSING ROOM 75M2; PMR. PROTOTYPE MANUFACTURING ROOM 175M2; TSR. TECHNOLOGY SUPPORTING ROOM 62M2;
P. PARKING 2425M2;

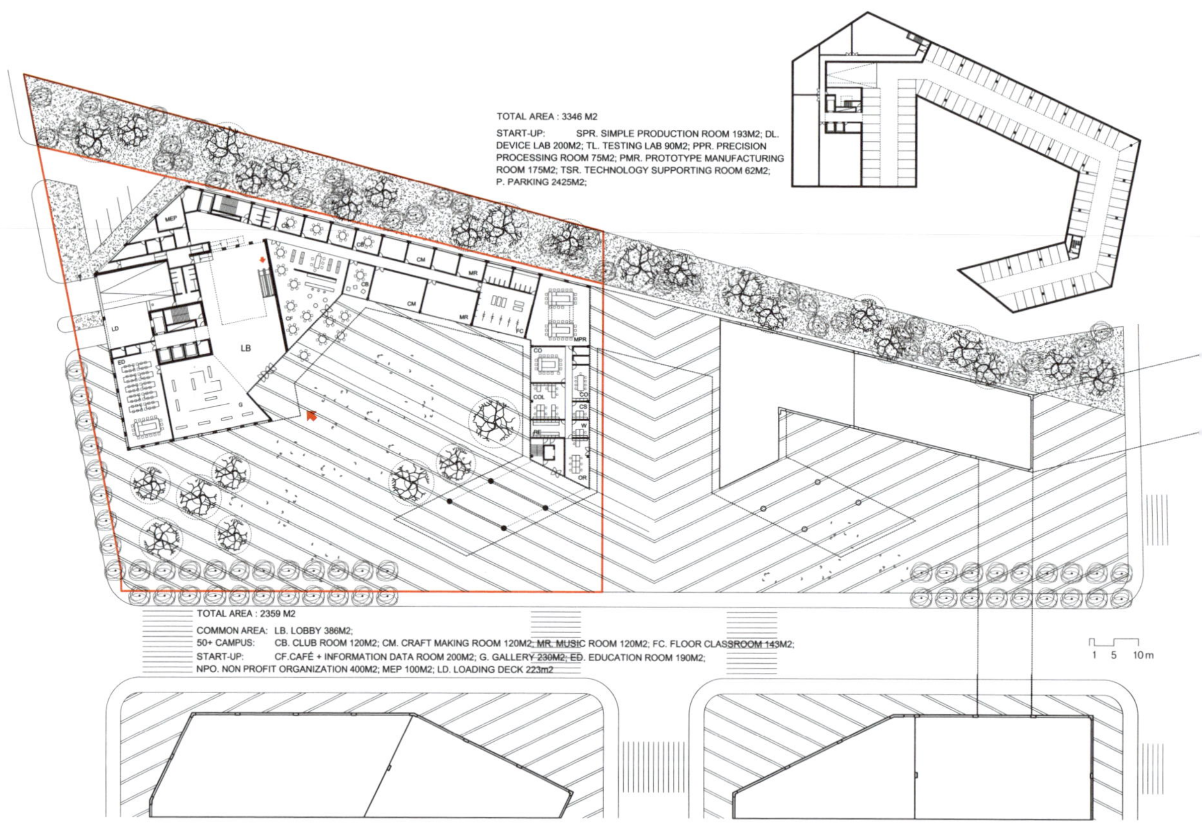

TOTAL AREA : 2359 M2

COMMON AREA: LB. LOBBY 386M2;
50+ CAMPUS: CB. CLUB ROOM 120M2; CM. CRAFT MAKING ROOM 120M2; MR. MUSIC ROOM 120M2; FC. FLOOR CLASSROOM 143M2;
START-UP: CF.CAFÉ + INFORMATION DATA ROOM 200M2; G. GALLERY 230M2; ED. EDUCATION ROOM 190M2;
NPO. NON PROFIT ORGANIZATION 400M2; MEP 100M2; LD. LOADING DECK 223m2

6

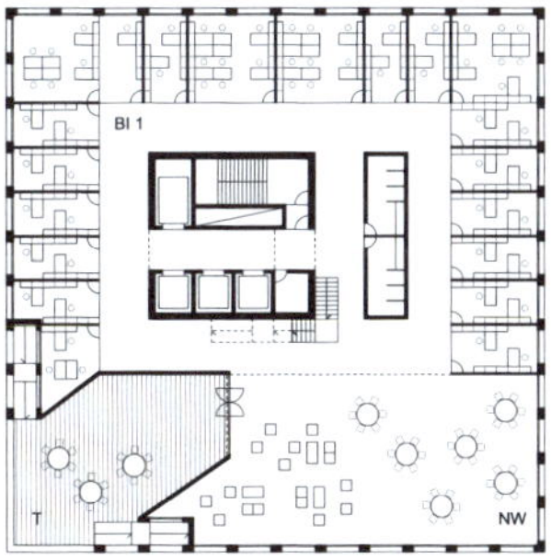

TOTAL AREA : 1002M2

START-UP: BI1. BUSINESS INCUBATOR INDEPENDENT TYPE STAGE 1 400M2; NW. NETWORKING SPACE 200M2; T. TERRACE 135M2;

9

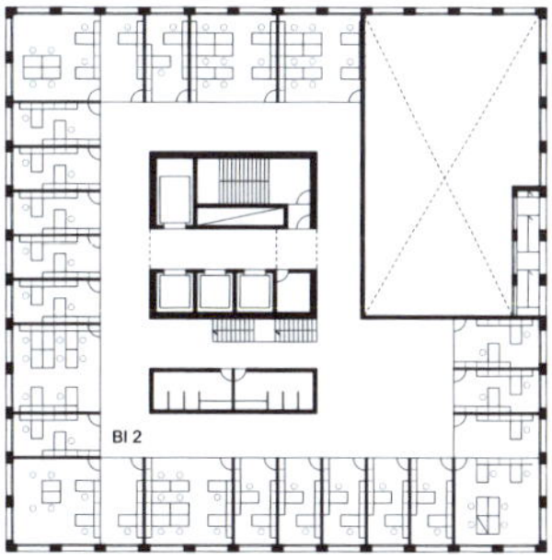

TOTAL AREA : 915M2

START-UP: BI2. BUSINESS INCUBATOR INDEPENDENT TYPE STAGE 2 600M2;

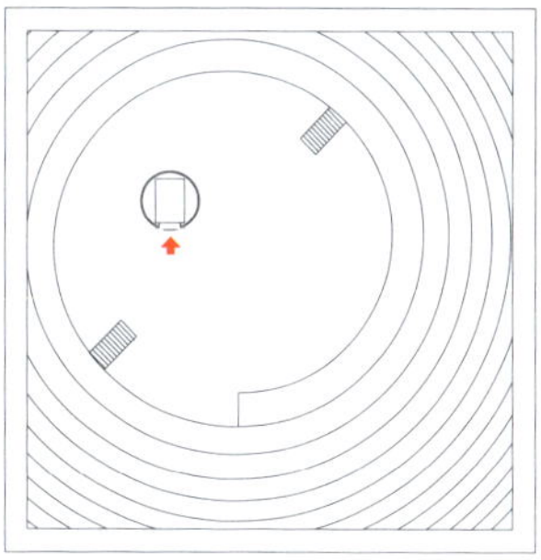

TOTAL AREA : 1248M2

COMMON AREA:
Rf. ROOF OBSERVATORY 1046M2;

5

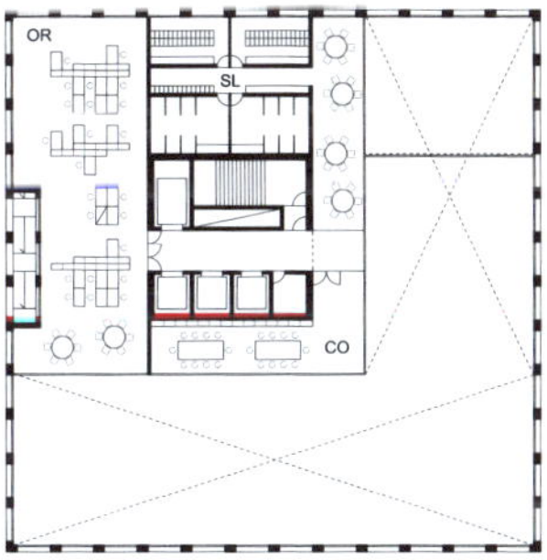

TOTAL AREA : 492M2

START-UP: OR. OPERATION ROOM 197M2; SL. SHOWER/LOUNGE ROOM 150M2; CS. CONSULTING ROOM 66M2

8

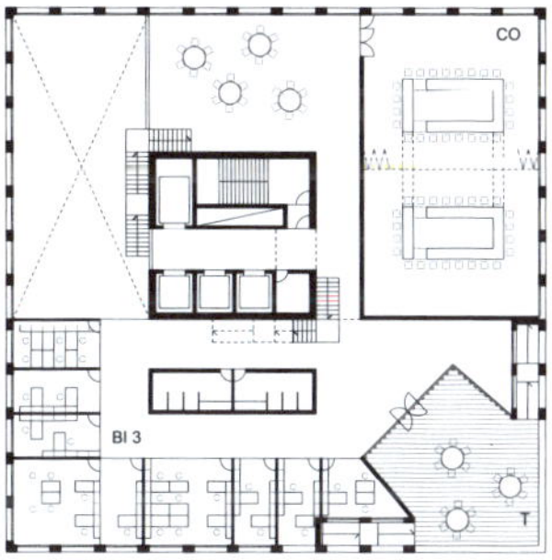

TOTAL AREA : 868M2

START-UP: BI3. BUSINESS INCUBATOR INDEPENDENT TYPE STAGE 3 180M2; CO CONFERENCE ROOM 238M2; T. TERRACE 103M2

11

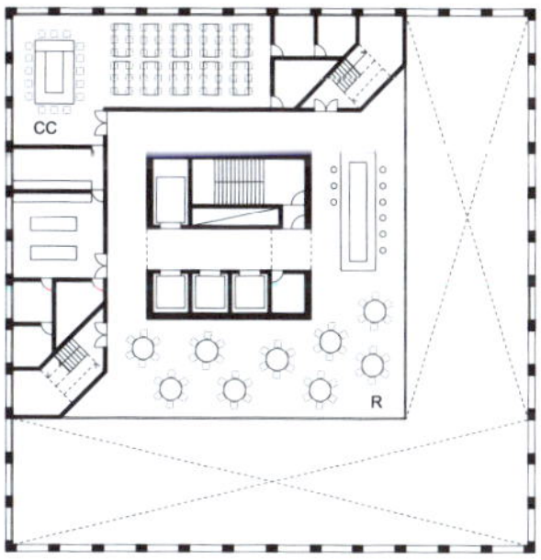

TOTAL AREA : 642M2

COMMON AREA:
R. RESTAURANT + CC. COOKING CLASS 528M2;

4

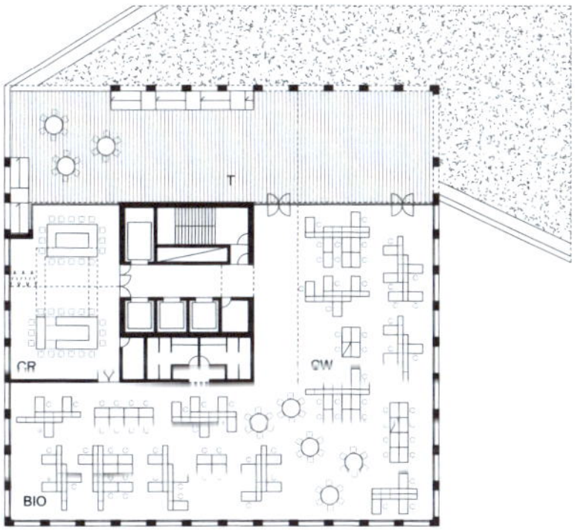

TOTAL AREA : 836M2

START-UP: BIO. BUSINESS INCUBATOR OPEN TYPE 320M2; CW. CO-WORKING SPACE 210M2; CR. CONFERENCE ROOM 120M2; T. TERRACE 338M2

7

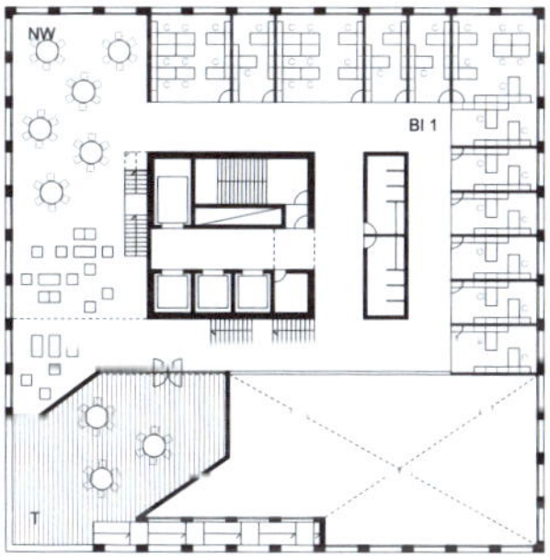

TOTAL AREA : 775M2

START-UP: BI1. BUSINESS INCUBATOR INDEPENDENT TYPE STAGE 1 250M2; NW. NETWORKING SPACE 120M2; T. TERRACE 131M2

10

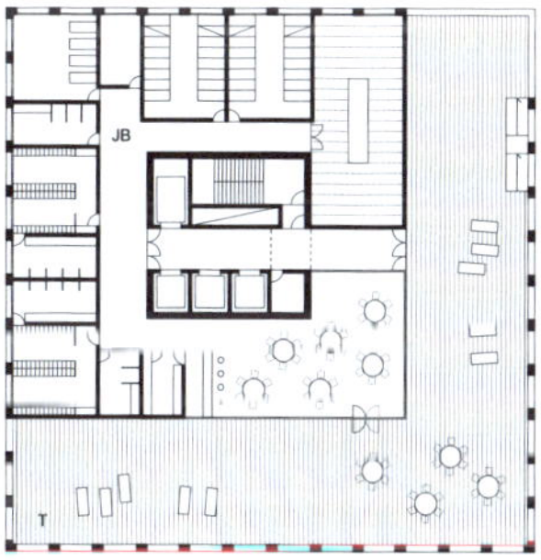

TOTAL AREA : 642M2

COMMON AREA:
JB. JIMJILBANG 563M2;

The New Primitivists

Who are the new primitivists? People who see the need to change the formulaic planning of today's cities and recover the intensity and spirit of other cultures; those striving to create a collaborative society that integrates life and work, brings different generations together and uses natural resources as efficiently and economically as possible. In architecture, new primitivism is about understanding all architecture, from every era, as part of a CONTINUOUS PRESENT, a source of inspiration to find new forms of organisation. New primitivists take a historical perspective: western and eastern monasteries; rural cooperatives or communes; vernacular dwellings where families, animals and workers live together in productive units. They realize, however, that a literal return to those models would be a naïve exercise in nostalgia. Instead, their architecture is a careful equation of form, matter and thermodynamic flows. It is based on material culture and state-of-the-art technology to achieve the utmost simplicity, simultaneously tackling both tectonic and thermodynamic issues.

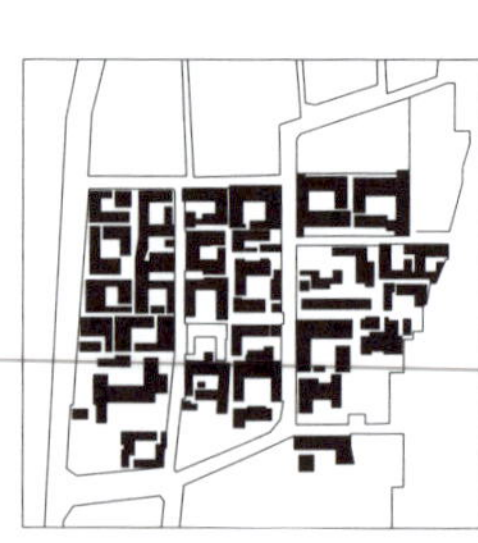

Vernacular

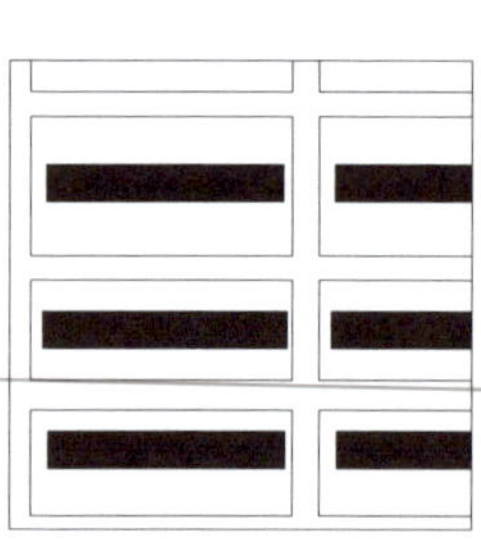

Modern

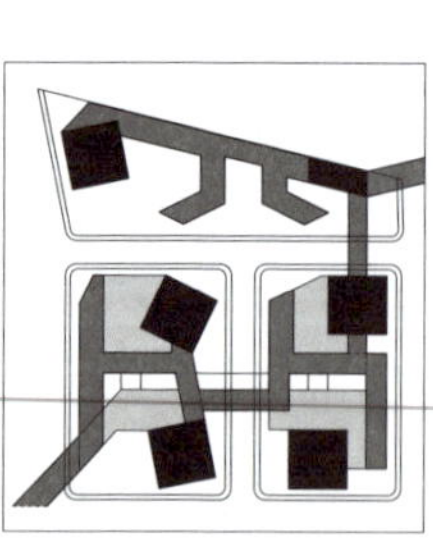

Present

Four thermodynamic systems

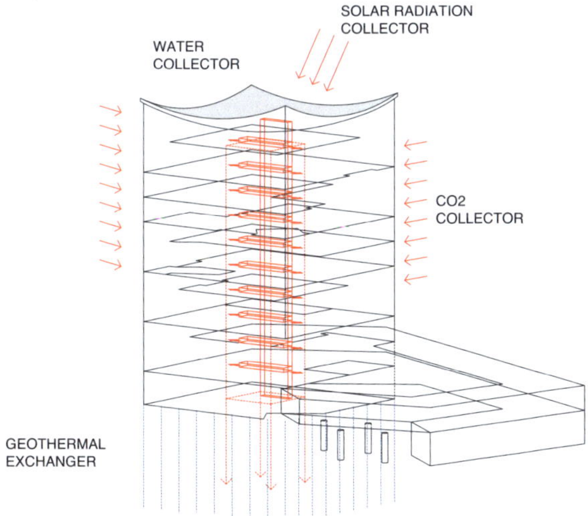

Internal tiered gardens

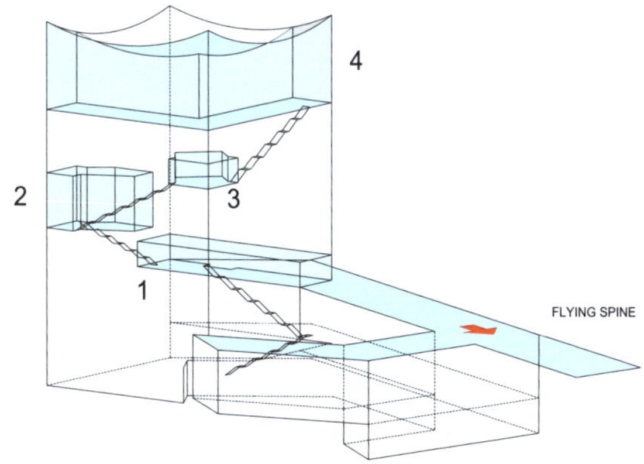

Vertical loads and percentages of voids

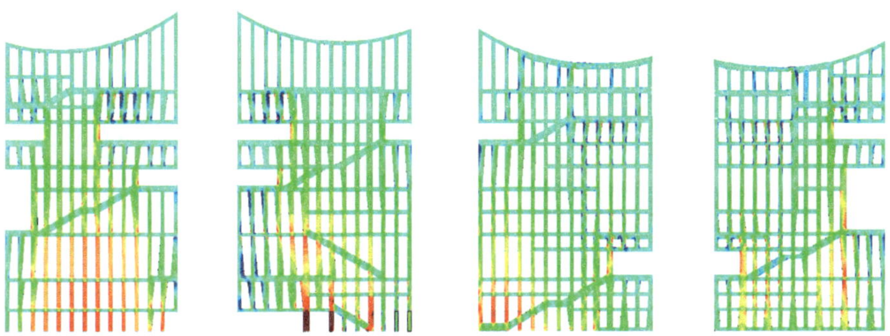

South façade **43%** East façade **40%** North façade **54%** West façade **32%**

Four Elements

Solar radiation and water harvesting are complemented by the capture of geothermal energy in the pile-driving and the treatment of the façade with GeoSilex (a CO_2 capture technology), meaning that Aristotle's four elements are integrated as landscaping and environmental resources. The building is also a landscape, a public-use structure and energy collector, whose iconic and primitive design emerges from the attempt to equalize solar radiation, natural lighting and the structural performance of the load-bearing façade. Environmental software has been combined with iterative processes evaluated at their first and most crucial phases, giving a reasonably accurate picture of the results. The concrete exoskeleton has been designed not only to meet the building's structural requirements but also to provide protection from solar gain on the sides most exposed to the sun, particularly on the west and east orientations, reducing transparent surfaces, while opening up to the south and north. This ensures a proper level of protection from the sun while maintaining natural light, creating a suitable environment for working, community events and education. Furthermore, the significant inertia of the concrete slabs absorbs the cold and heat, thus lowering the peaks in energy demand.

San Antonio Urban Regeneration. Historic Centre of Medellín, Colombia. 2015-

After years of focusing on mitigating the problems on Medellín's outskirts with a series of high-value interventions, the city is now also setting out to revive the centre as a key element in the city's economic development. It has identified the San Antonio district as one of the few large-scale and strategically located public spaces in the historic centre with access to public transport, the central market and the city's administrative hub. Although this was the space chosen for a competition to create a large green area three decades ago, the monumental design was out of proportion with the local urban topography and lacked a security policy, leading to considerable degradation to the area over time. AS+ has submitted a proposal in conjunction with Medellín's EDU government-run urban development firm, is based on thermodynamic and social design principles applied to public space and building, and incorporating the disciplines of architecture and landscaping to create a new microclimate with economic, ecological, social and cultural impact in the heart of the city.

The Cathedral

San Antonio Park

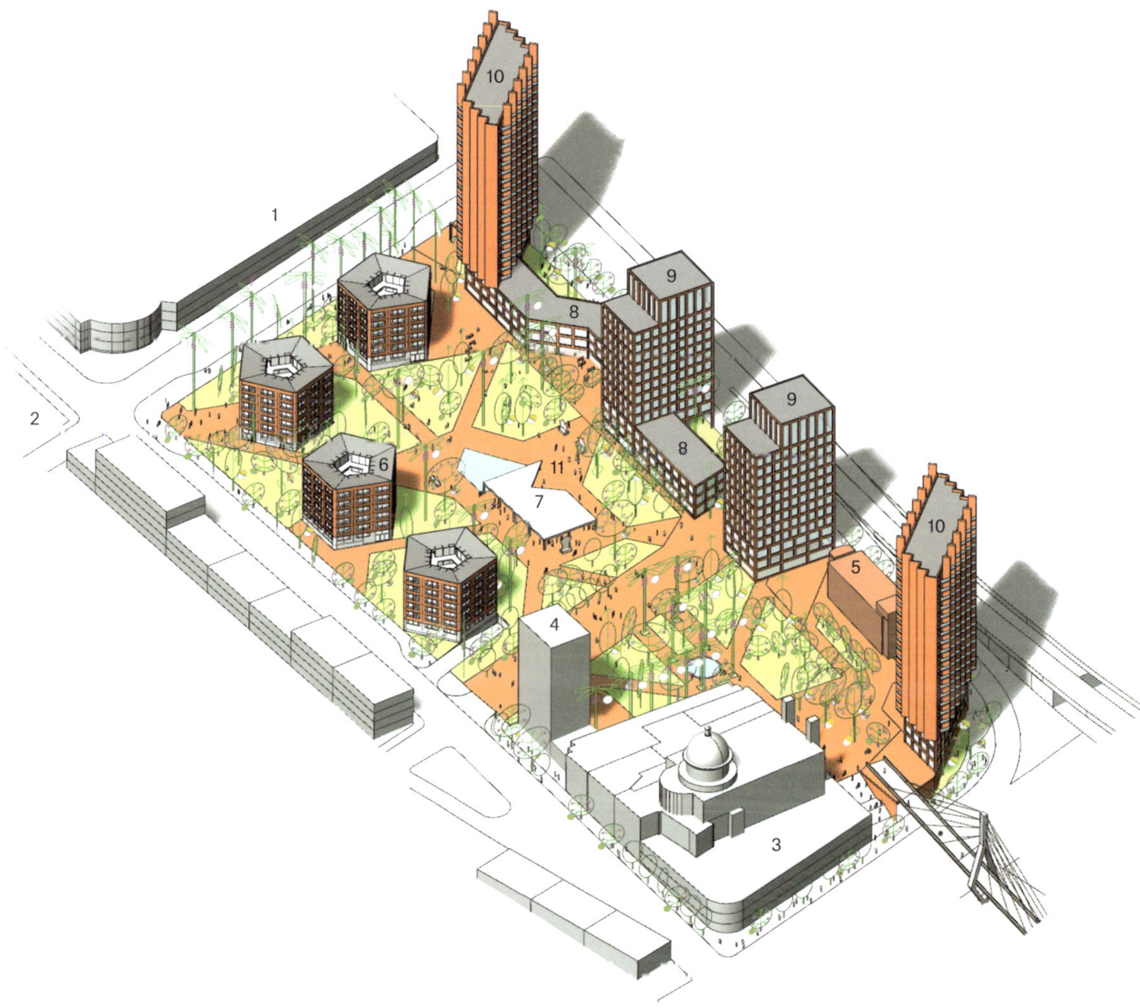

1. Central Market
2. Central Metropolitan Station
3. San Antonio Church
4. EDU
5. French Institute
6. Youth Housing
7. Playful Pavilion (Flowers, crafts and restoration)
8. Commercial Zocalo
9. Offices
10. Mixed-Use
11. San Antonio Park with Botero sculptures

Current Situation

A lack of local community activity or commerce, and a disconnect from the topography of the rest of the city creates insecurity and sucks life out of the area.

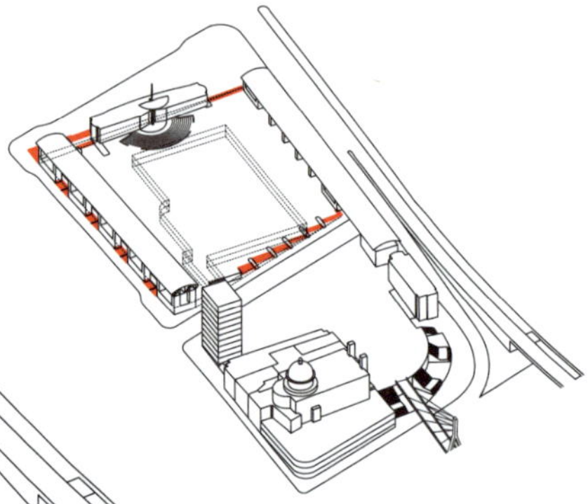

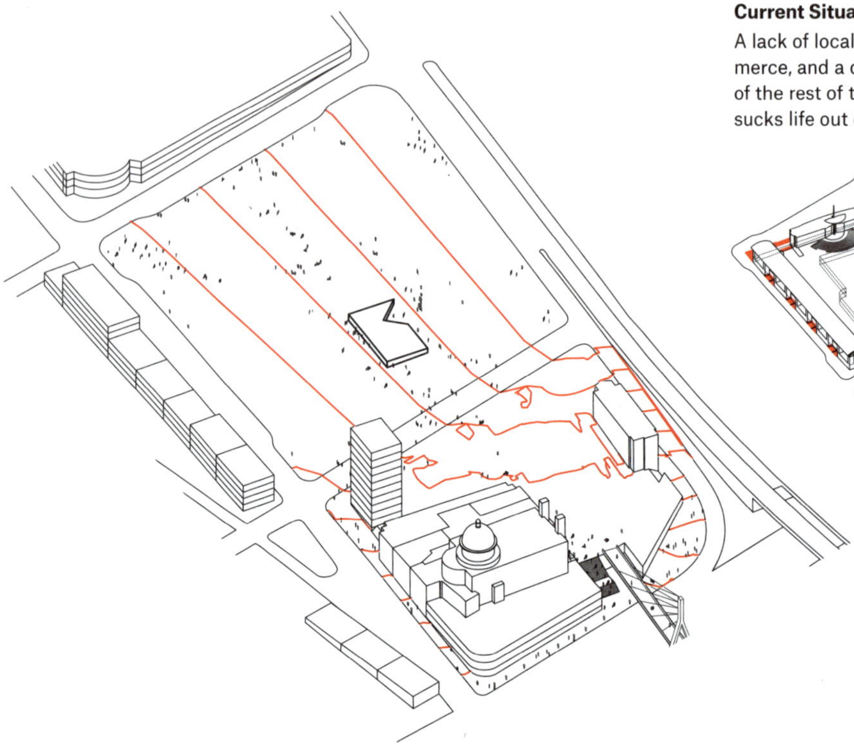

Proposal. Restoration of the urban topography.

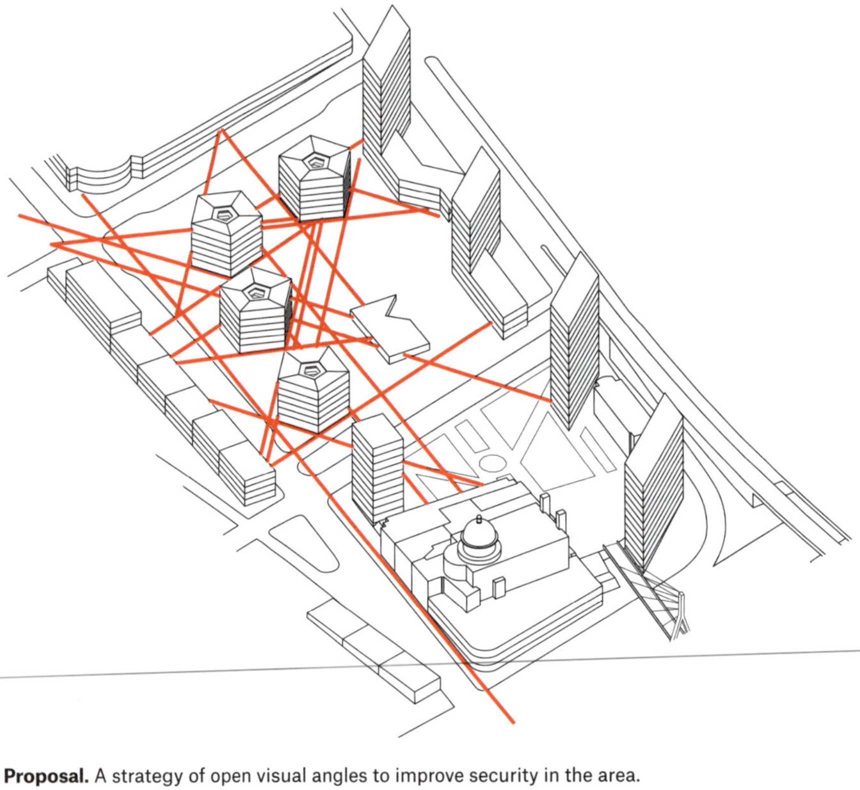

Proposal. A strategy of open visual angles to improve security in the area.

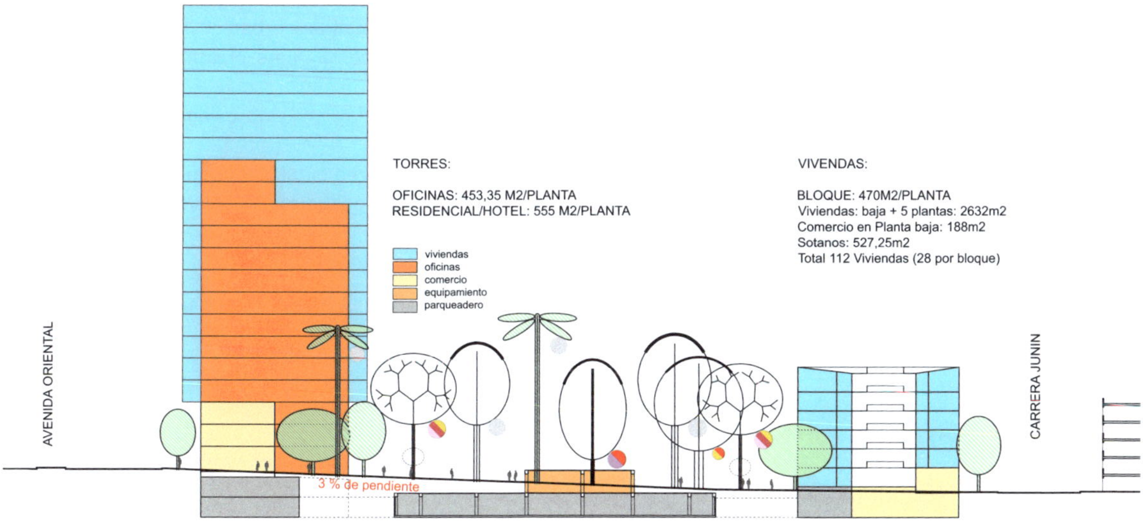

Proposal. Transversal section

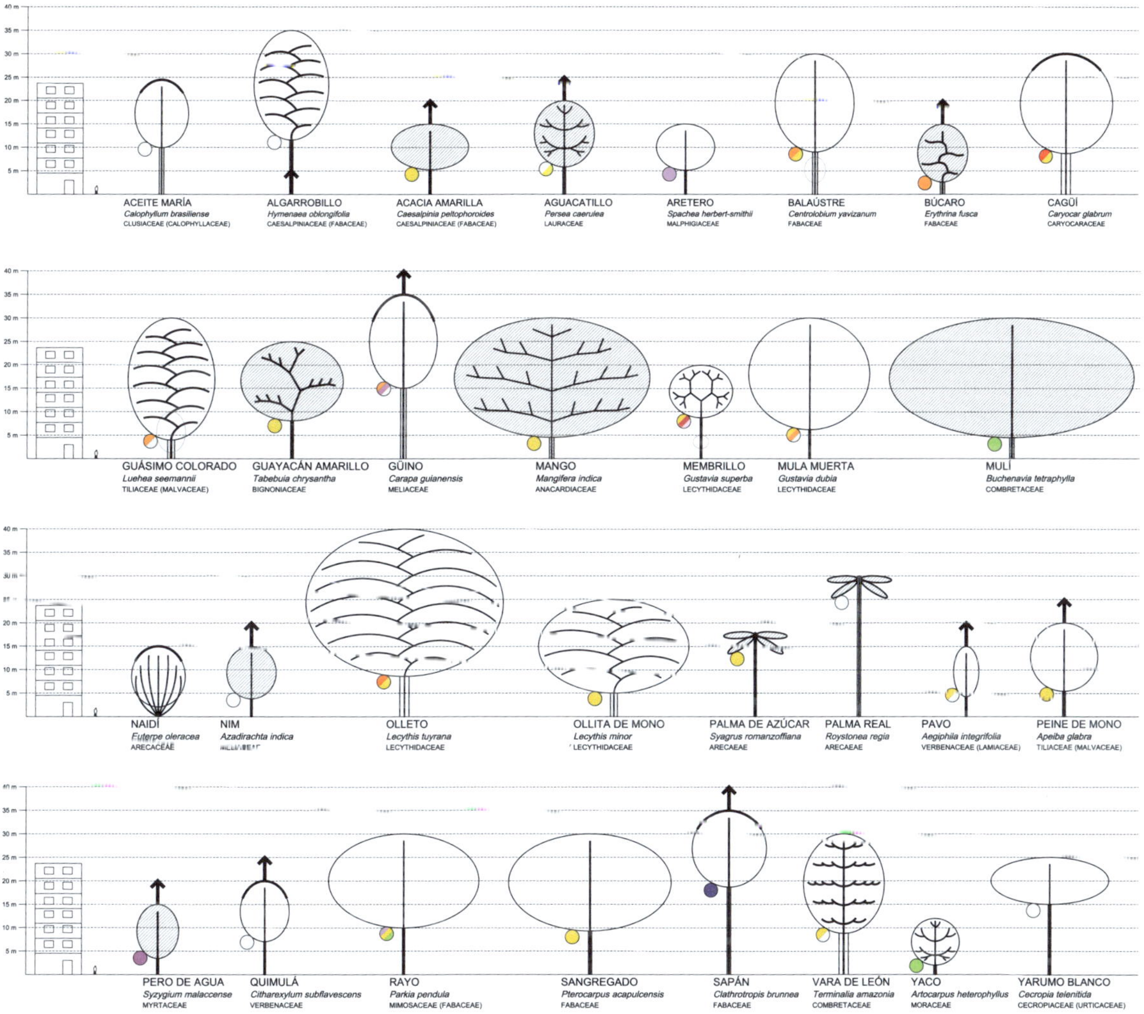

The core strategies are to:

- Restore the green and wooded areas as a key element for improving the comfort of this urban environment.
- Provide protection from atmospheric and noise pollution from the Vía Oriental thoroughfare, creating a barrier in the form of a commercial podium.
- Increase natural ventilation by studying prevailing winds at different times of day, and improving air flow through the area.
- Create homes for young people, to help populate an area that is currently deserted outside working hours.
- Devise straightforward typological and material layouts that are oriented to reduce the costs of residential and office building construction by maximizing their energy efficiency.
- Establish a centre for handcrafts, flowers and gastronomy with the pavilion of the "emerged" parking area by restoring the urban topography.

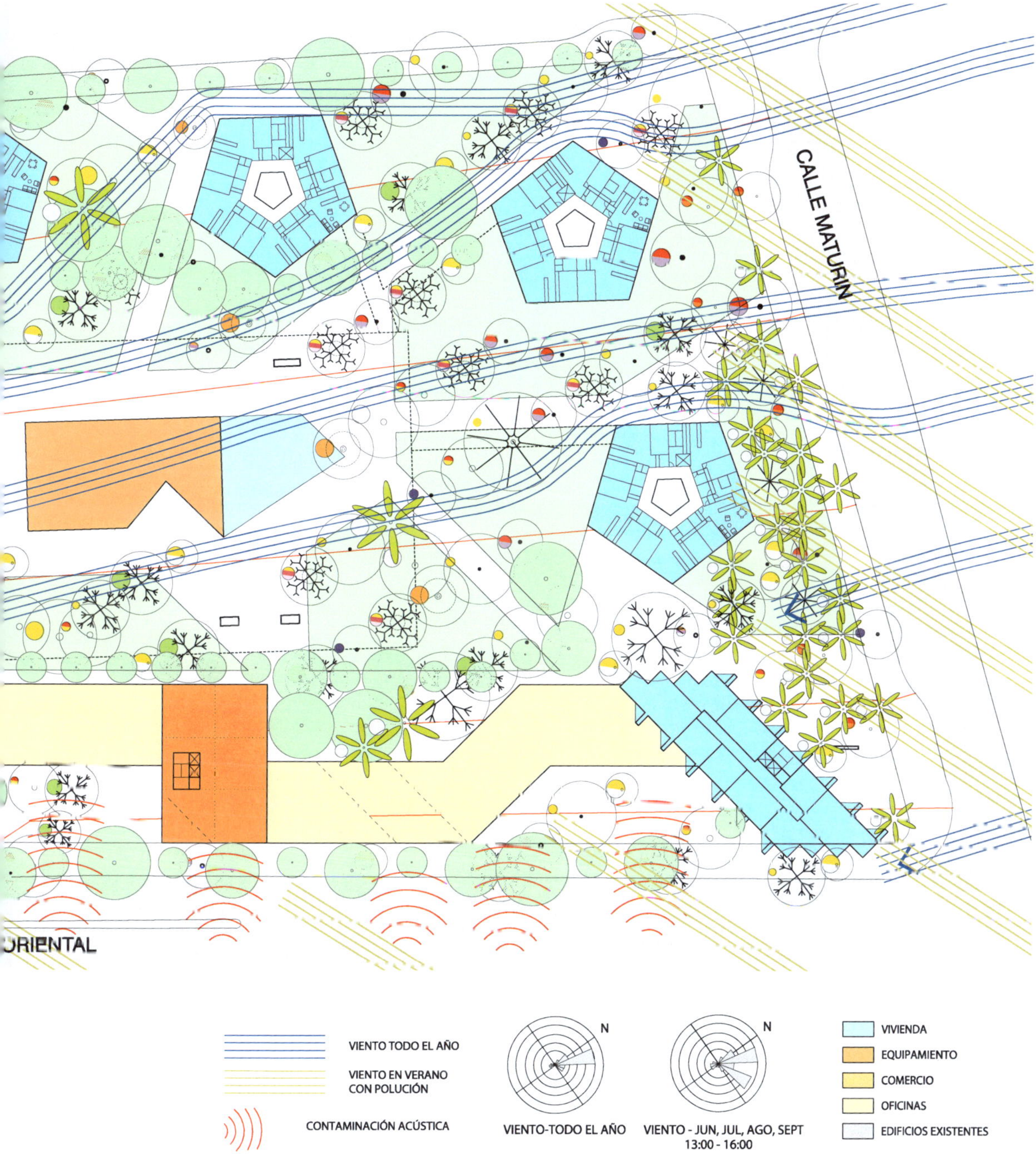
CALLE MATURIN
ORIENTAL
VIENTO TODO EL AÑO
VIENTO EN VERANO CON POLUCIÓN
CONTAMINACIÓN ACÚSTICA
N
VIENTO-TODO EL AÑO
N
VIENTO - JUN, JUL, AGO, SEPT 13:00 - 16:00
VIVIENDA
EQUIPAMIENTO
COMERCIO
OFICINAS
EDIFICIOS EXISTENTES

Strategies for Breathing Buildings: Orientation and Ventilation

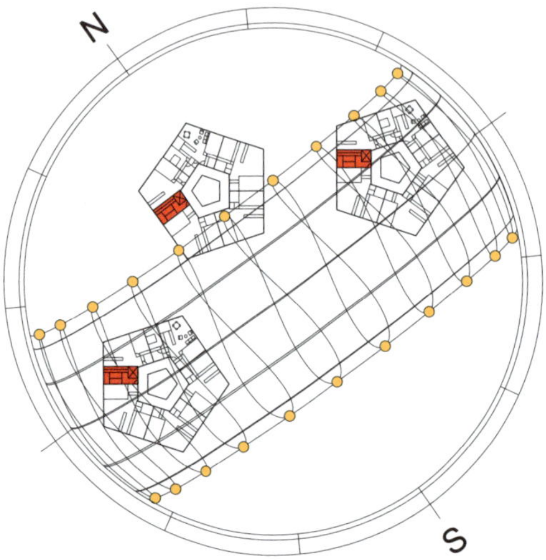

The entrance faces west to mitigate solar radiation.

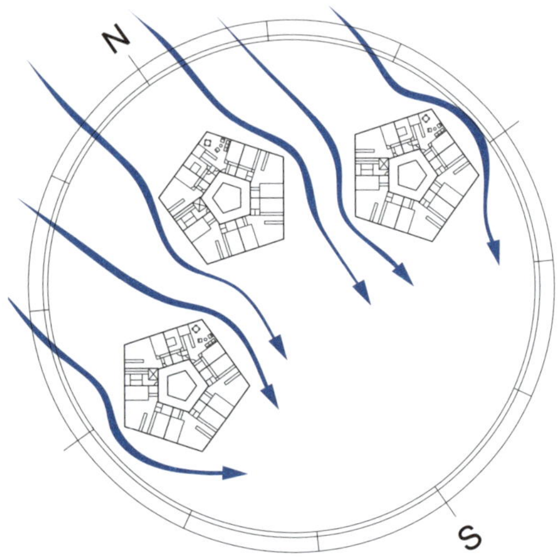

The form minimizes the impact of the wind on the public space.

Strategies for Breathing Office Buildings: Sun and Wind

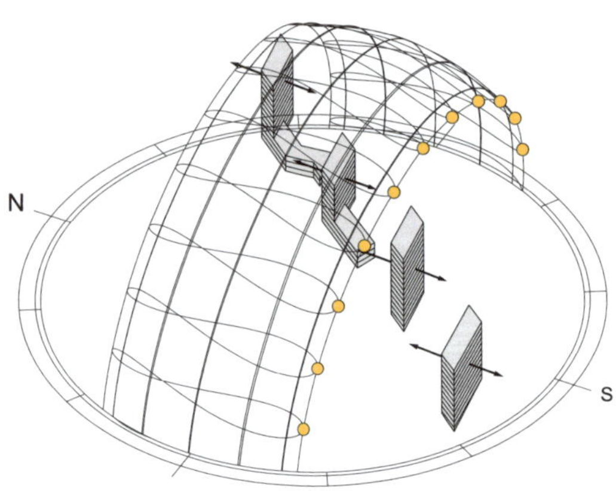

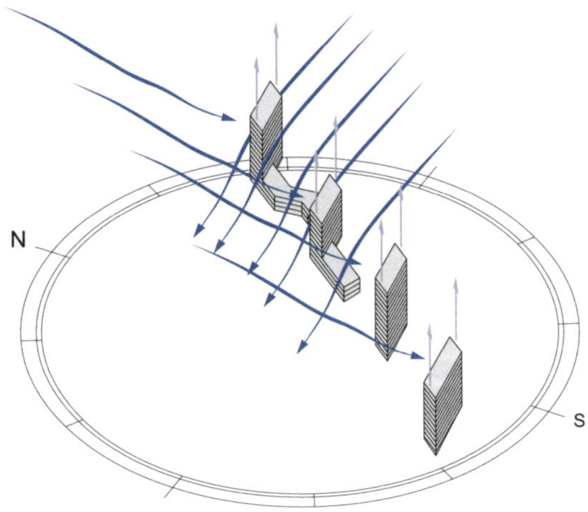

A north-south orientation is ideal for offices, as the brise-soleils provide shade for office spaces exposed to direct sunlight, and the depth makes natural ventilation possible. Buoyancy-driven ventilation is permanently active and the wind direction also allows cross-ventilation whenever possible.

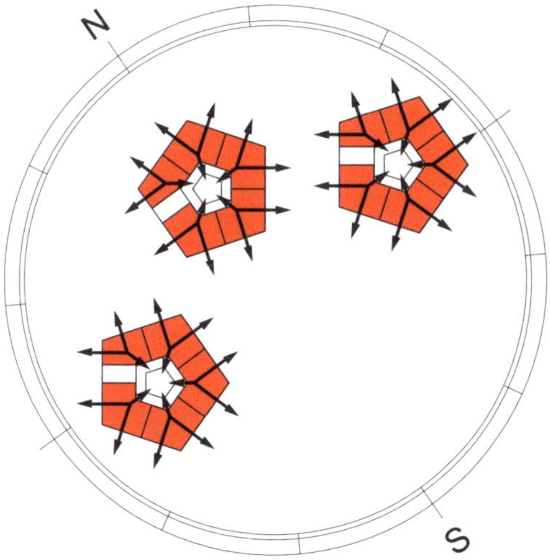

Apartments open on three sides.

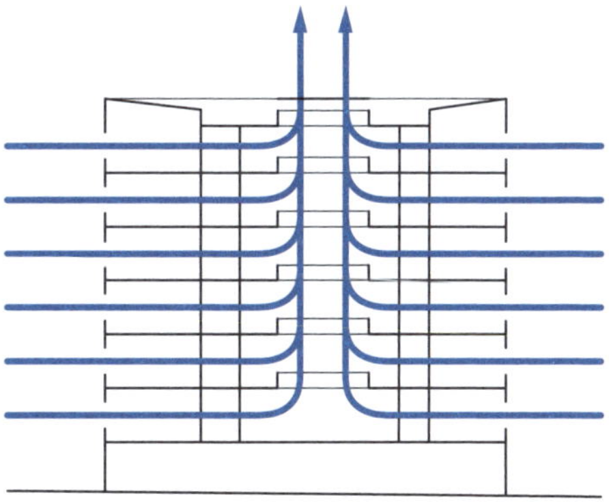

Buoyancy-driven ventilation through the courtyard.

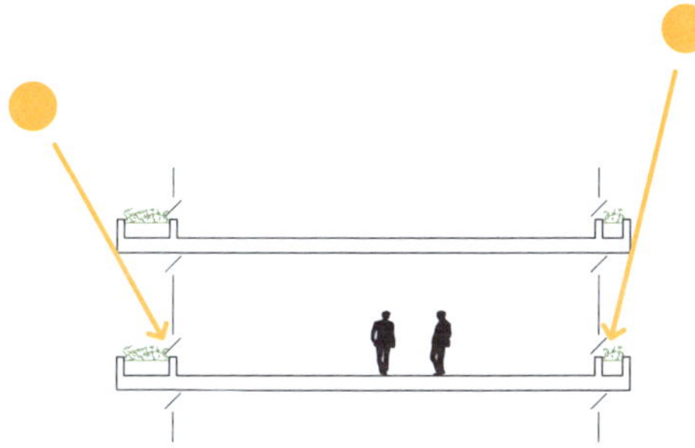

The brise-soleils shade office spaces, protecting them from direct sunlight in both summer and winter months.

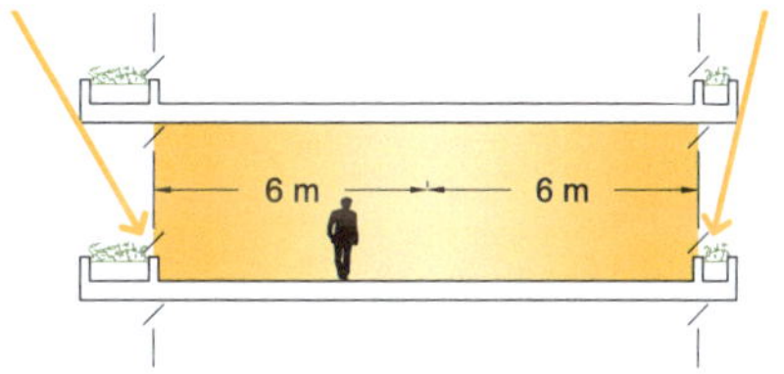

The depth of the building ensures offices receive natural lighting.

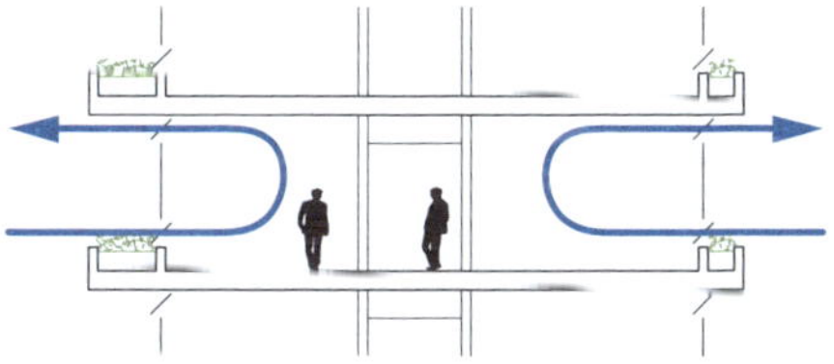

With a corridor, buoyancy-driven ventilation circulates air, whether or not there is a breeze.

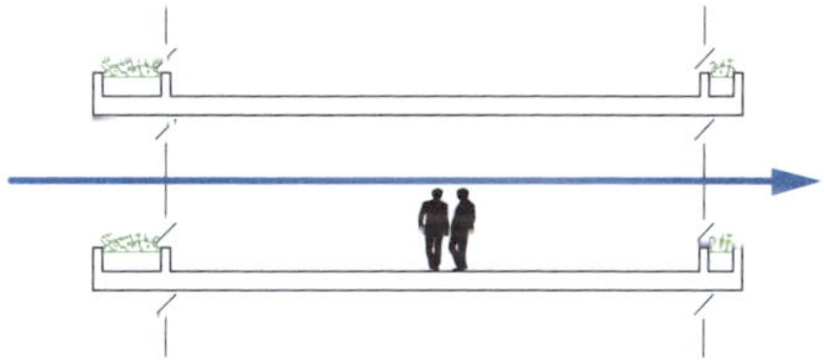

Without a corridor, the north-south wind direction creates cross-ventilation.

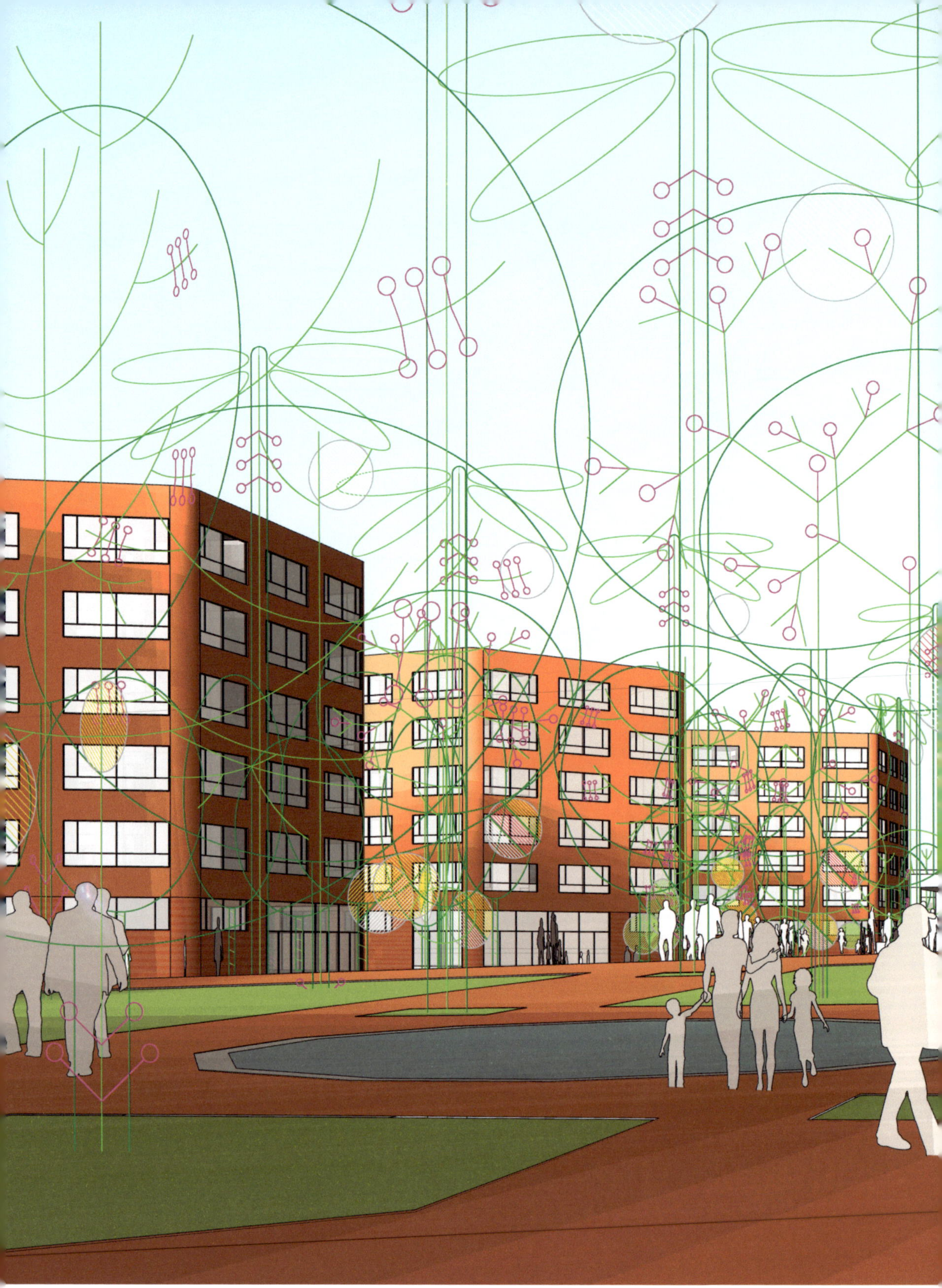

Felipe VI City Park. Logroño, La Rioja, Spain. 2008-2020

Placing the railway tracks underneath the intermodal station offered an opportunity to restore the connection between areas previously cut off from each other, creating a large, central public park, with the station roof establishing its geometric and topographical pattern. In this way, the different surfaces create both sides of a folded shell, with the exterior forming a small mound or observation deck looking out over the city, while the interior takes on the shape of a cave

or grotto. The park itself—created in collaboration with Arquitectura Agronomía—leaves large, flat green spaces, with the geometry and vegetation becoming more complex as it rises. A pergola with a pool, a tribute to Max Bill, shows the geometric matrix of the whole, and the pergola and skylights of the platforms of the high-speed train (TAV) station are the only architectural elements to emerge above ground level in the park.

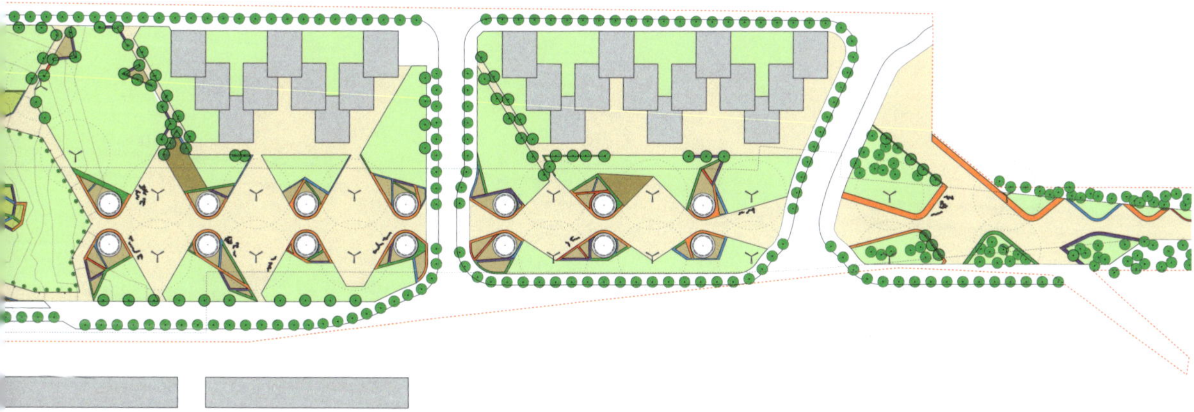

Torre Spina. Turin, Italy. 2008

The flatness of the Turin region and the contrast with the crystal-like geometric contour of the Alps form the backbone of our proposal. These mineral forms are the sole elements used to form a crown, the outline of which strikes up a dialogue with Turin's most significant natural and artificial landmarks. In this way the project seeks an effect of unity or totality, inspired less by the usual vertical competitiveness of skyscrapers than by the effect of an integrated, massive, solid volume that both emerges from and generates the urban fabric. The colossal, triangulated geometry is useful both to minimize the wind effect on the structure and to optimize energy. This determines the orientation of the housing volumes, which rise up toward the south to provide shade for the office buildings, while leaving the rooftops exposed for photovoltaic installations and machinery. The triple glazing used for the envelope includes a ventilated chamber and screen-printed exterior glass with variable density depending on its orientation. This generates an almost snow-like presence or atmospheric halo that is suitable both from a compositional and a thermodynamic perspective.

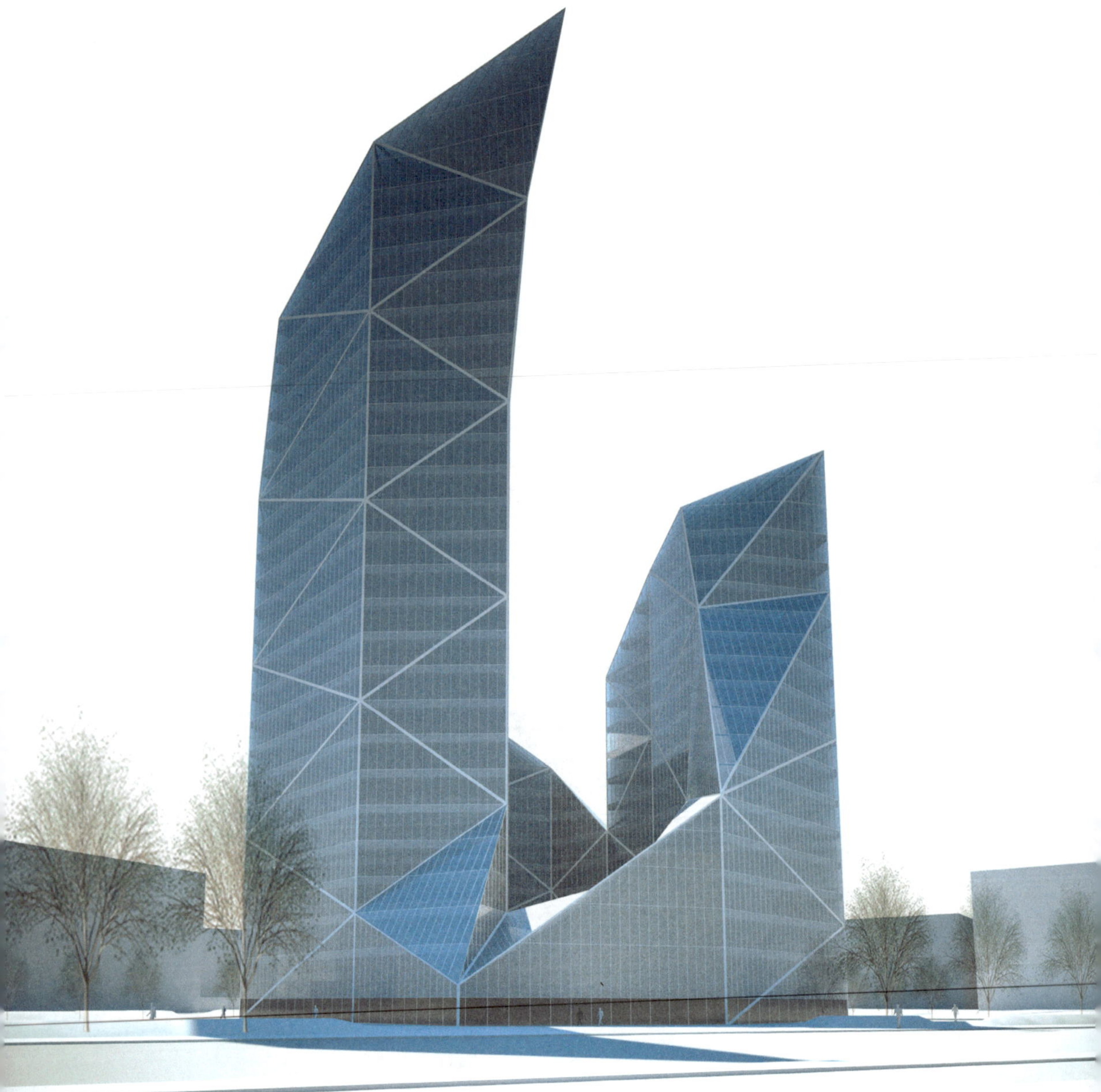

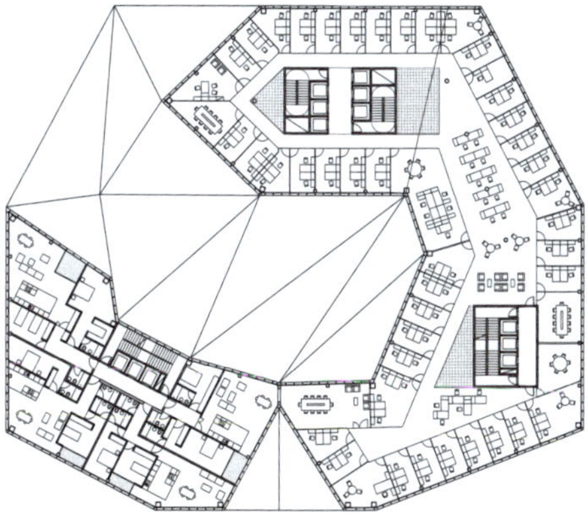

Level 6

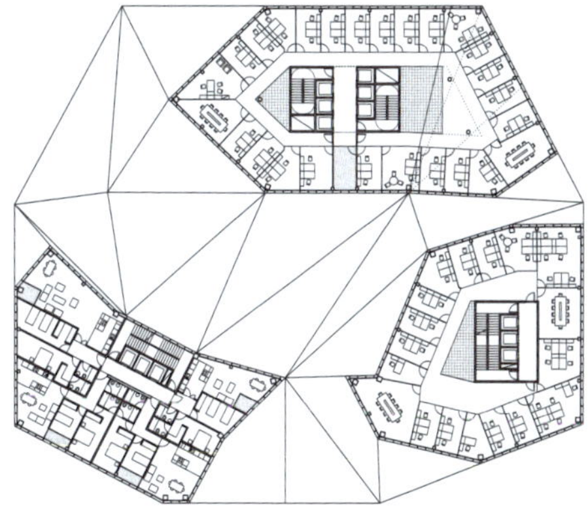

Level 9

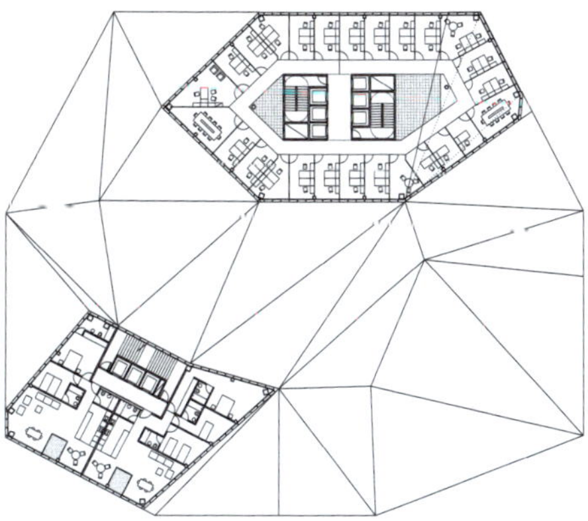

Level 13

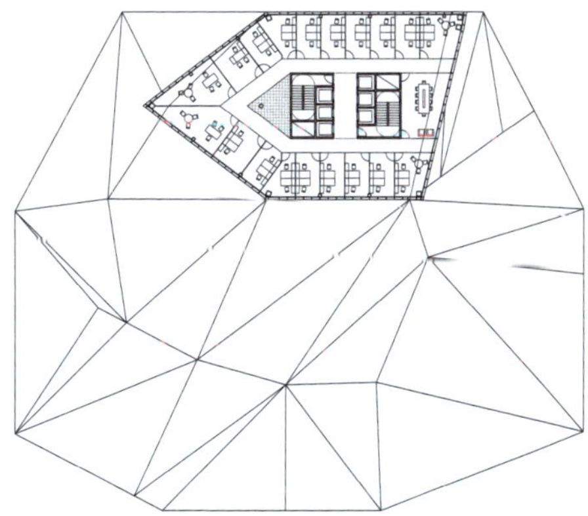

Level 24

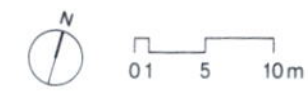

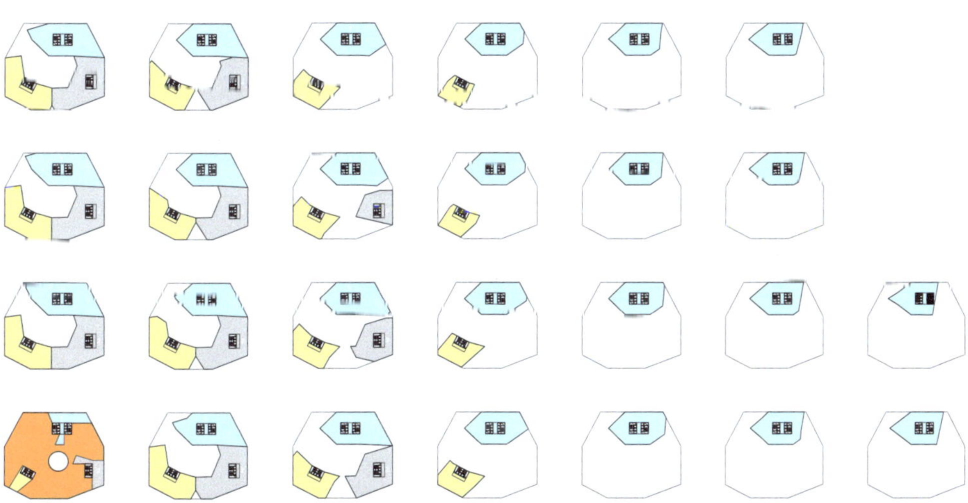

Contemporary Art Museum. Zhuhai, China. 2013-

The design museum takes both the location and the programme as its central theme, introducing a tension between the characteristically solid and closed typology of the museum, and the will to create an unique and festive open space for the museum, that also emerges onto the exterior of the building, turning it into a panoramic observation deck. A contrast is established between an open space or landscape and a protective building wrapped around a series of central patios. This duality produces the seed of a new museum prototype, not only adapted to local climatic conditions but also responding to the need to offer new ways of bringing culture closer to China's new middle classes. This duality or compositional contrast becomes an opportunity to try out new air conditioning techniques, based precisely on the interaction between one or the other type of space in the building's composition.

ZHUHAI
珠海市
1
2
MACAO
澳門

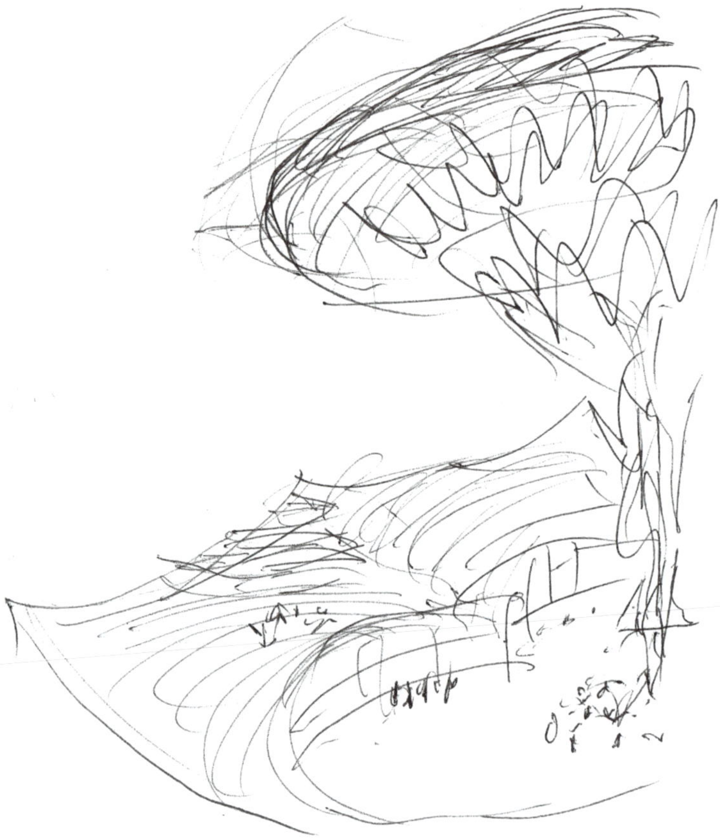

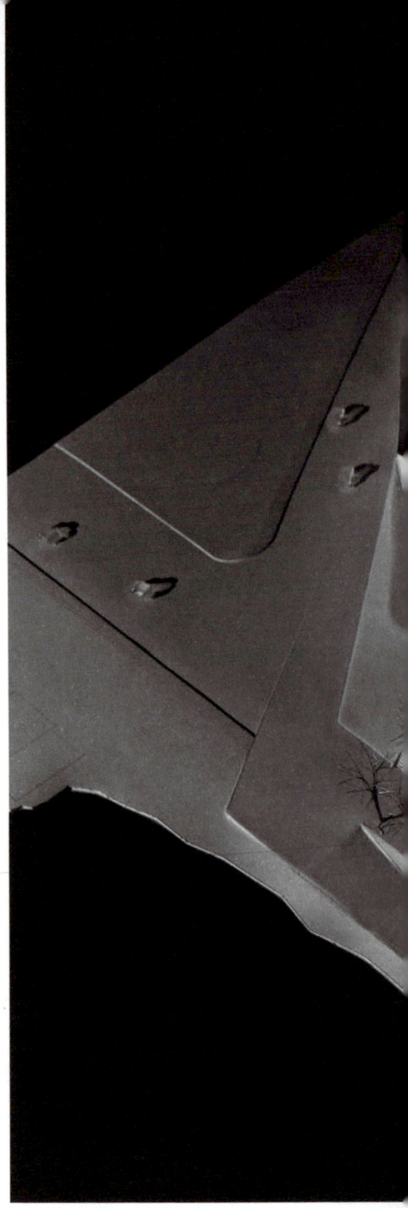

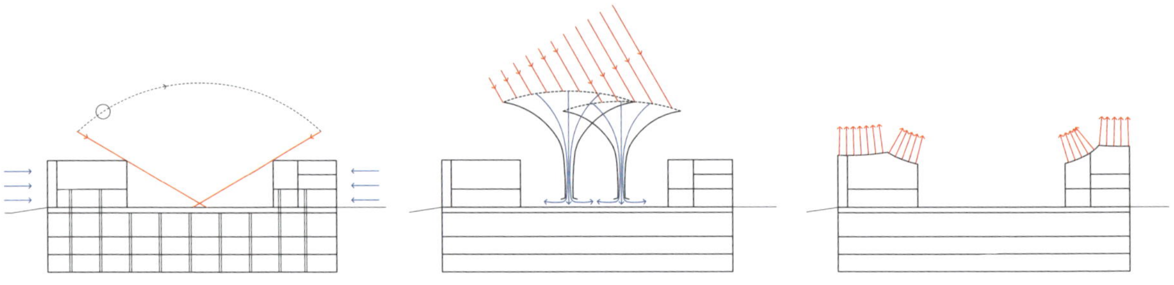

1. **Courtyard and extension of the parking structure.** Protection against damp and strong winds. Limited shade.

2. **Tree awning.** Efficient shade. Atmospheric radiative cooling. Water collector. Convective flow toward the patio. Fresh and dry air.

3. **Waves.** Underground mass stabilizes temperature. Radiative cooling at night. Dehumidification by concrete (porous material).

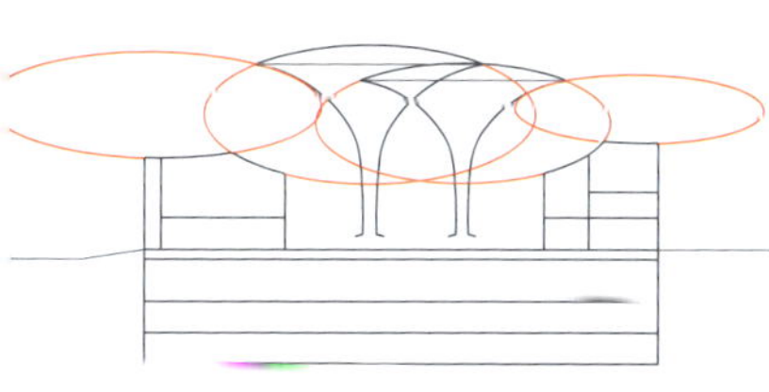

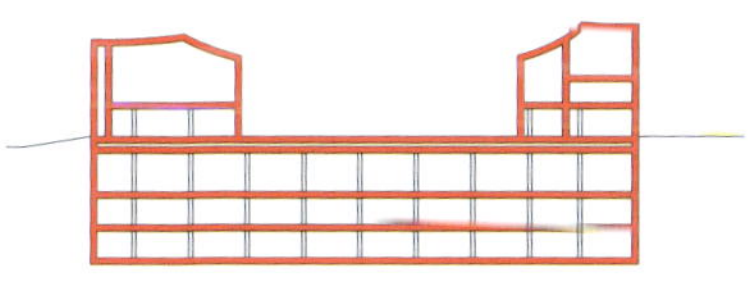

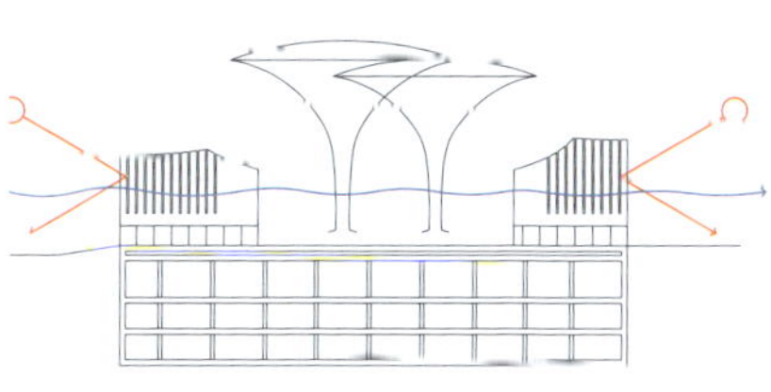

4. **Bubbles.** Spatial unit. Virtual and unified experience in external environments.

5. **Thermal mass.** The conductivity of concrete uses the stable temperature of the ground as a passive measure. The external cladding of white concrete reflects direct sunlight.

6. **Cross-ventilation.** The fluted windows minimize solar gain and allow natural ventilation by preventing exposure to direct sunlight.

Artificial Trees

Six artificial convective trees are arranged inside the patio, controlling the dew, humidity and sunlight to cool and dry the space (like trees' natural behaviour; the dragon tree obtains its nourishment from night-time condensation). The trees act as a thermodynamic mechanism to significantly extend the number of hours of passive comfort throughout the year through various cooling methods.

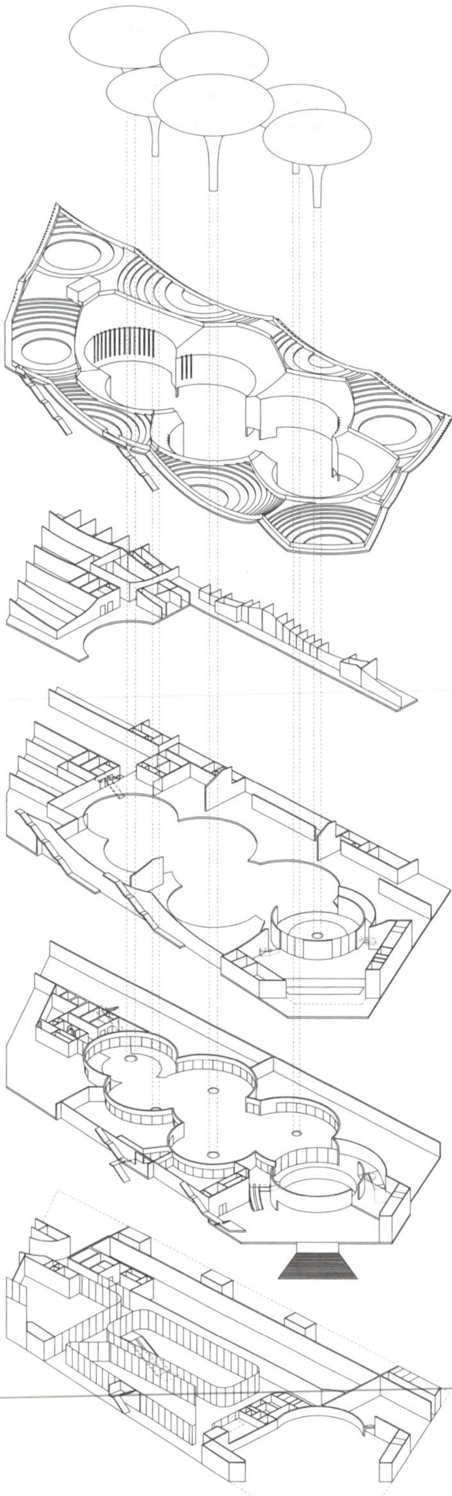

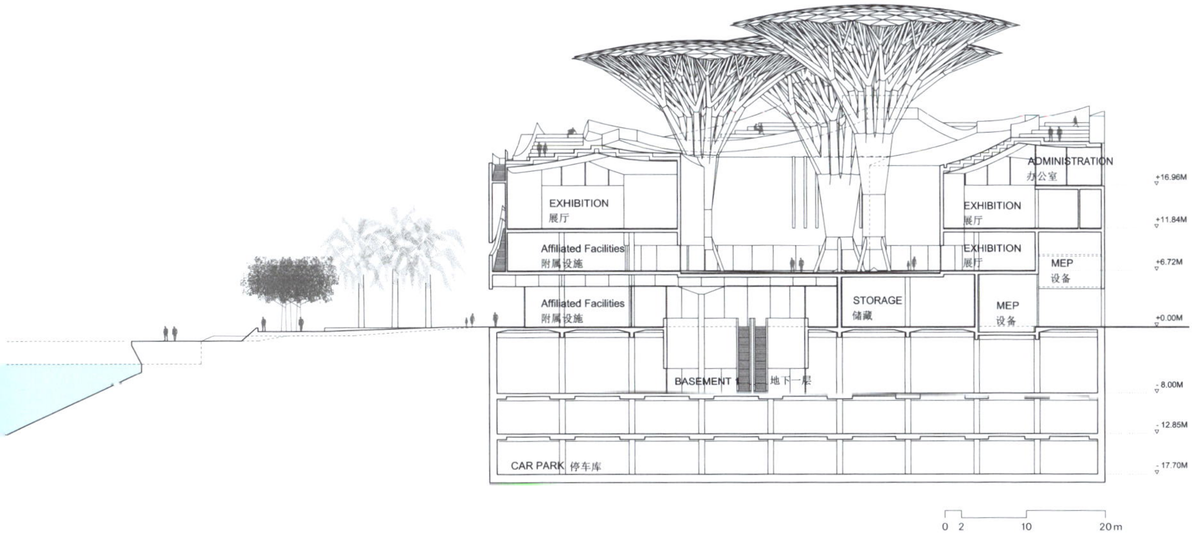
ADMINISTRATION
办公室
EXHIBITION
展厅
Affiliated Facilities
附属设施
EXHIBITION
展厅
EXHIBITION
展厅
MEP
设备
Affiliated Facilities
附属设施
STORAGE
储藏
MEP
设备
BASEMENT 1 地下一层
CAR PARK 停车库
+16.96M
+11.84M
+6.72M
+0.00M
-8.00M
-12.85M
-17.70M
0 2 10 20m

Form

The vertical composition of the tree is divided into levels that emerge from the base of the tree, levels one to four and the rooftop surface. The number of structural branches increases at each level, so that the height increases with a 1:2 ratio at the first two levels and 1:3 at the last two. The resulting process ranges from 10 branches at level one, 20 at level two, 60 at level three, and finally 180 at level 4. The rate of forking will be used to precisely calculate a balance between the branches' diameters.

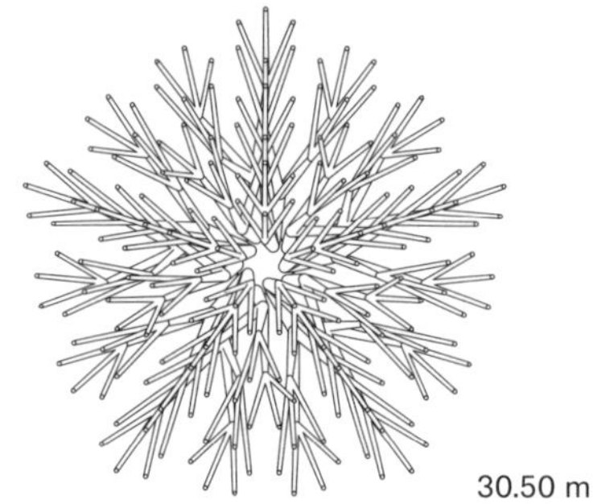

Materials

Fed by its thermal mass, stainless steel is one of the few metals that can handle the corrosive conditions of coastal sites. It is one of the densest metals, and also one of the worst conductors of energy. Therefore it has a very high capacity for storing heat during daily fluctuations in temperature.

Flow

The thermodynamic trees' three cooling effects are:

- Radiative Cooling Downshaft (RCD) (night-time). The tree crowns' surface is cooled by atmospheric radiation. These surfaces then cool the air around them, and gravity drags this heavier air toward the inside of the tree, creating a downward air flow.
- Evaporative Cooling Downshaft (ECD) (daytime). The condensation within the tree evaporates, humidifies and cools the air, creating a downward air flow.
- Solar Upshaft (SU) (daytime). The sun heats the surface of the crown. The air in contact with the tree's surface heats up, creating an upward air flow, sucking up the tree's air.

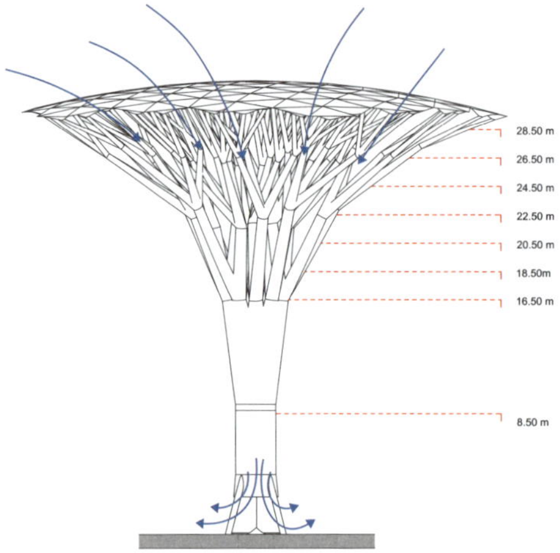

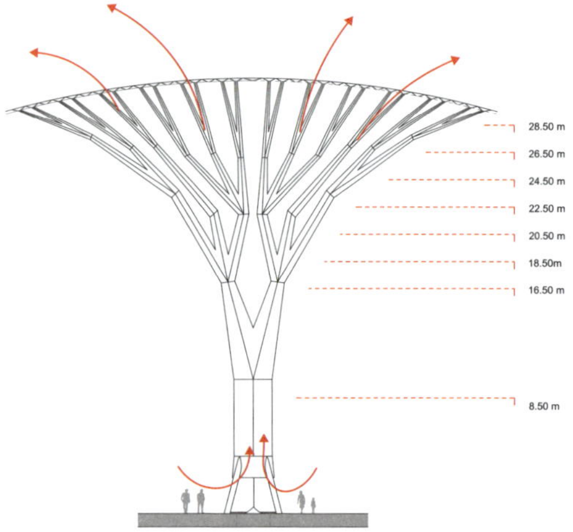

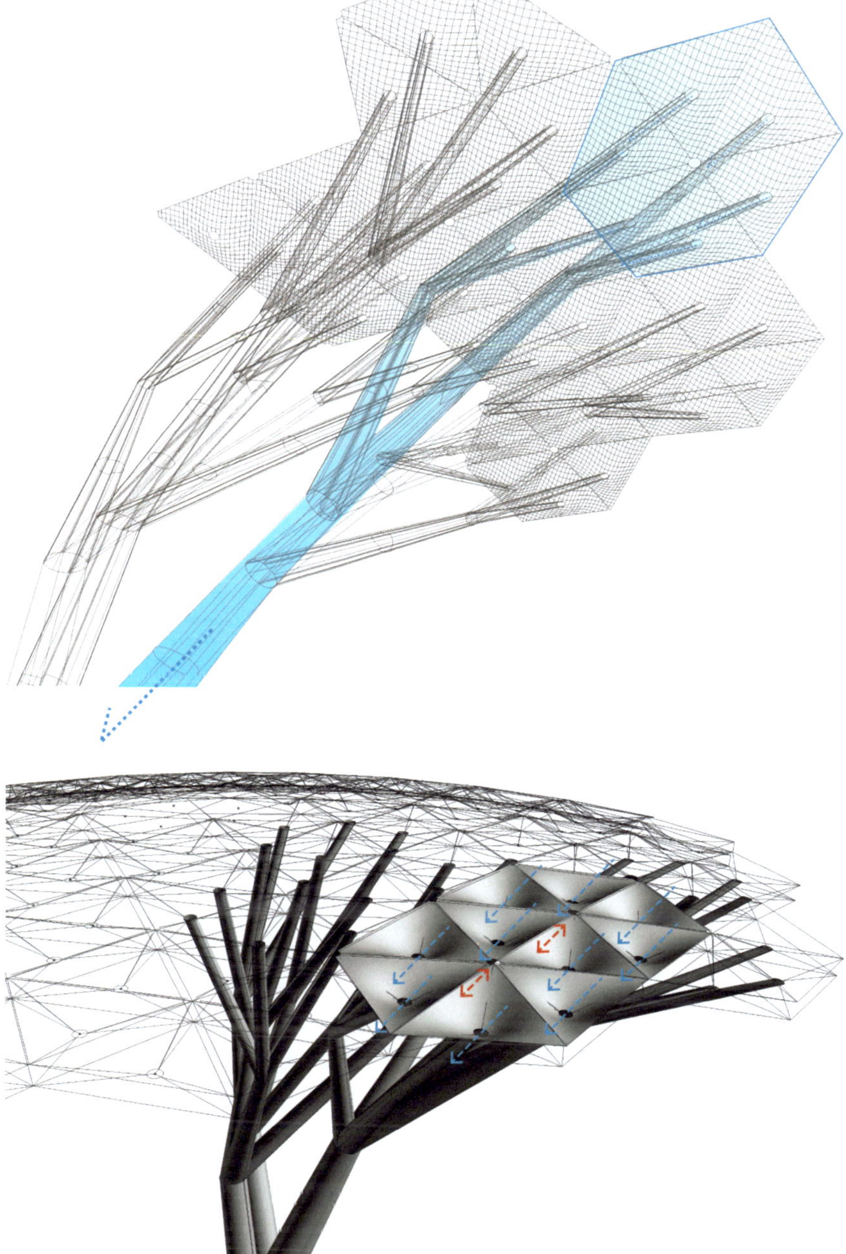

Rainwater and Dew Harvesting
During the monsoon season, the crown channels rainfall along the hollow branches and the trunk to the storage level of water underneath the patio. This water is kept cool and is used in the summer. During cloudless and humid nights, the crown's surface becomes cooler than dew point due to the atmospheric radiative cooling. The vapour condenses on the crown like dewdrops, which link up, run along the hollow branches and flow down the trunk. Our experiments have shown that this can produce up to half a litre of dew per square meter, per night.

Lugar de Lutos, año 793.

Mendaza, invierno de 1834.

Ante la mesa del rey, Las Navas de Tolosa, verano de 1212.

Mirando hacia el campamento de Peña Redonda, Numancia, 133 a J.C.

Ocaña, 19 de noviembre de 1809.

Hacia el desfiladero de Valcarlos, Roncesvalles, 778.

Sagunto, primavera del 219 a J.C.

Entre Toro y Peleagonzalo, primero de marzo de 1476.

Próximos del castillo de Ucles, año 1108.

Puente de fierro, Villalar de los Comuneros, primavera de 1521.

Images from the series *Battlefields,* donated by Bleda and Rosa

Battlefields. Masters' at the Laboratory of Contemporary Techniques and Landscapes, ETSAM. 2002–2003 (Research) / Colegio de Arquitectos de Cataluña (COAC), Barcelona. 2004 (Exhibition)

A battlefield is a sudden, instantaneous discharge of energy (a deployment of fluids and energy) that catalyses all temporal projections on a place. Its cultural impact is the same as that of a volcanic eruption on geology, irreversibly polarizing space and time. And just as a single volcano can become a natural monument or create a national park (for example, Las Cañadas del Teide, Timanfaya and the Caldera de Taburiente in Spain), major battles can produce monuments that are simultaneously natural and artificial, not only because of the projection of memory and culture onto the territory but also because, in the absence of physical traces, the site's geography and ecology (which were strategic at some point in history) become elements in which we stage a space of re-enactment that can convey and evoke this instant discharge of energy in terms of landscape.

Detail of *The Surrender of Breda* (1634) by Velázquez

Theoretical model of a battle

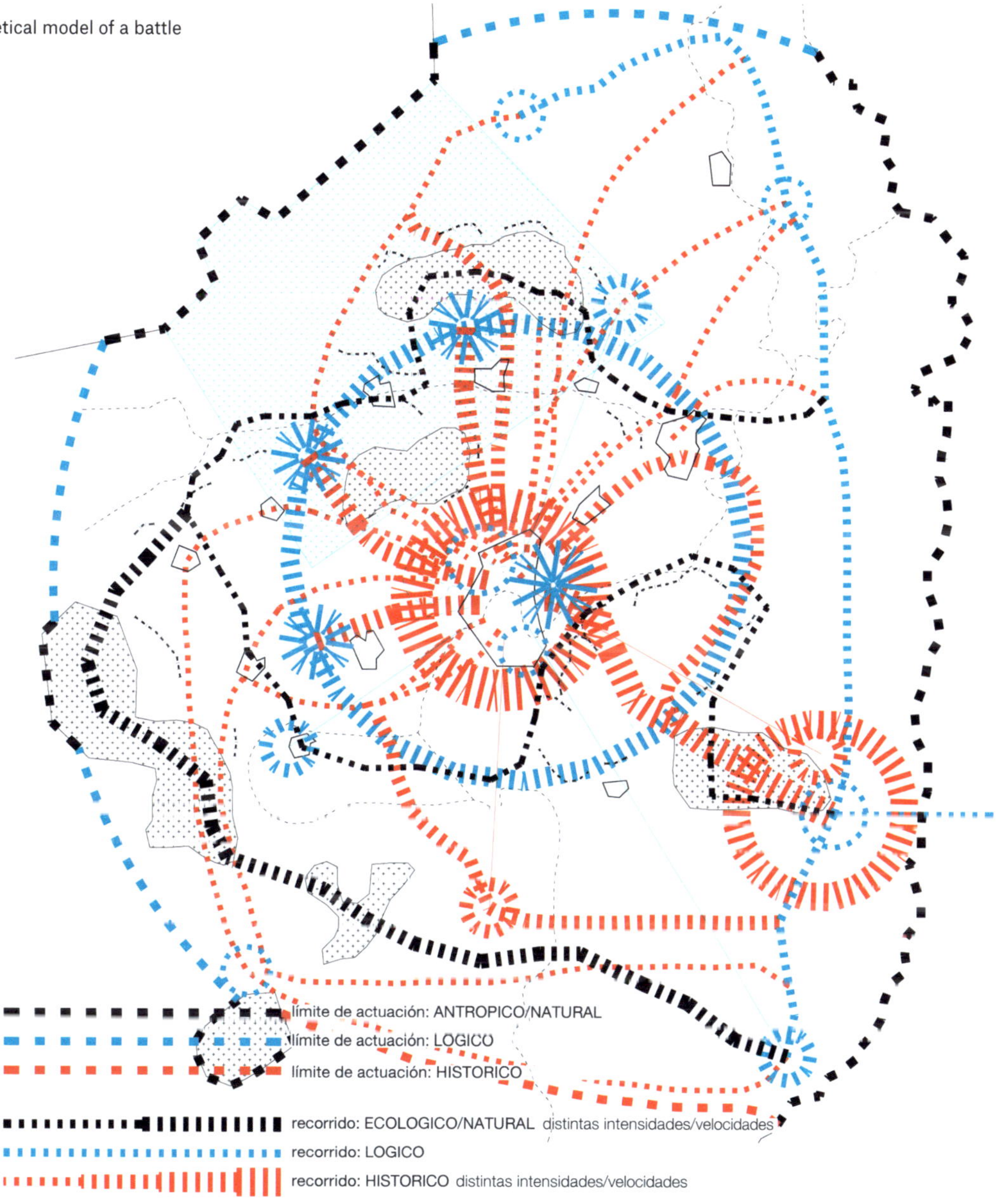

Catalogue of Iberian Battlefield Landscapes

Together with the battlefields, the Iberian peninsula's landscapes are essential objects in the network. We developed a (subjective) tool for selecting landscapes, which we may be able to use to define, applying various criteria, the minimum and maximum number of landscapes that could belong to the network. This produced a catalogue with which to build sequenced spectra of landscapes on the Iberian Peninsula that, like a film, could explain the character of a specific route.

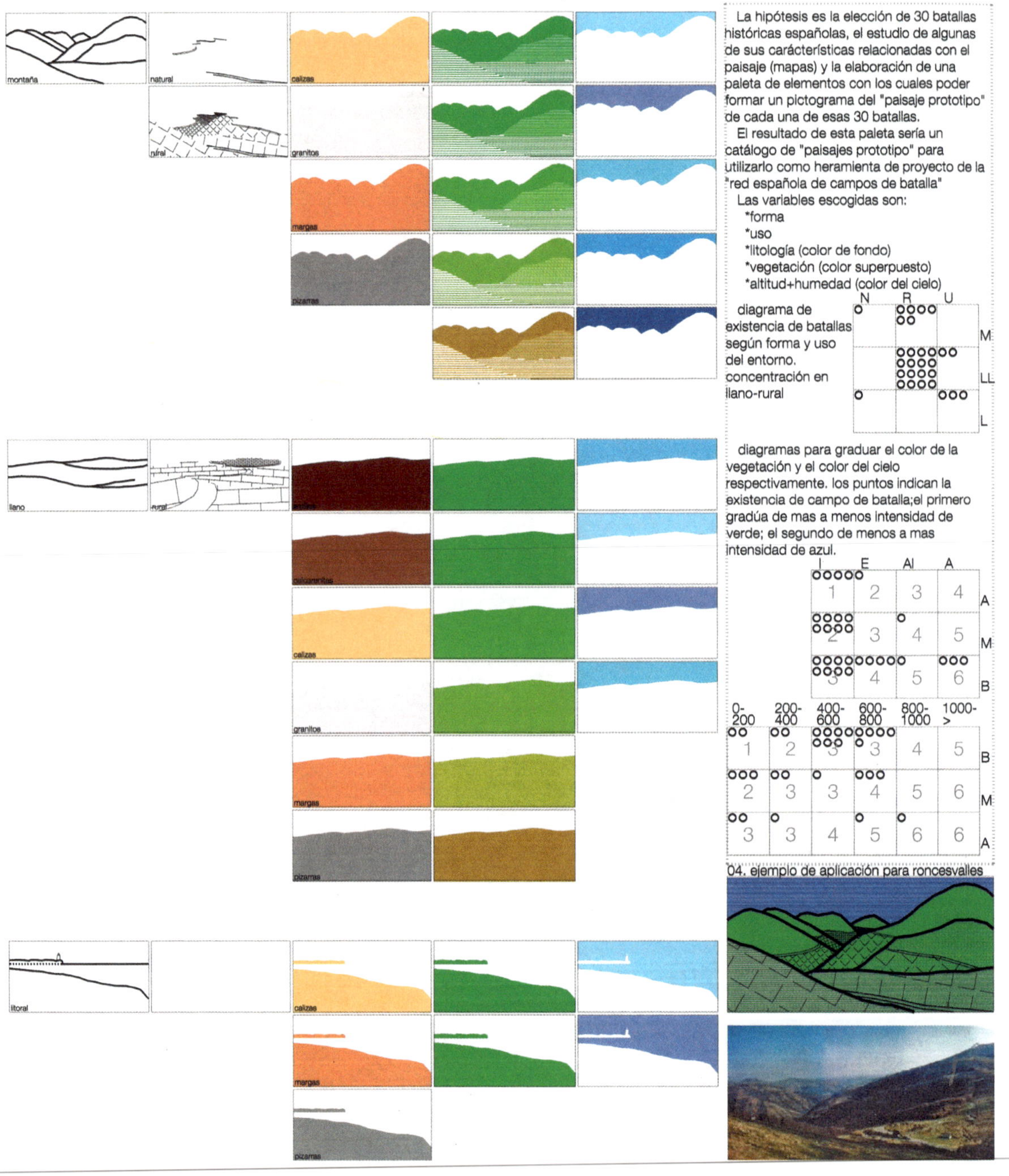

01. numancia, s.II a.c

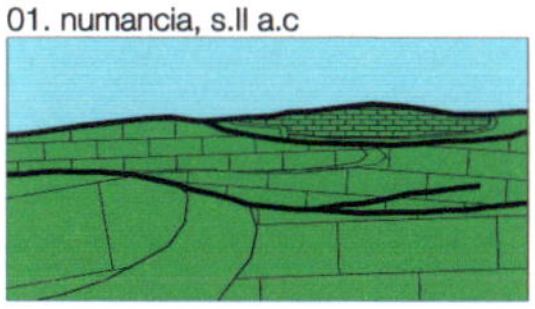

02. guadalete, 711

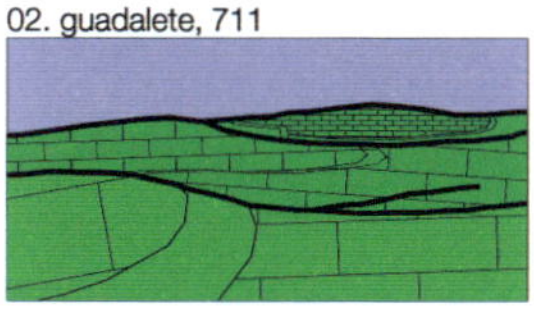

03. covadonga, 722

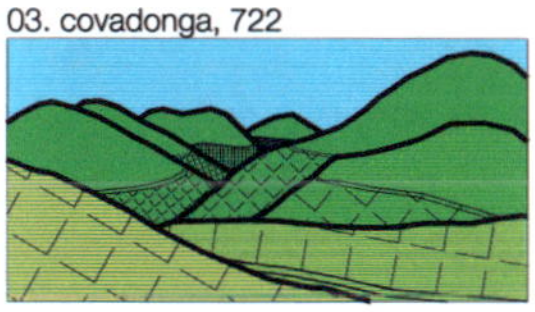

04. roncesvalles, 778

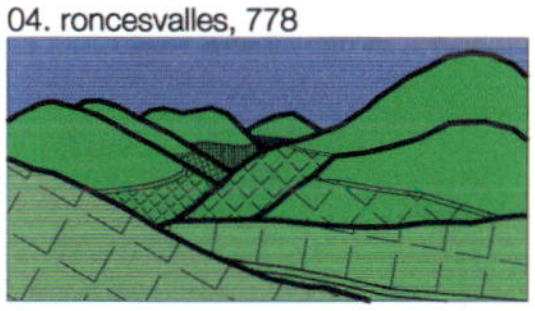

05. clavijo, 859

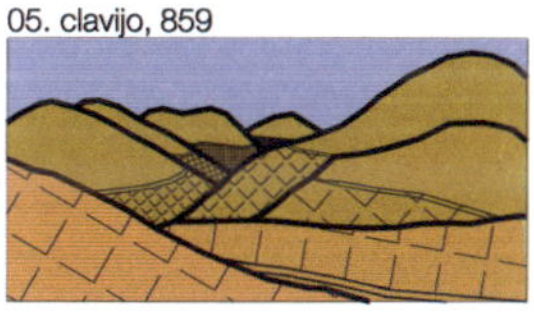

06. nájera, 1367

07. rebelión:`umar ibn hafsun`, 880-917

08. saqueo de santiago, 997

09. calatañazor, 1000-1002

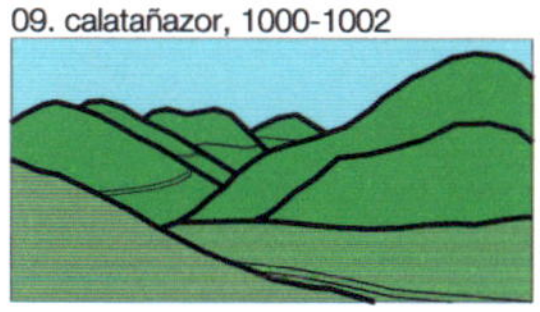

10. sagrajas, 1086

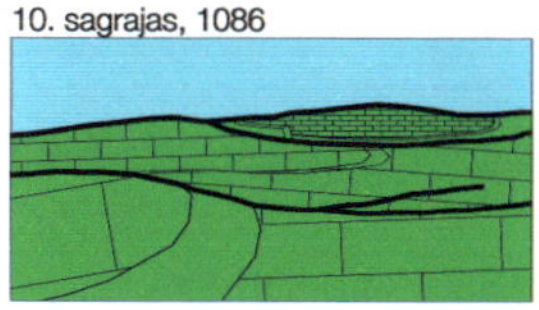

11. alarcos, 1197

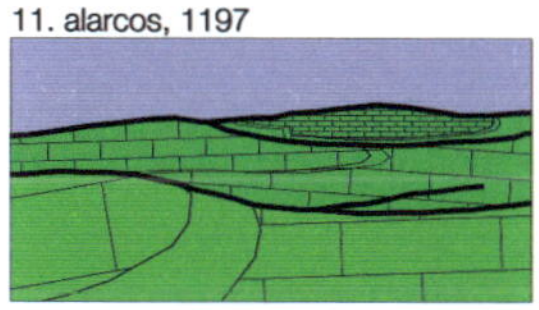

12. las navas de tolosa, 1212

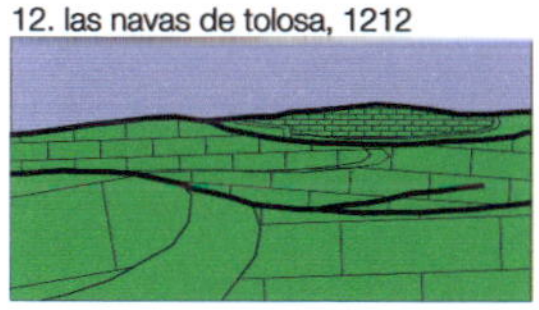

13. conquista de mallorca, 1229

14. el salado, 1340

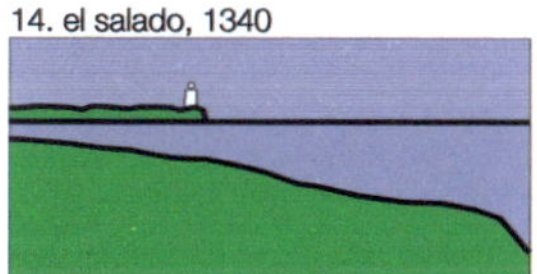

15. trafalgar, 1805

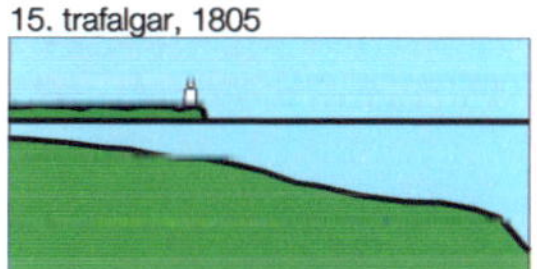

16. conquista de granada, 1491-1492

17. toro, 1476

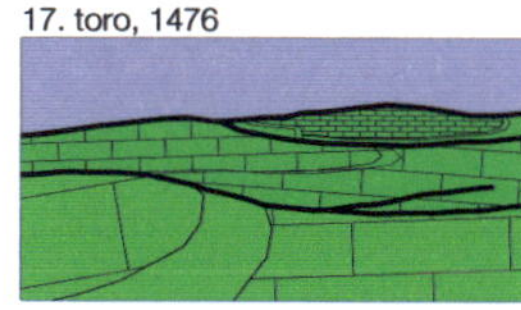

18. villalar de los comuneros, 1520

19. menorca, 1708-1782 y 1798-1802

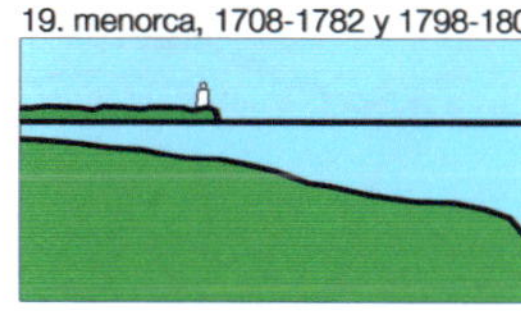

20. almansa, 1707

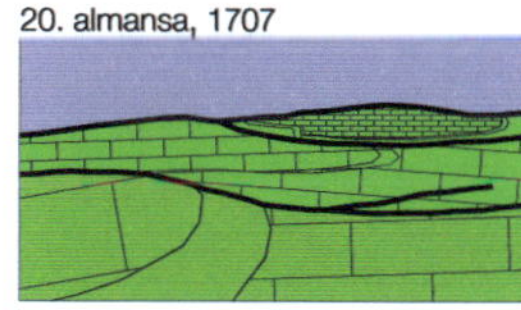

21. brihuega y villaviciosa,1710

22. bailén, 1808

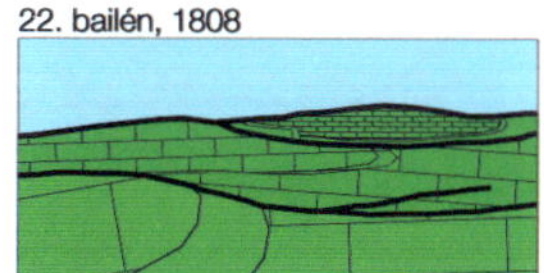

23. bruc, 1808

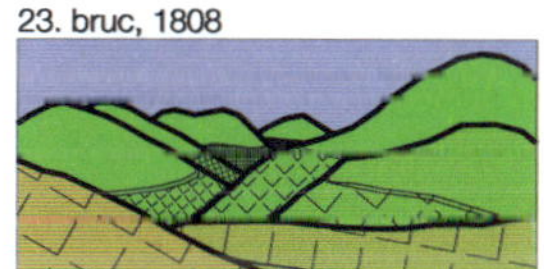

24. talavera de la reina, 1809

25. puente del arzobispo, 1809

26. vitoria y san marcial, 1813

27. retuerta, 1837

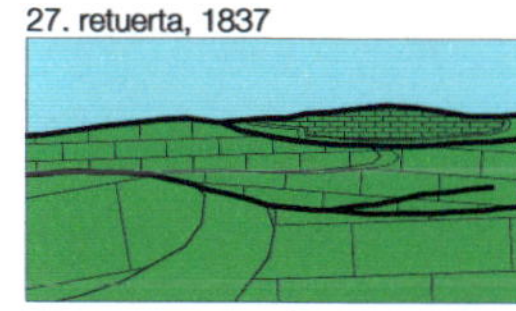

28. el maestrazgo, 1835-1840

29. el ebro, 1938

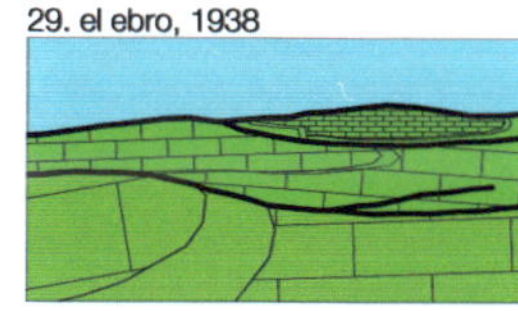

30. madrid, 1939

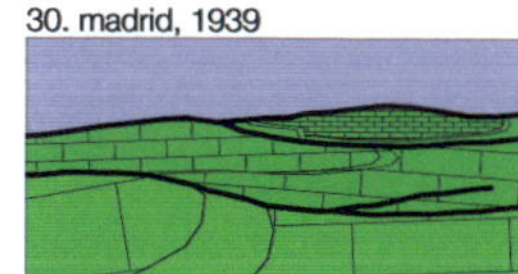

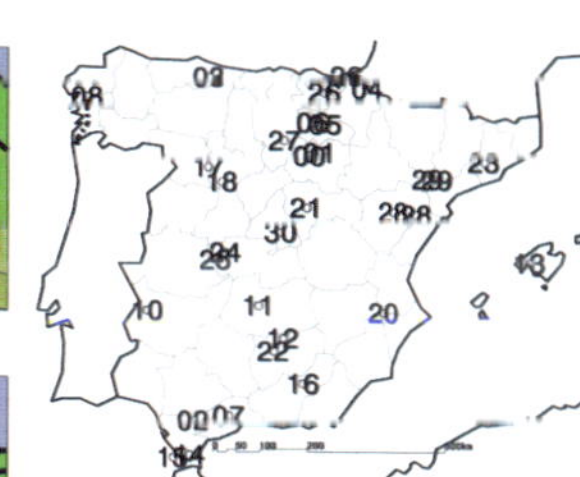

catálogo de paisajes de batallas ibéricas

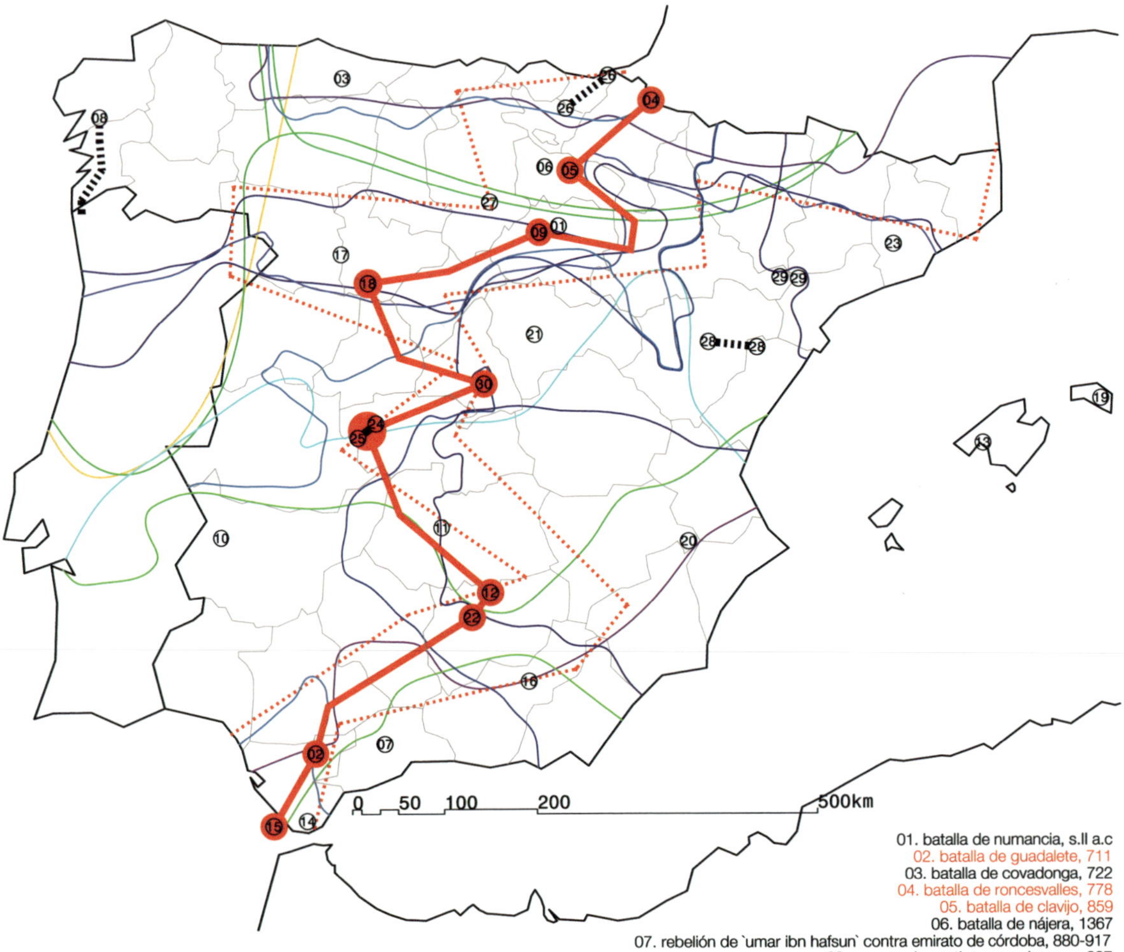

01. batalla de numancia, s.II a.c
02. batalla de guadalete, 711
03. batalla de covadonga, 722
04. batalla de roncesvalles, 778
05. batalla de clavijo, 859
06. batalla de nájera, 1367
07. rebelión de `umar ibn hafsun` contra emirato de córdoba, 880-917
08. saqueo de santiago por almarzor, 997
09. victoria ficticia sobre almanzor en calatañazor, 1000-1002
10. batalla de sagrajas, inauguración del período almorávide, 1086
11. batalla de alarcos, 1197
12. batalla de las navas de tolosa, 1212
13. conquista de mallorca por jaime I, 1229
14. batalla de el salado, 1340
15. batalla de trafalgar, 1805
16. conquista de granada, 1491-1492
17. batalla de toro, 1476
18. batalla de villalar de los comuneros, 1520
19. dominación inglesa en menorca, 1708-1782 y 1798-1802
20. batalla de almansa, 1707
21. batallas de brihuega y villaviciosa,1710
22. batalla de bailén, 1808
23. batalla de bruc, 1808
24. batalla de talavera de la reina, 1809
25. batalla del puente del arzobispo, 1809
26. batalla de vitoria, incendio de san sebastian y batalla de san marcial, 1813
27. batalla de retuerta, 1837
28. campañas de cabrera en el maestrazgo, 1835-1840
29. batalla del ebro, 1938
30. batalla de madrid, 1939

Spinal Cord. Lower limit of the battlefield network

By adding the first and second planes of action, we find the lower limit of the interval of the battlefield network—the minimum number of battlefields that make the network meaningful. For this we used the two aforementioned tools: through a subjective (pictorial) analysis of the battlefield landscapes, we obtained a tool that helps us decided which battlefields within the zone of "greatest danger" are going to form the minimum number of battlefields. Therefore we decided that two battlefields with a similar landscape cannot coexist with this group, thus ensuring the "exclusive landscape" of each element making up the lower limit of the battlefield network.

15. trafalgar, 1805

T C

Batalla táctica de persecución. Guerra entre la Francia napoleónica (con España como aliada) e Inglaterra por el dominio de Europa.

12. las navas de tolosa, 1212

D C

Batalla decisiva de combate. Batalla definitiva con victoria cristiana sobre los almohades.

02. guadalete, 711

D C

Batalla decisiva de combate. Batalla que dio pie a la ocupación árabe de la península, y casi 8 siglos de civilización islámica en Al-Ándalus.

04. roncesvalles, 778

M S

Batalla mítica de escaramuza. Emboscada librada por los vascones sobre el ejército de Carlomagno en su retirada a través de este paso natural.

05. clavijo, 859

M C

Batalla mítica de combate. Victoria de Ramiro I sobre Abd al Rahmán II, con la supuesta intervención de Santiago.

09. calatañazor, 1000-1002

M C

Batalla mítica de combate. Inexistente derrota de Almanzor en su regreso hacia Medinaceli.

18. villalar de los comuneros, 1520

D C

Batalla decisiva de combate. Derrota comunera a manos del Conde de Haro, resultando prisioneros Padilla, Bravo y Maldonado.

30. madrid, 1939

D C

Batalla decisiva de combate. Levantamiento de la ciudad de Madrid contra la dominación francesa.

22. bailén, 1808

D C

Batalla decisiva de combate. Primera victoria del ejército español sobre las tropas francesas durante la guerra de la Independencia

24. talavera de la reina, 1809

T C

Batalla táctica de combate. Batalla librada por las mejores tropas inglesas, francesas y españolas, en las guerras napoleónicas.

Church in the New Bund District. Pudong, Shanghai, China. 2016-2018

The construction of a church funded by the Shanghai government in the New Bund district is a first in China, a country where the persecution of Christian (and in particular Catholic) communities has made them similar to those built by NGOs in other parts of the world. AS+ was commissioned to integrate ecclesiastical uses into the public space, creating a portal into the district's green areas, at the same time as giving the community new public spaces in the interior and exterior. Because of the metro line, the church sits on a long, narrow strip of land, defining the footprint of the church's nave and using a broad set of stairs to expand the public space to the green roof, the site for a variety of ceremonies. An unbuilt project, the Green House (1997), provided a model for understanding the complex as an organic volume that reconnects all existing parts into the place and creates a landmark in the new urban landscape.

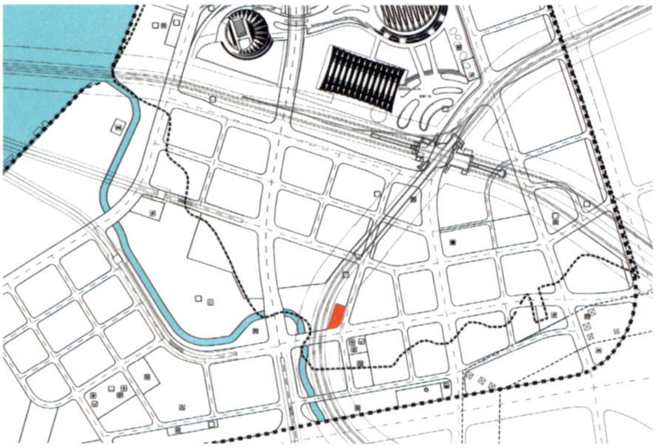

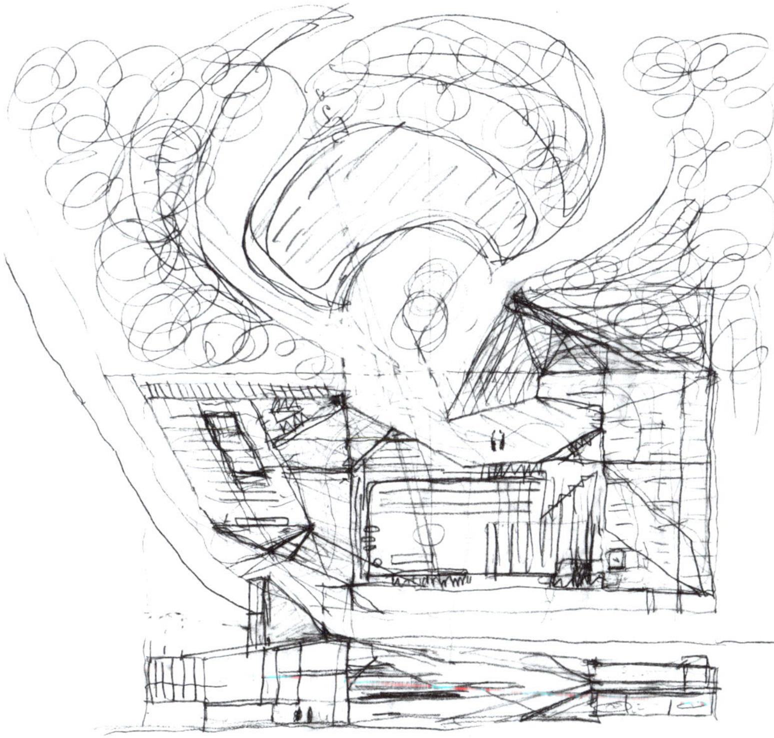

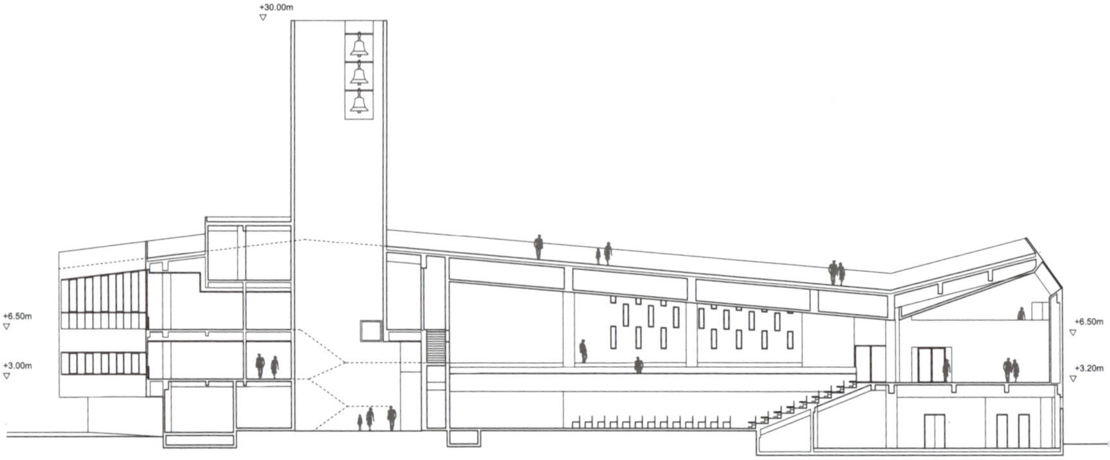
+30.00m
+6.50m
+3.00m
+6.50m
+3.20m

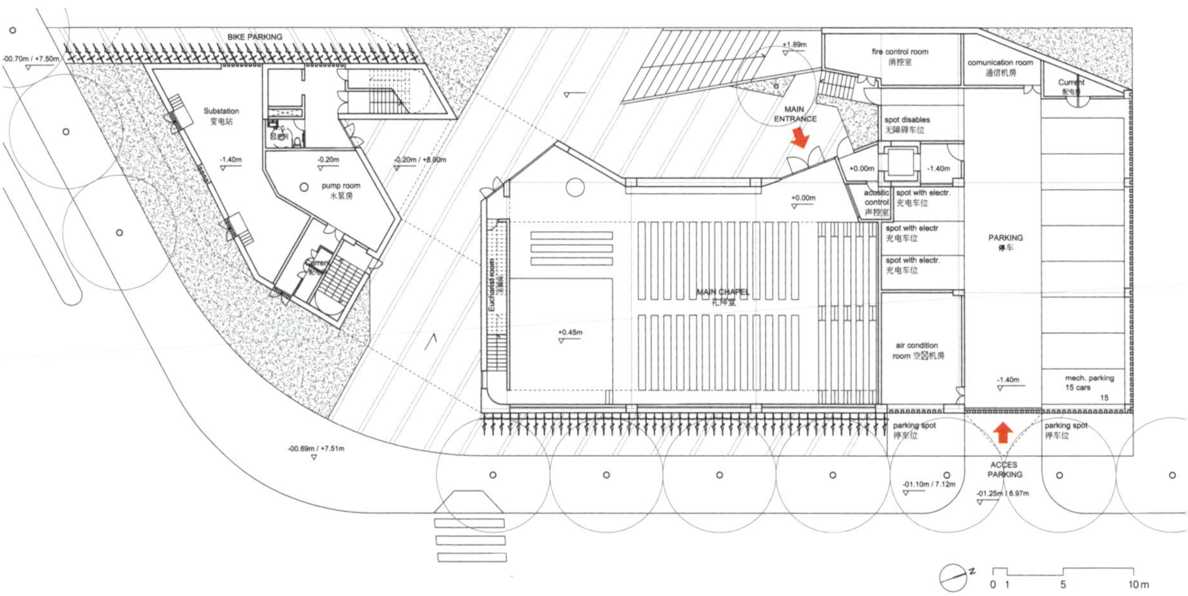
BIKE PARKING
-00.70m / +7.50m
Substation
变电站
-1.40m
-0.20m
pump room
水泵房
-0.20m / +8.00m
+1.89m
MAIN
ENTRANCE
fire control room
消控室
comunication room
通信机房
Current
spot disables
无障碍车位
+0.00m
-1.40m
acustic
control
声控室
spot with electr.
充电车位
+0.00m
spot with electr
充电车位
spot with electr.
充电车位
PARKING
停车
Eucharist room
MAIN CHAPEL
礼拜堂
+0.45m
air condition
room 空调机房
-1.40m
mech. parking
15 cars
15
parking spot
停车位
parking spot
停车位
ACCES
PARKING
-00.69m / +7.51m
-01.10m / 7.12m
-01.25m / 6.97m
0 1 5 10 m

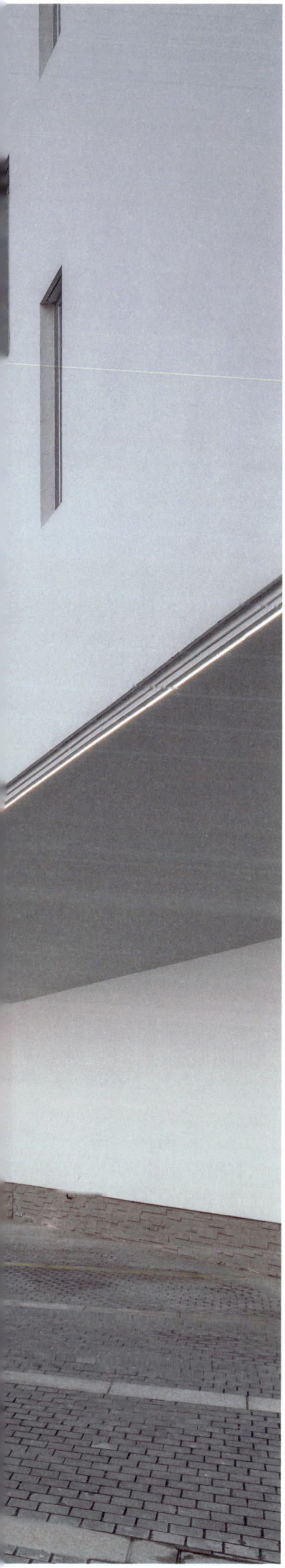

Yangpu Bridge Area Riverside Development Plan. Shanghai, China. 2018–

After competing against five of the largest international architecture firms, our winning proposal is for a new, large-scale, multi-use, 2.5-million-square-meter urban centre by the Huangpu River, near the centre of Shanghai. Our plan had two major points of reference: the bridge and the river (along with the important industrial buildings by the river), with the idea of creating a dual composition for the visual magnetism of the bridge to be reflected in the incline of the three tallest skyscrapers. In plan view, a compositional tension exists between symmetry and organic intrusions, with a route evoking well-known artistic creations, giving structure to this complex programme.

Complementing the composition, the programme's various elements are arranged according to technical criteria, as an open system that forms an ecosystemic metabolism based on the interaction of five sub-systems: a Green System, a Memory System, a Water System, a Knowledge System and an Infrastructure System, turning this area into a cohesive urban system controlled by flows of matter, energy and information that meet all current environmental requirements (Sponge City, Smart City, Near-Zero Emissions...), while adding order, rhythm, integration, memory and urban structure.

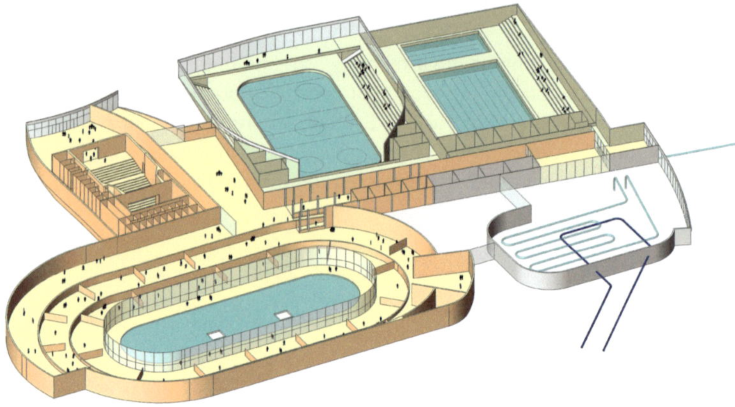

1. **Water System**
   - Public Centre for Water Infrastructure + Washrooms + District Cooling System

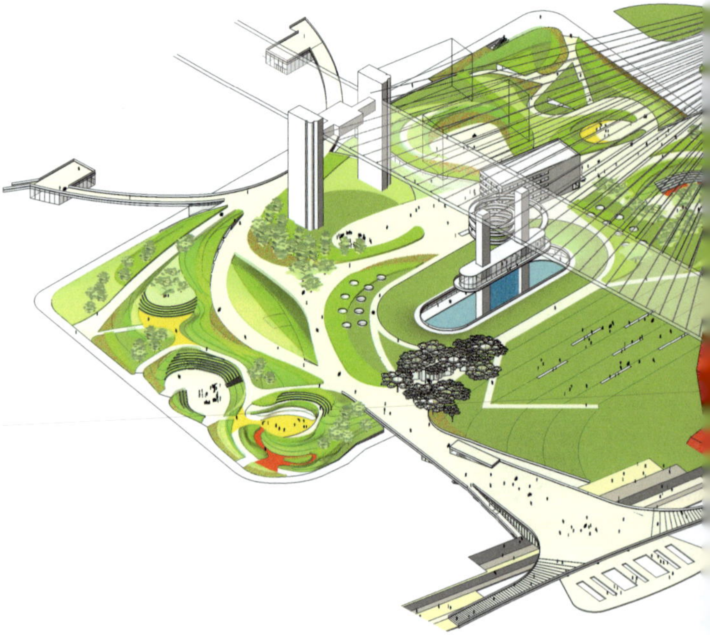

4. Knowledge System
   - Block M2-1 and M3-1. Technological Innovation and Creativity Zone

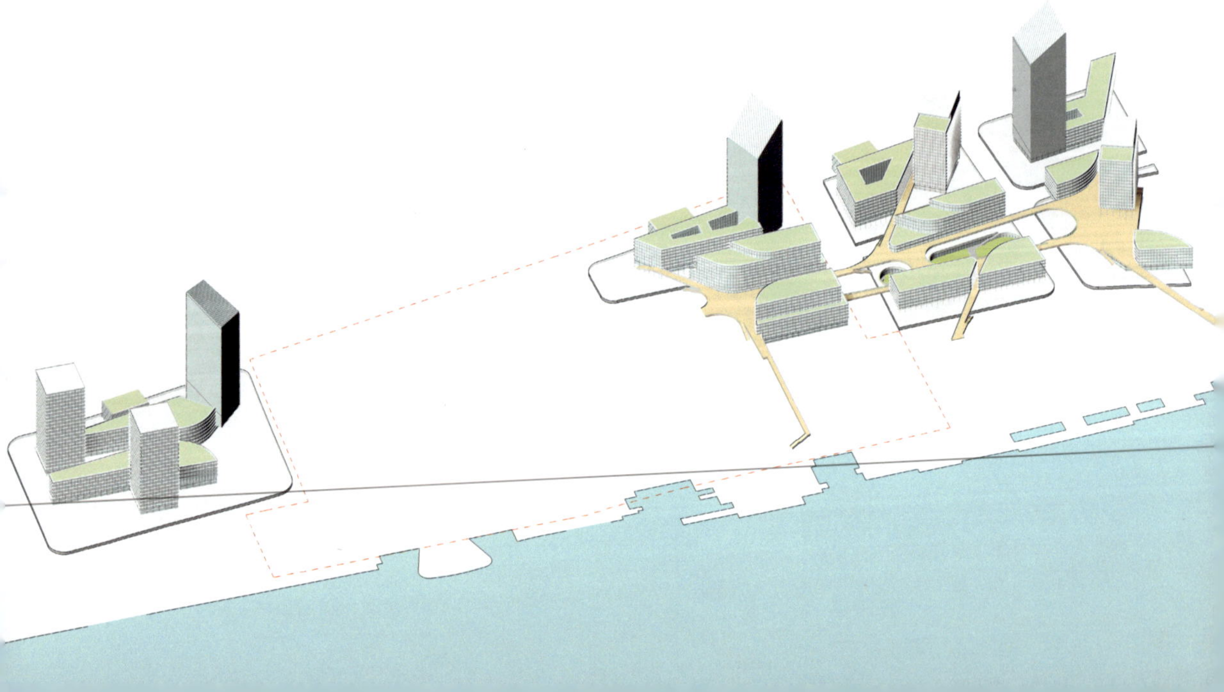

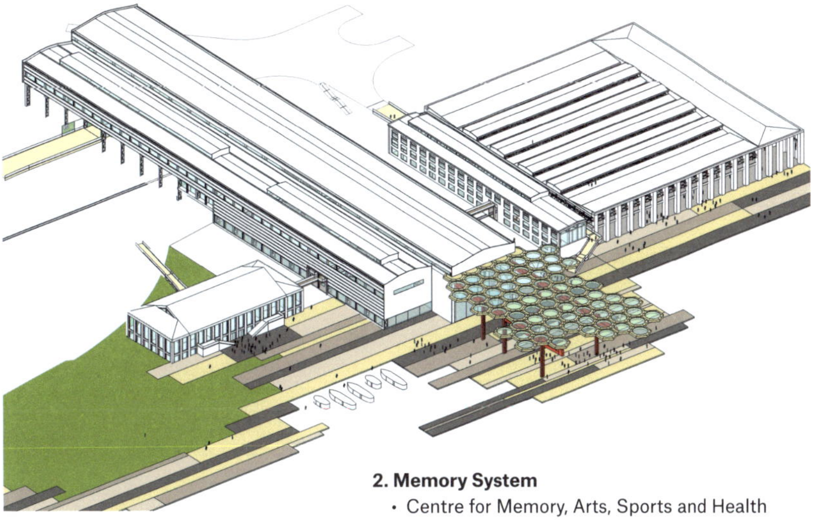

2. Memory System

- Centre for Memory, Arts, Sports and Health

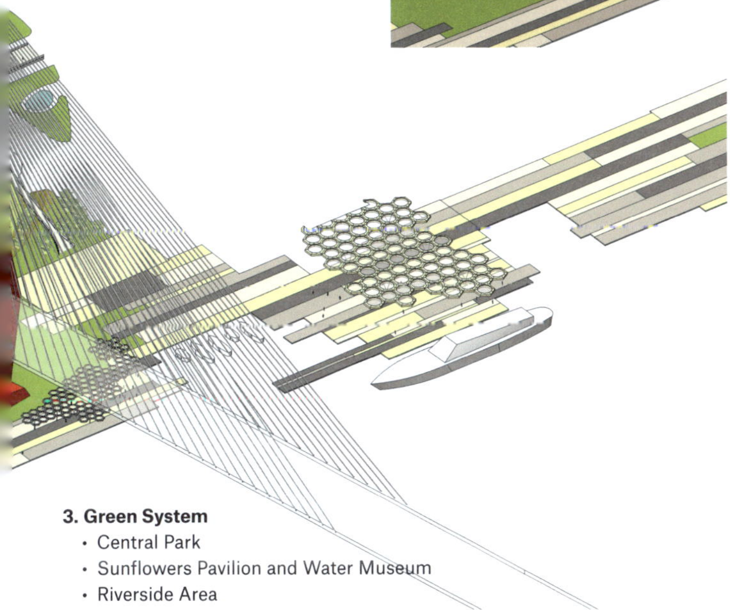

5. Infrastructure System

- Ningguo Road Ferry Station and underground pedestrian connections
- Photovoltaic solar installation
- District Cooling closed-loop system

3. Green System

- Central Park
- Sunflowers Pavilion and Water Museum
- Riverside Area

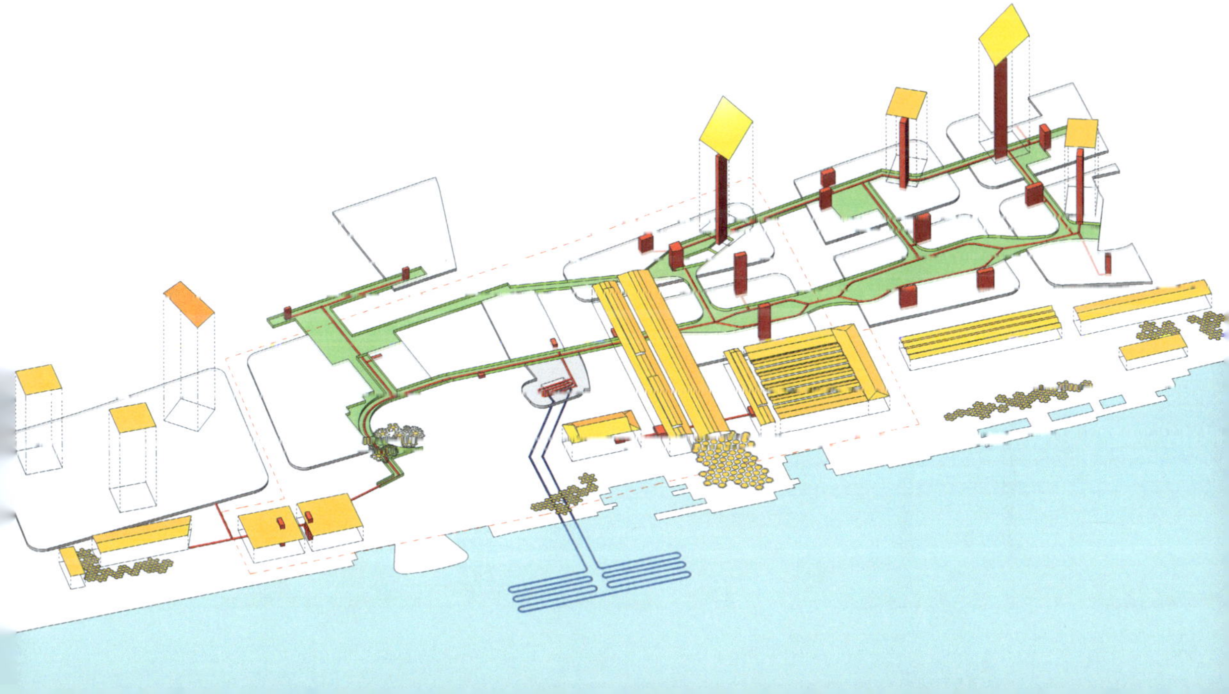

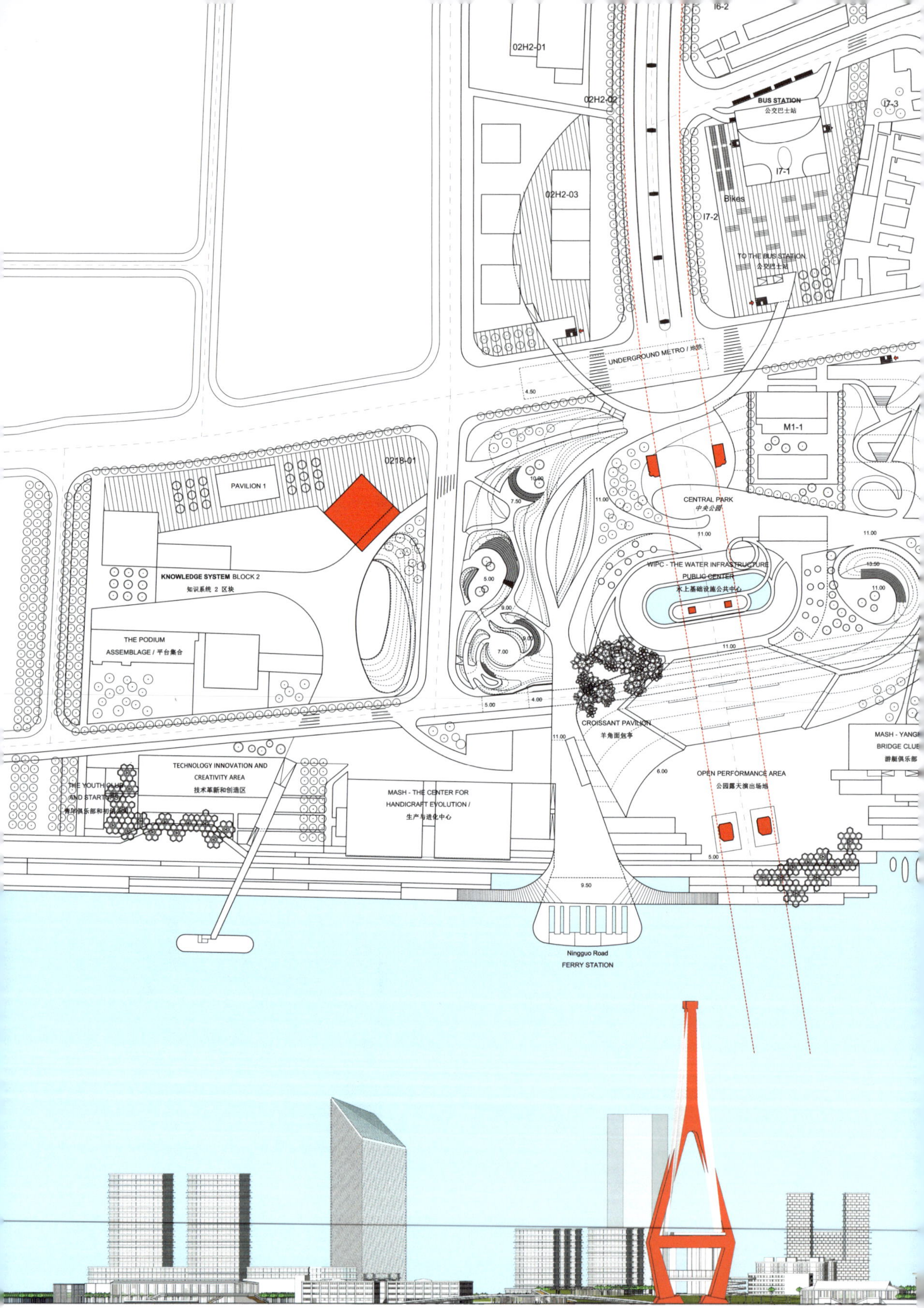
I6-2
02H2-01
02H2-02
BUS STATION
公交巴士站
I7-3
I7-1
02H2-03
Bikes
I7-2
TO THE BUS STATION
公交巴士站
UNDERGROUND METRO / 地铁
4.50
M1-1
0218-01
PAVILION 1
10.00
7.50
11.00
CENTRAL PARK
中央公园
11.00
11.00
KNOWLEDGE SYSTEM BLOCK 2
知识系统 2 区块
5.00
WIPC - THE WATER INFRASTRUCTURE
PUBLIC CENTER
水上基础设施公共中心
13.50
11.00
9.00
THE PODIUM
ASSEMBLAGE / 平台集合
9.00
7.00
11.00
5.00
4.00
CROISSANT PAVILION
羊角面包亭
11.00
MASH - YANG
BRIDGE CLUB
游艇俱乐部
TECHNOLOGY INNOVATION AND
CREATIVITY AREA
技术革新和创造区
6.00
OPEN PERFORMANCE AREA
公园露天演出场地
MASH - THE CENTER FOR
HANDICRAFT EVOLUTION /
生产与进化中心
5.00
9.50
Ningguo Road
FERRY STATION

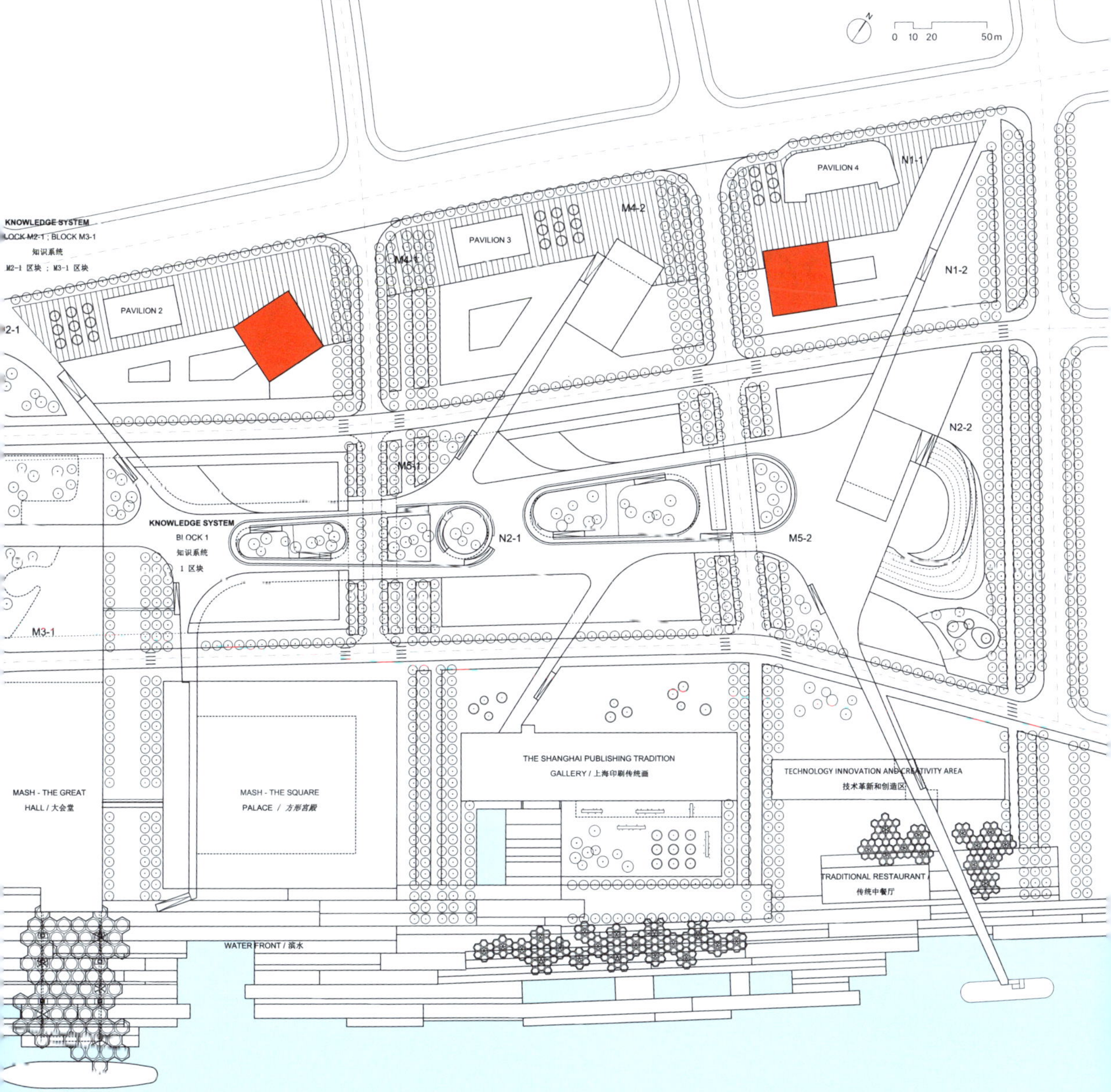
0 10 20 50m
KNOWLEDGE SYSTEM
LOCK M2-1 ; BLOCK M3-1
知识系统
M2-1 区块 ; M3-1 区块
PAVILION 2
PAVILION 3
PAVILION 4
M4-1
M4-2
N1-1
N1-2
N2-2
M5-1
N2-1
M5-2
KNOWLEDGE SYSTEM
BLOCK 1
知识系统
1 区块
M3-1
MASH - THE GREAT
HALL / 大会堂
MASH - THE SQUARE
PALACE / 方形宫殿
THE SHANGHAI PUBLISHING TRADITION
GALLERY / 上海印刷传统画
TECHNOLOGY INNOVATION AND CREATIVITY AREA
技术革新和创造区
TRADITIONAL RESTAURANT /
传统中餐厅
WATER FRONT / 滨水

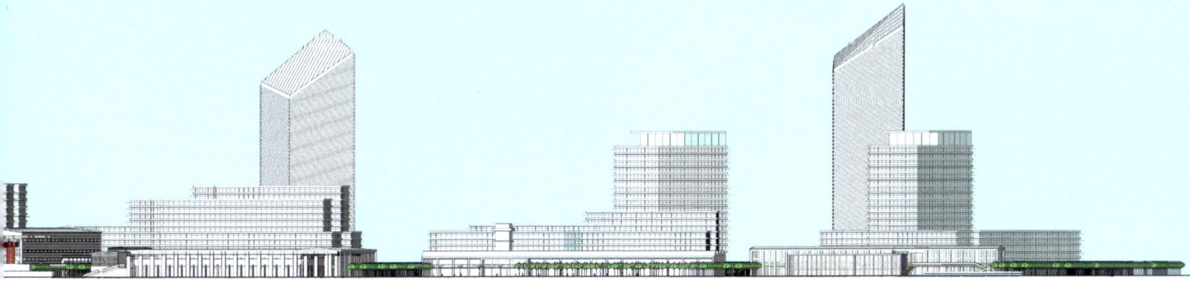

Heritage / 遗产

DETAILED DESIGN SCOPE / 详细设计范畴

BUILDING 1 (B1). THE SQUARE PALACE / *方形宫殿*.

BUILDING 2 (B2). THE CLUB / 游艇俱乐部.

BUILDING 3 (B3). THE GREAT HALL / 大会堂

BUILDING 5 (B5). THE CENTER FOR HANDICRAFT EVOLUTION / 生产与进化中心.

PLANNING RESEARCH SCOPE / 规划研究范围

C1. THE SHANGHAI PUBLISHING TRADITION GALLERY / 上海印刷传统画

F1. THE YOUTH CLUB AND STARTUPS / 青年俱乐部和初创公司

A1,2,3,4. THE FOUR PAVILIONS AT YANGPU ROAD / 杨树浦路沿街四座亭

E1, 2, 3. THE PODIUM ASSEMBLAGE / 平台集合

C2. TRADITIONAL RESTAURANT (CHINESE) / 传统中餐厅

K1, K2. KNOWLEDGE SYSTEM / 知识系统

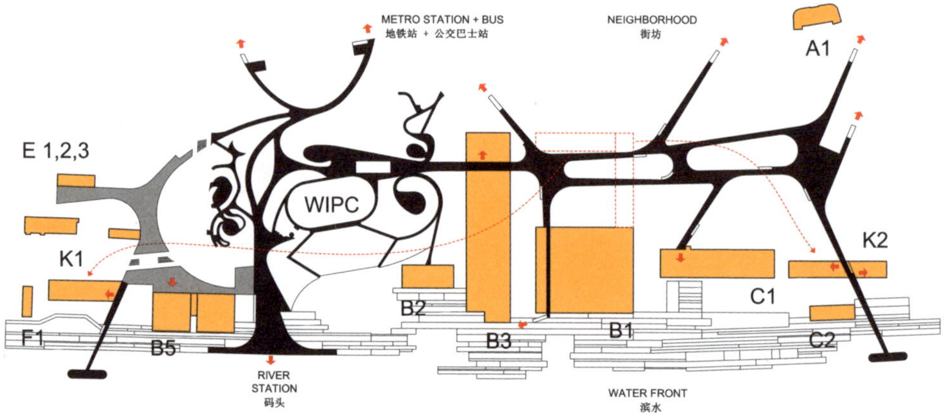

Basement / 地下室

-1

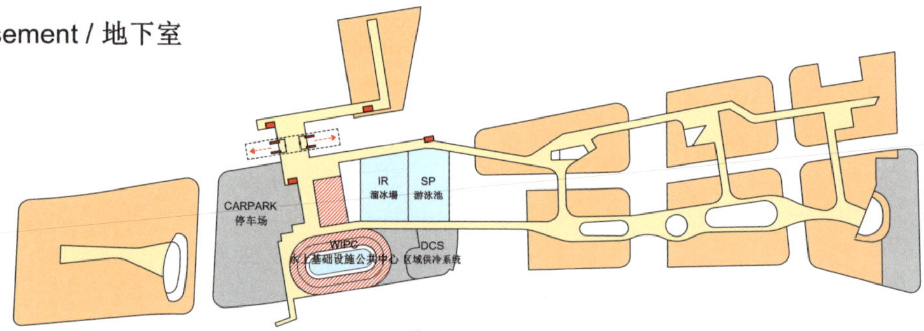

BLOCK 1 / 街区1
(M2-1, M3-1, M4-2, M5-2, N1-1, N2-1)

Commercial / Retail
商业 / 零售

Carpark / 停车场

WATER SYSTEM / 水系统

WIPC / 水上基础设施公共中心

IR / 溜冰場 + SP / 游泳池

DCS / 区域供冷系统

-2

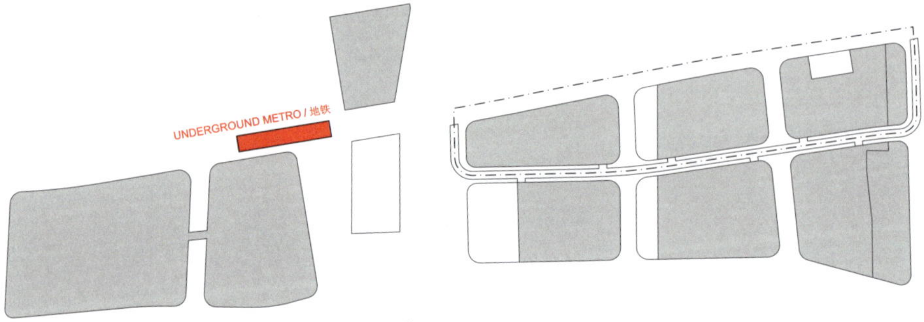

BLOCK 1 / 街区1
(M2-1, M3-1, M4-2, M5-2, N1-1, N2-1)
Carpark / 停车场

-3

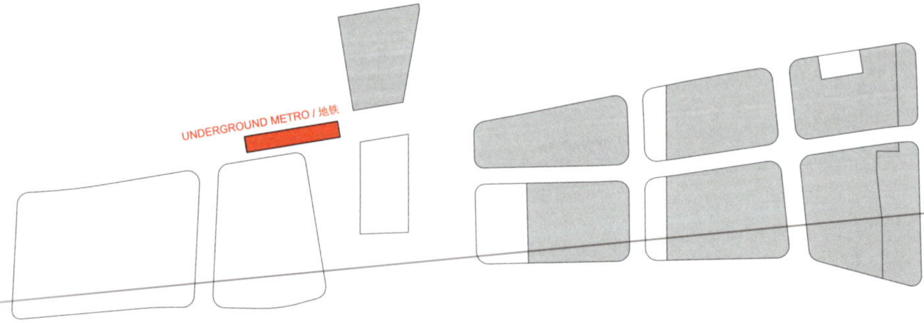

BLOCK 1 / 街区1
(M2-1, M3-1, M4-2, M5-2, N1-1, N2-1)
Carpark / 停车场

Towers / 塔

BLOCK 2 (02I8-01)
- Business Offices
- Science and Technology Innovation
- Creative and Cultural Spaces
- Finance Activities
- Science and Technology Spaces
- +Specific program for the elderly

号街区 2 (02I8-01)
- 商务办公
- 科技创新空间
- 创意与文化空间
- 金融活动
- 科技空间

MIXED USE / 混合功能 (02H2-03)
Residencial + Office Space
居住和办公空间

MIXED USE / 混合功能 (16-3)
Residencial + Office Space 居住和办公空间

MIXED USE / 混合功能 (17-1)
HUB + PIAZZA / 合的中枢和广场：
Two Towers - Studios + Small offices + Showrooms / 两座塔：工作室+小型办公+展示间
Curved Slab - Small Officces + Startup / 波形板：小型办公和初创公司

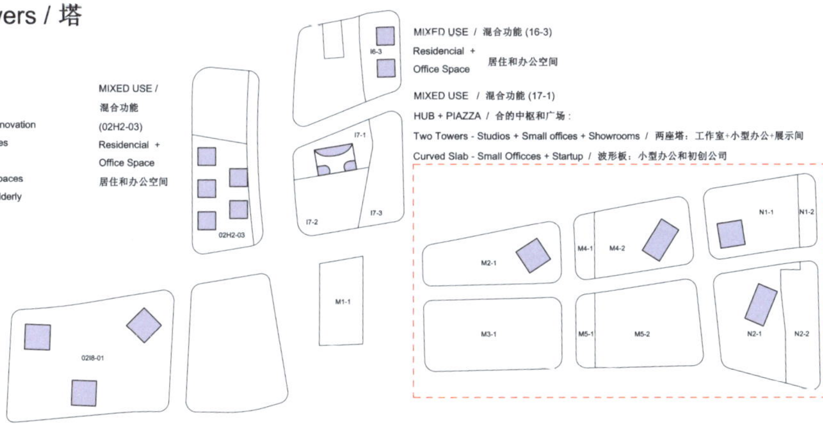

BLOCK 1 (M2-1, M3-1, M4-2, M5-2, N1-1, N2-1)
- Business Offices
- Science and Technology Innovation
- Creative and Cultural Spaces
- Finance Activities
- Science and Technology Spaces

街区1 (M2-1, M3-1, M4-2, M5-2, N1-1, N2-1)
- 商务办公
- 科技创新空间
- 创意与文化空间
- 金融活动
- 科技空间

Podium / 裙房

BLOCK 2 (02I8-01)
- Business Offices
- Science and Technology Innovation
- Creative and Cultural Spaces
- Finance Activities
- Science and Technology Spaces
- +Specific program for the elderly

号街区 2 (02I8-01)
- 商务办公
- 科技创新空间
- 创意与文化空间
- 金融活动
- 科技空间

+上为该建筑内老年人设置的特别计划

MIXED USE (02H2-03)
Commercial / Retail
混合功能 (02H2-03)
商业和零售

MIXED USE / 混合功能 (16-3)
Commercial / Retail
商业和零售

MIXED USE / 混合功能 (17-1)
Library + Bookshop and Multimedia (kind of FNAC)
图书馆+书店+多媒体 （电子产品零售企业）

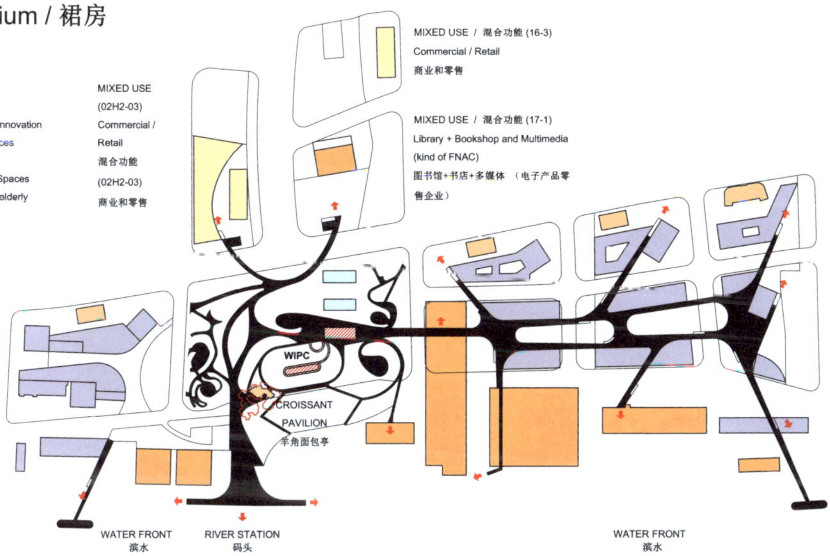

BLOCK 1 (M2-1, M3-1, M4-2, M5-2, N1-1, N2-1)
- Commercial - Level +6.00m

upper floors:
- Business Offices
- Science and Technology Innovation
- Creative and Cultural Spaces
- Finance Activities
- Science and Technology Spaces

街区1 (M2-1, M3-1, M4-2, M5-2, N1-1, N2-1)
- 商业 +6.00m

上层:
- 商务办公
- 科技创新空间
- 创意与文化空间
- 金融活动
- 科技空间

COMMERCIAL / RETAIL
商业 / 零售

KNOWLEDGE / 知识系统

MEMORY SYSTEM / 记忆系统

WATER SYSTEM / 水系统
- WIPC / 水上基础设施公共中心
- IR / 溜冰场 + SP / 游泳
- DCS / 区域供冷系统

Ground level / 地面层

1 - 4 PAVILIONS / 四座亭子
Leisure and cultural activities / 休闲和文化活动:
- Art Galleries / 艺术画廊
- Restaurants / 餐厅
- Bookshops / 书店
- Shops, Contempory craftmanship: Silk; Porcelain; Wood; Jade
/ 当代手工艺专卖商店：丝绸 / 陶瓷 / 瓷器 / 木制品 / 玉器。。。

MIXED USE / 混合功能 (02H2-03)
Commercial / Retail
商业和零售

MIXED USE / 混合功能 (16-3)
Commercial / Retail
商业和零售

MIXED USE / 混合功能 (17-1)
HUB + PIAZZA / 合的中枢和广场：
Piazza + Bus Station + Bikes
广场 + 公交巴士站 + 自行车

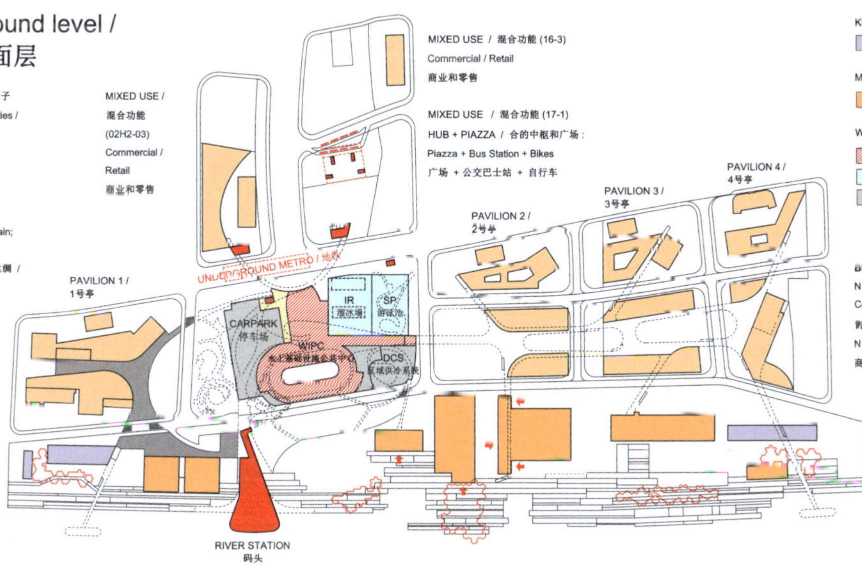

BLOCK 2 / 号街区 2 (02I8-01)
Commercial / Retail
商业和零售

BLOCK 1 (M2-1, M3-1, M4-2, M5-2, N1-1, N2-1)
Commercial / Retail
街区1 (M2-1, M3-1, M4-2, M5-2, N1-1, N2-1)
商业和零售

Yangpu Memory Park. Shanghai, China. 2019–

Yangpu Memory Park develops landscaped and public spaces as well as heritage industrial buildings that form the large central park as proposed in the winning submission for the Yangpu Bridge Area Riverside Development Plan international competition. The park is laid out as a Green System around a central valley that revives the original mangroves, a densely wooded area with species noted for their large root systems that are visible above ground. This central valley is surrounded by gardened, curvilinear areas which create various routes, sports and recreational areas, as well as scenic spots of different sizes. The central valley leads onto a waterfall fountain and a lake that will be refreshing in the summer months, and in the winter can be used as an ice rink. Both the lake and the fountain, together with the storm reservoir and the District Heating & Cooling (both underground but visitable), form the development's Water System, using

river water as the urban area's passive resource. The Infrastructure System principally consists of the underground link to the ferry, metro and bus stations, together with shopping and parking areas. The Memory System—designed as an Integrated Centre of the Arts, Traditional Sports and Health—consists of the three heritage buildings and exterior spaces between them that connect the riverside area to the city. Elements of local history and culture inspire the formal appearance, as well as the Integrated Centre's programme; core aspects of the park's composition include the central valley's original tree species, women's contributions to Shanghai's industrialisation, from the river transport of goods and raw materials to the floral motifs in the local textile industry.

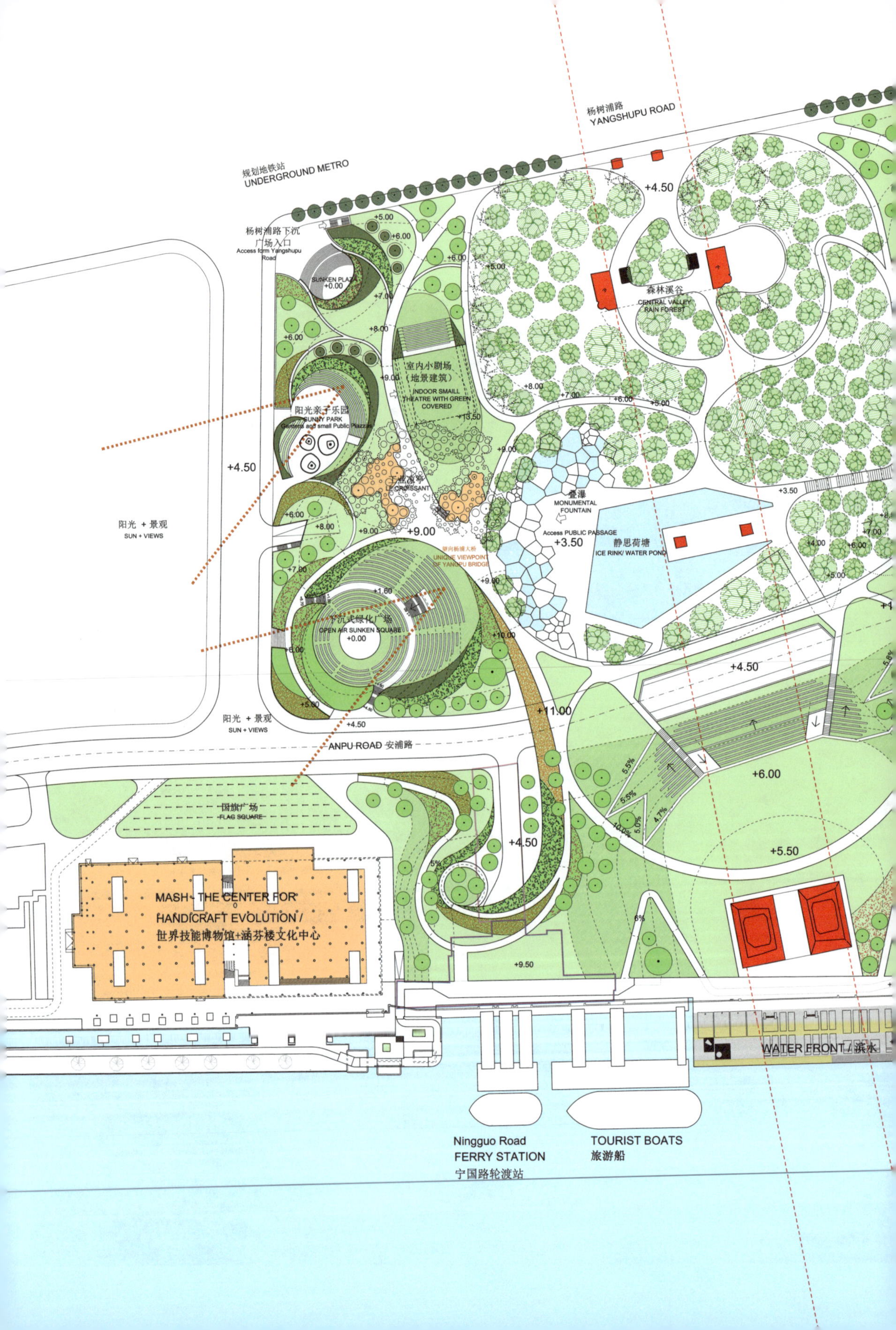

杨树浦路
YANGSHUPU ROAD
规划地铁站
UNDERGROUND METRO
杨树浦路下沉
广场入口
Access form Yangshupu Road
SUNKEN PLAZA
室内小剧场
(地景建筑)
INDOOR SMALL THEATRE WITH GREEN COVERED
阳光亲子乐园
SUNNY PARK
Gardens and small Public Plazzas
CROISSANT
森林溪谷
CENTRAL VALLEY RAIN FOREST
叠瀑
MONUMENTAL FOUNTAIN
Access PUBLIC PASSAGE
静思荷塘
ICE RINK/ WATER POND
阳光 + 景观
SUN + VIEWS
UNIQUE VIEWPOINT OF YANGPU BRIDGE
下沉式绿化广场
OPEN AIR SUNKEN SQUARE
ANPU ROAD 安浦路
国旗广场
FLAG SQUARE
MASH - THE CENTER FOR HANDICRAFT EVOLUTION /
世界技能博物馆+涵芬楼文化中心
WATER FRONT / 滨水
Ningguo Road
FERRY STATION
宁国路轮渡站
TOURIST BOATS
旅游船

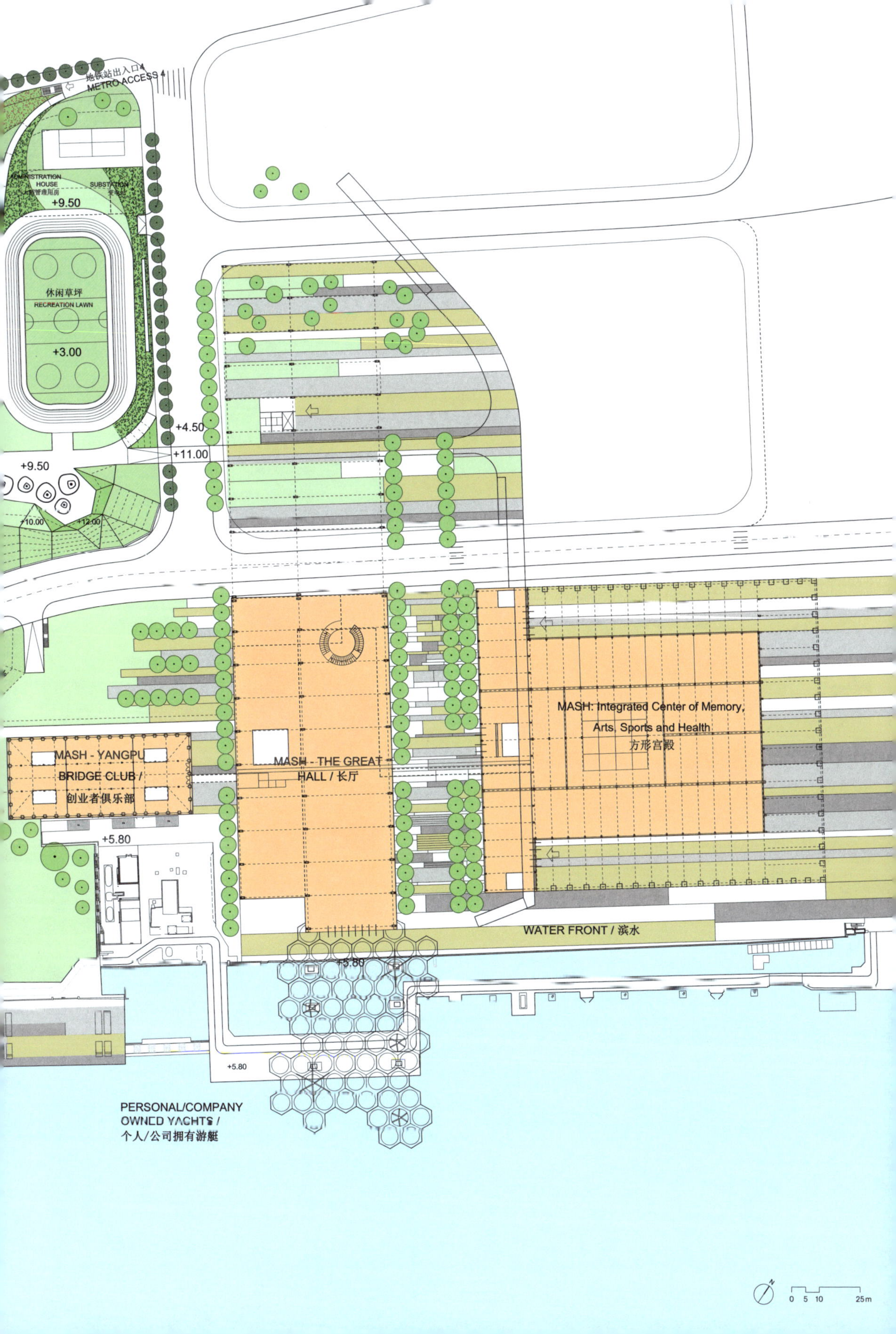
地铁站出入口4
METRO ACCESS 4
ADMINISTRATION HOUSE
SUBSTATION
+9.50
休闲草坪
RECREATION LAWN
+3.00
+4.50
+11.00
+9.50
+10.00
+12.00
MASH - YANGPU BRIDGE CLUB /
创业者俱乐部
MASH - THE GREAT HALL / 长厅
MASH: Integrated Center of Memory, Arts, Sports and Health
方形宫殿
+5.80
WATER FRONT / 滨水
+5.80
+5.80
PERSONAL/COMPANY OWNED YACHTS /
个人/公司拥有游艇
0 5 10 25m

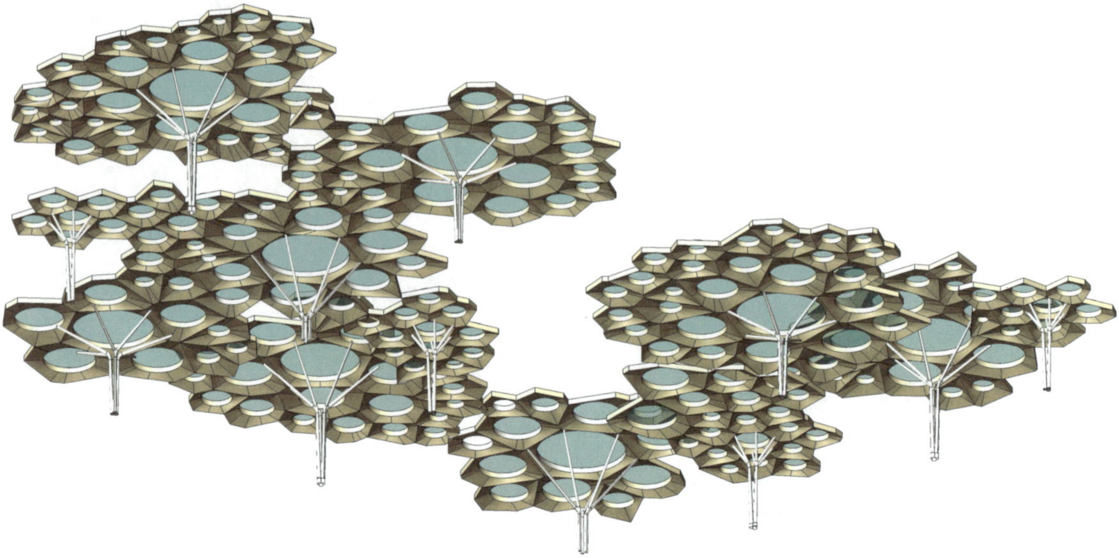

The Sunflowers Pavilion is located in the part of the park with the most spectacular panoramic views over the bridge, the river and the city, making it a must-see for tourists and a landmark where people can gather. This shows the project's overall ambition of visualising a construction aesthetic for the area, based on parametric patterns (Voronoi) that represent the Sponge City / Near-Zero Emissions model.

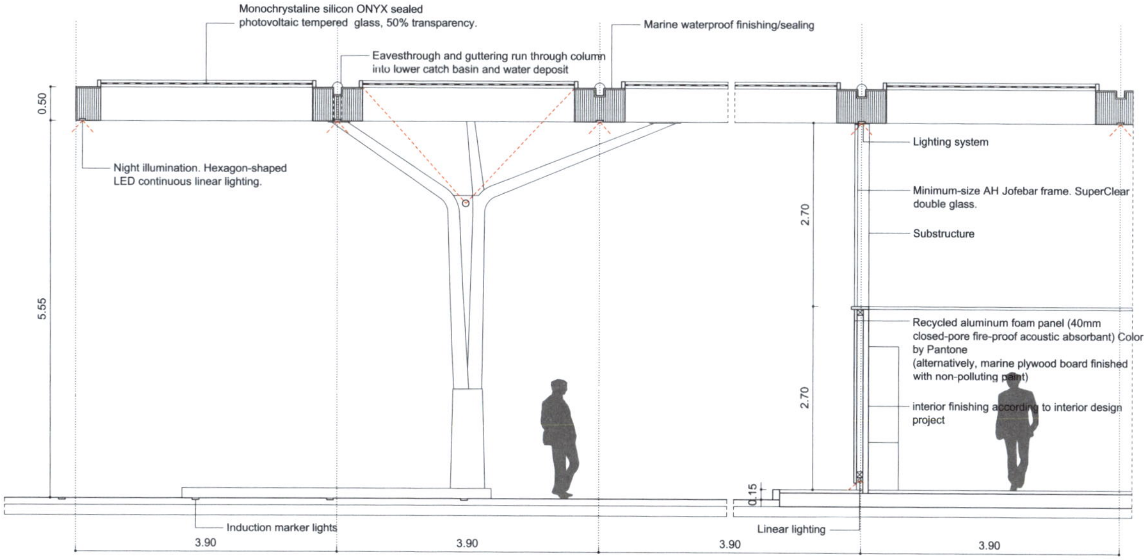

Construction section

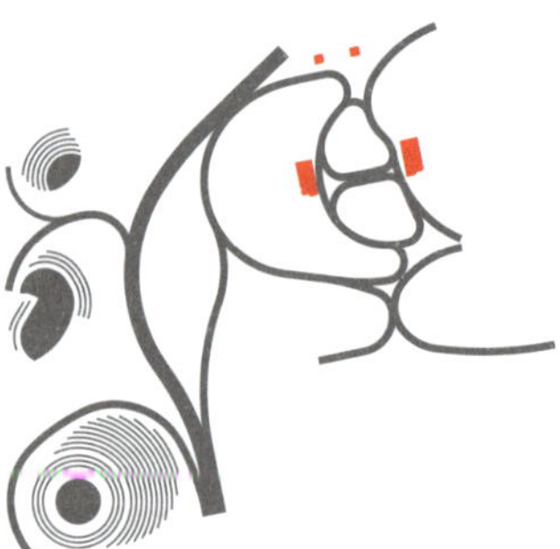

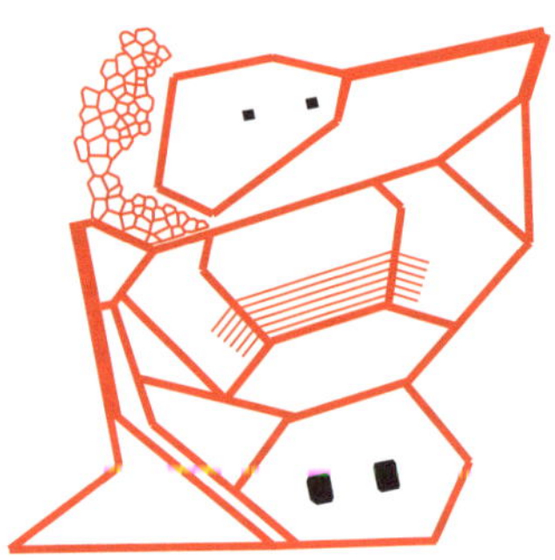

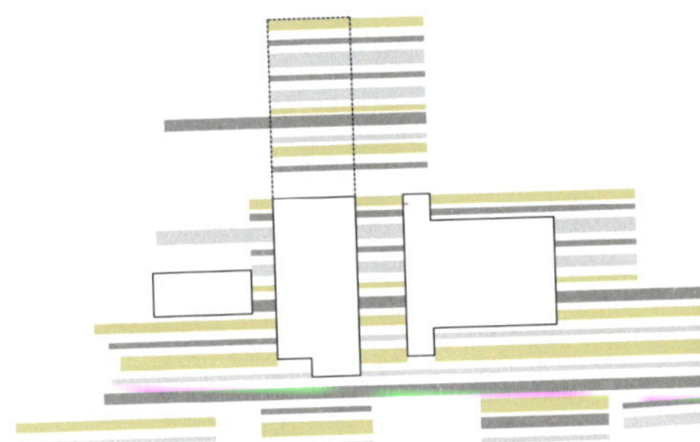

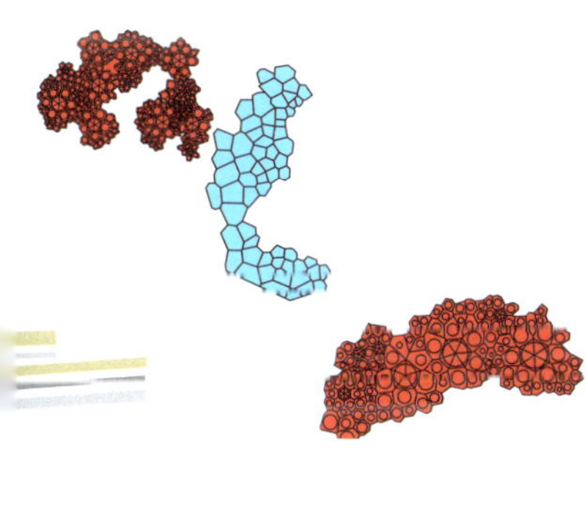

1. The central valley recalls the river's original, geological and biological formation, represented by the mangrove trees' extensive, exposed root system, and by the presence of water in various forms.
2. In ancient China, wood was used to create original shapes when building arches, ships and other elements of river infrastructure, drawing linear connections in complex connections that inspire some of the park's facilities.
3. The park's recreational areas have sinuous contours that not only emulate the gentle shapes of traditional Chinese landscaping and its interlocking effects, but also reflect the beauty of the organic patterns of the local textiles and pay tribute to the role played by women as the force that made it possible.
4. The river's industrialization and the trading along its route led to an important shift in the patterns and methods of urbanisation, shipping containers and shed roofs took over the riverside, providing inspiration for the choice of paving and gardens with fluid lines surrounding the historic buildings and along the riverside.
5. Other natural features are inspired by a fifth geometry, based on biological and biomimetic studies that view nature on a micro and macro scale, using Voronoi parametric geometry.

These patterns provide geometric support, connecting the park to the past, present and future, interconnecting the various patterns of material culture, whose evolution has helped the city's economic development.

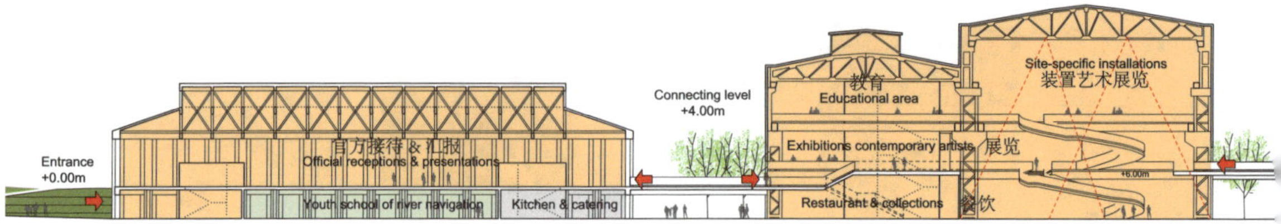

Yangpu Bridge Club

The Great Hall

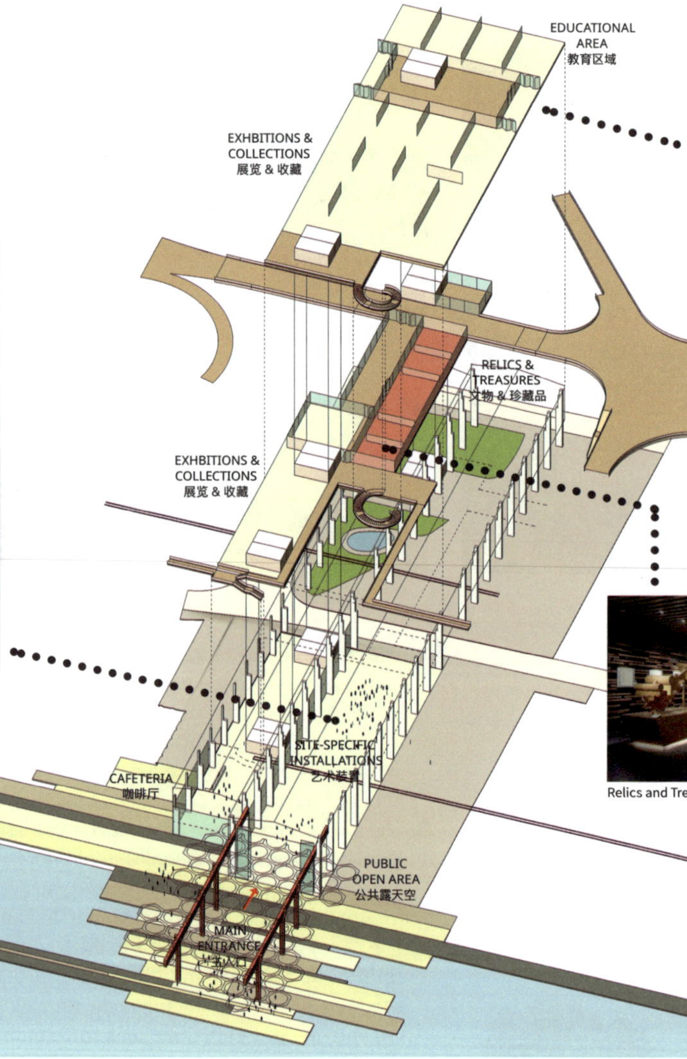

Educational Area for Kids. 优

Site Specific Installations. 装置艺术。

Relics and Treasures. 高度保护的历史文物的

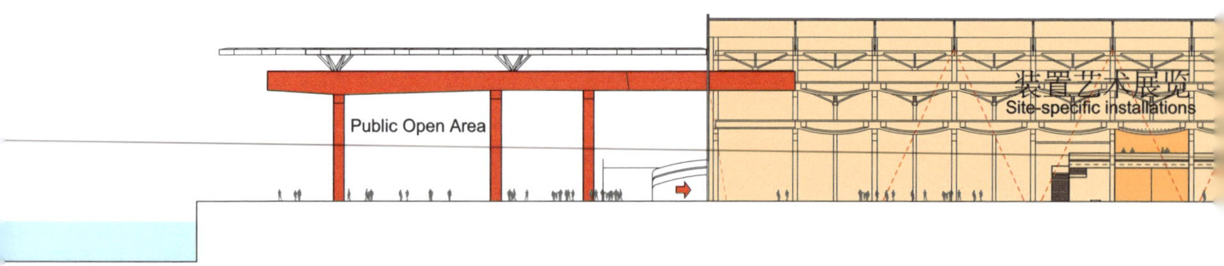

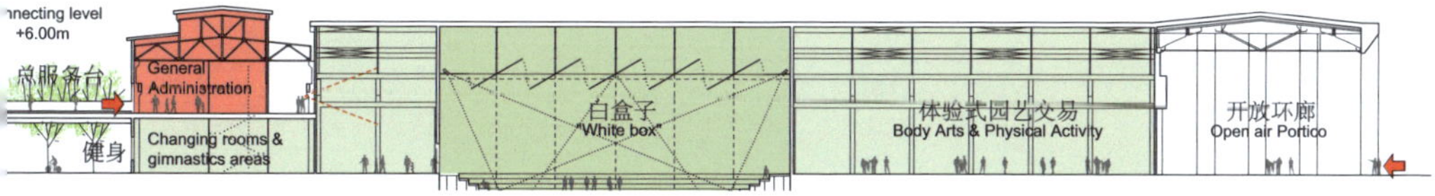

General Administration

Integrated Centre of the Arts, Traditional Sports and Health

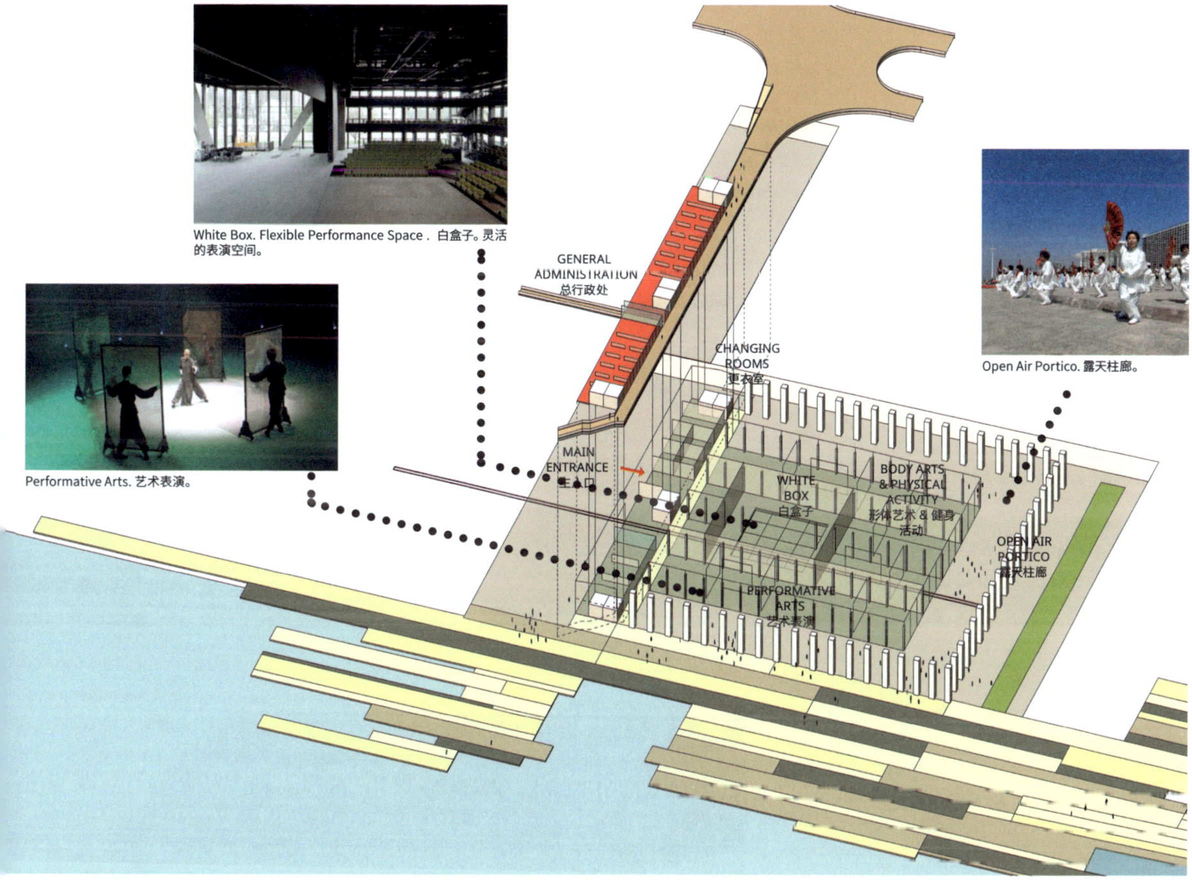

White Box. Flexible Performance Space . 白盒子。灵活的表演空间。

Performative Arts. 艺术表演。

Open Air Portico. 露天柱廊。

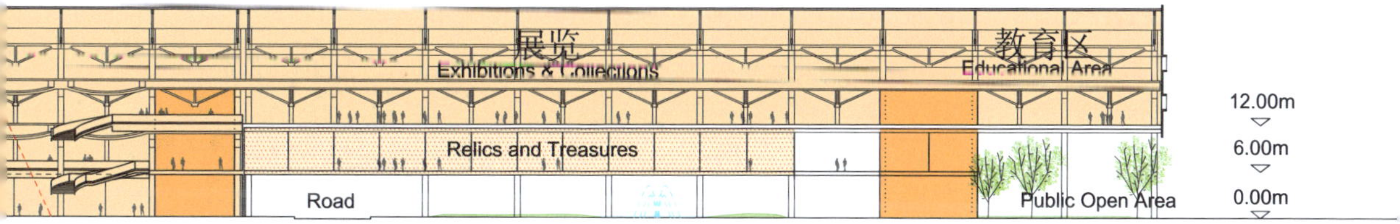

2

Integrated Centre of the Arts, Traditional Sports and Health
1. View of the new perimeter entrance for open-air sports activities. 2. View of the current façade. 3. View of the interior (current state).

1

3

Intermodal Station and Urban Railway Integration. Logroño, La Rioja, Spain. 2008-2020

The AS+ design won this major international competition by prioritizing the green belt created by the new train line's route underneath the city, knitting together a previously fragmented urban area and turning it into a new, green pedestrian route. The stations change from iconic and somewhat "original" constructions to become a "mound" along the linear green route that characterises the park, giving both stations their own identity as "public cellars" evoking the many warehouses in the Rioja wine region. This was all delivered within the original budget (the only TAV station to achieve this), and even the cost of the park—which proved very popular—was included within the budget. Once the bus station and the dome are finished, the urban operation begins, which includes the new residential neighbourhood connecting the city's northern and southern districts. The complex's faceted appearance uses natural materials for the roof, and man-made ones inside both stations.

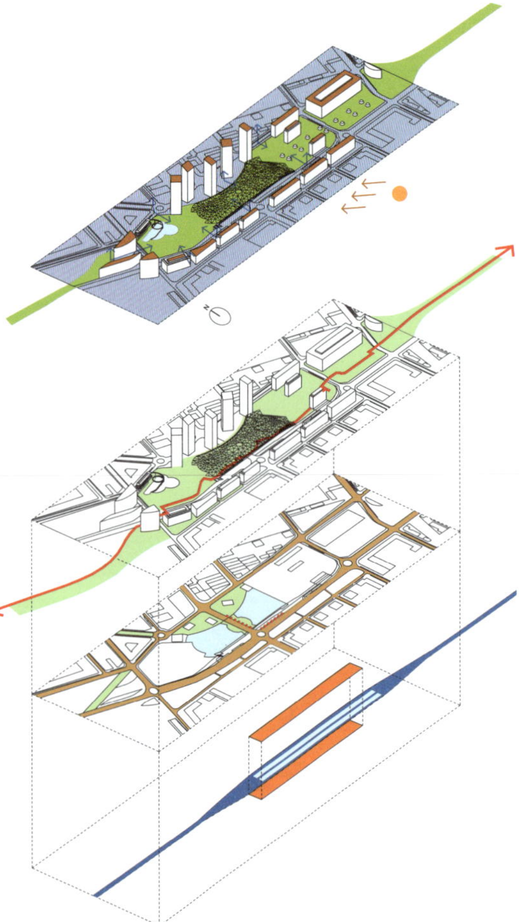

The train station and underground platforms were built between 2010 and 2013, the bus station between 2017 and 2020, and the dome that links them to form a great urban gateway in 2020. While the design of the train station focuses on the transition between the entrance and the platforms, the bus station, with its typical horseshoe shape, emphasizes the link with the park on its deck (see Felipe VI City Park, pp. 72-79) through a staircase that seeks the light and orients the entire space. The central dome spans a space of 60 meters between stations. The complex is the first intermodal public transport structure to obtain a BREEAM Urbanism certification in Spain for its sustainability.

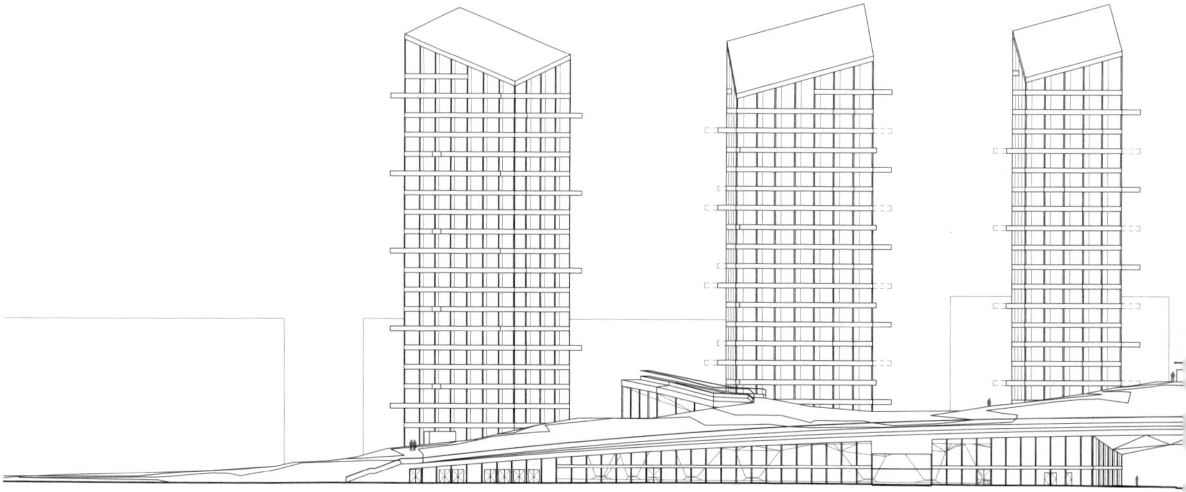

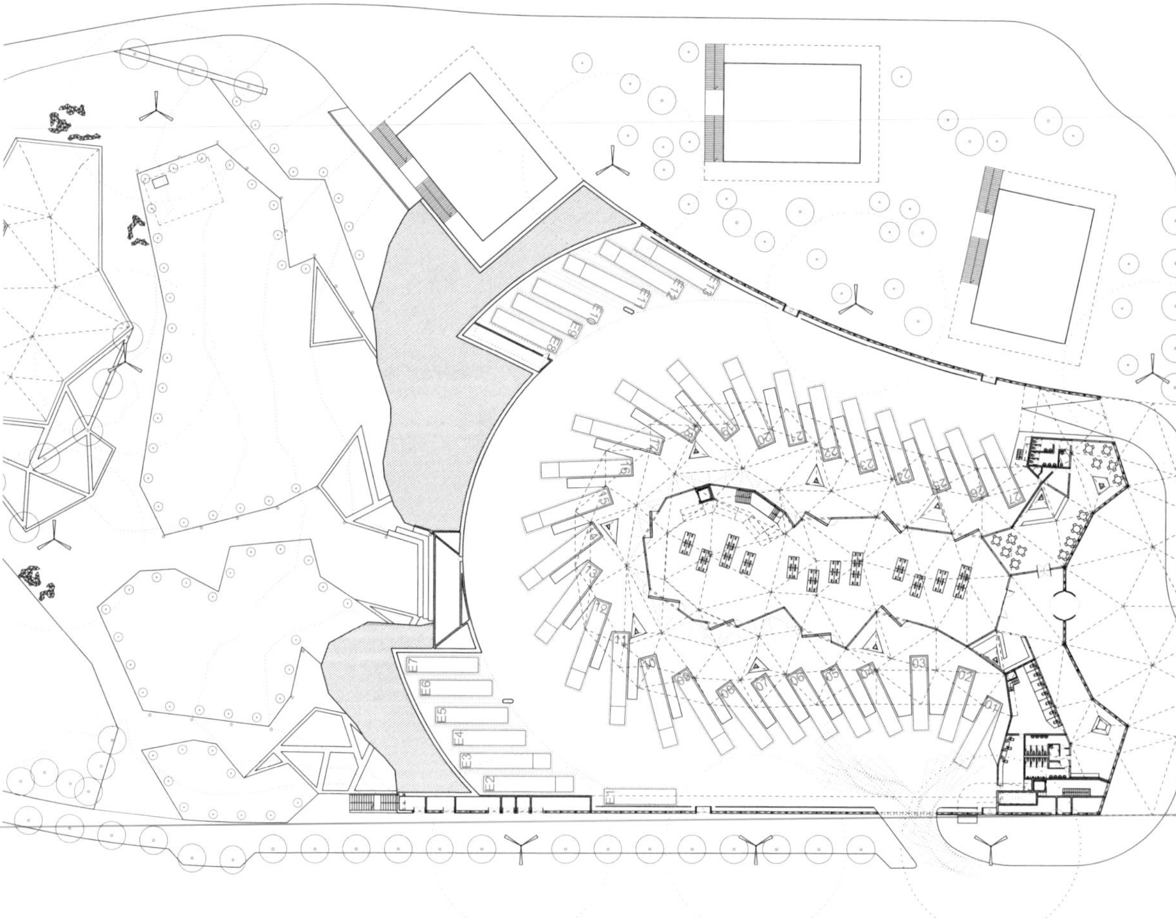

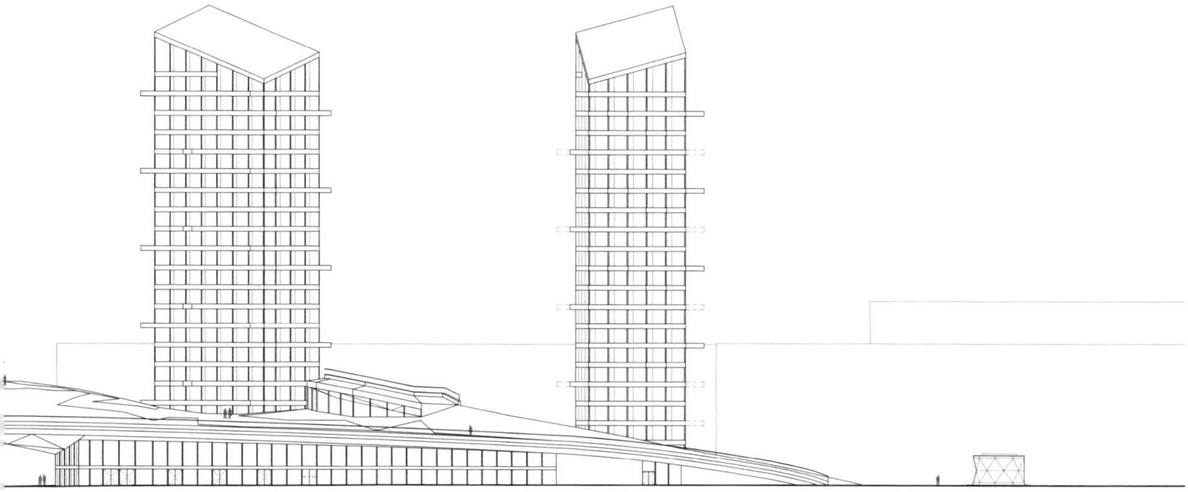

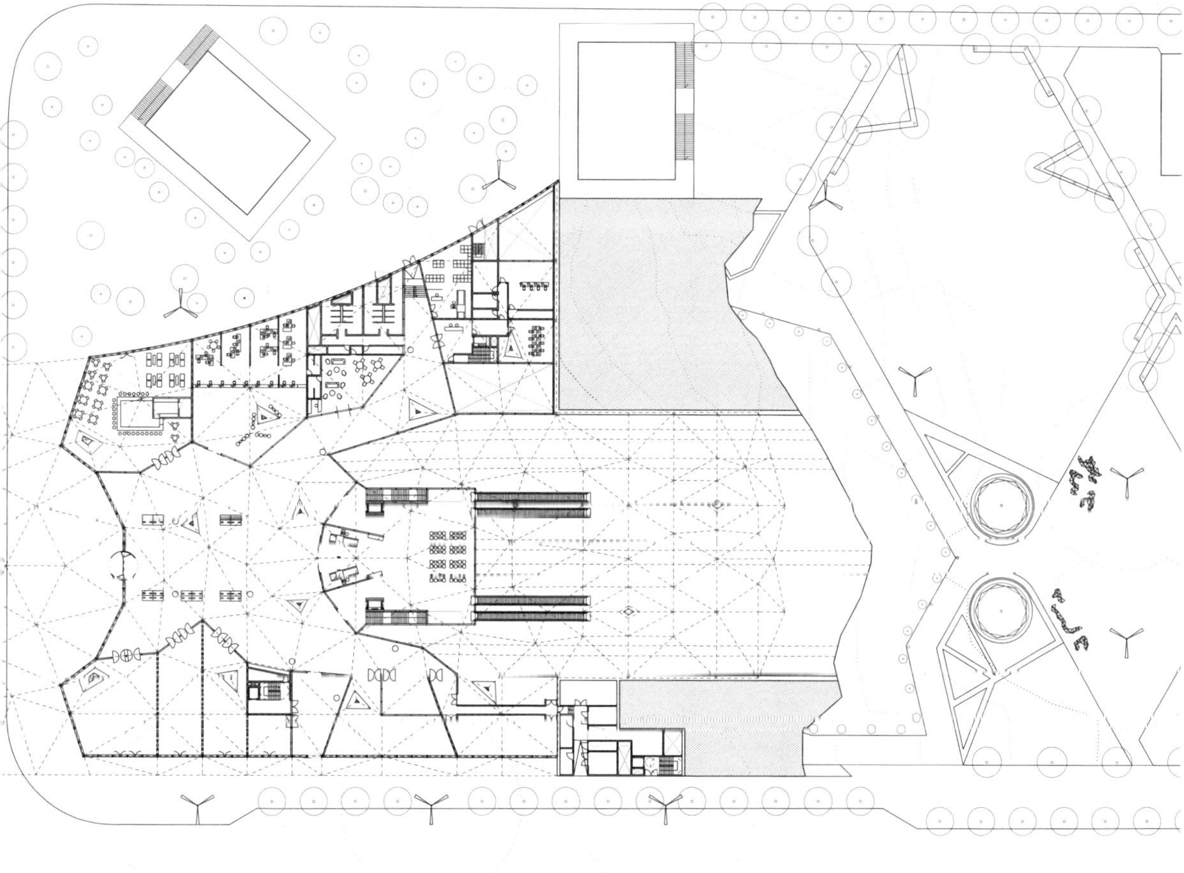

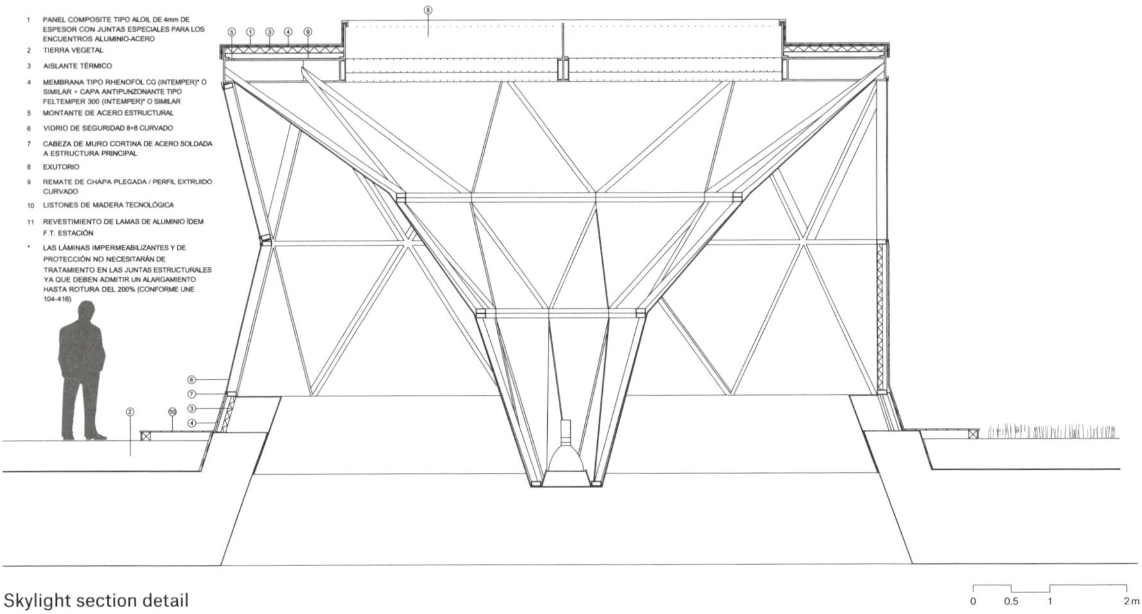

Skylight section detail

902 888 830

LOG

estilo

DOCUMENTALISM AND MATERIAL CULTURE

Abalos+Sentkiewicz interviewed by Plácido González

The intersections between heritage and contemporary architecture constitute one of the most prolific fields of study in our time. Particularly after intense debates like the introduction of contemporary architecture in historic environments, which crystallized in the 2005 Vienna Memorandum, and Rem Koolhaas' warning in 2014 about how 'preservation is overcoming us', it is necessary to study the spaces where the symbiosis between the past and the future is offering new opportunities to rethink both disciplines.

The recent work by Iñaki Ábalos and Renata Sentkiewicz illustrates the richness of this discussion. Founders of the studio AS+, based in Madrid, they have played a key role in the internationalization of Spanish architecture in the recent years, applying their conception of material culture as a fundamental key for interpretation and design in varied contexts like Europe, the Americas and China. This search is based in a solid academic background: Professor at the School of Architecture of Madrid Polytechnic University, Iñaki Ábalos served as Chair of the Department of Architecture at Harvard University's Graduate School of Design (GSD) between 2013 and 2016. A Visiting Critic in Harvard GSD, Renata Sentkiewicz holds together with Iñaki Ábalos a long track record of research on design, landscape and thermodynamics that they have consistently applied in their practice since it was founded in 2006.

This conversation offers an insight into their approach to heritage, memory and recreation, rooted in concepts like documentalism and metaphors like still life painting and self-portraits, which appear as useful tools for their contemporary definition of today's heritage through the practice of architecture. With such references, the dialogue will focus on two cases of intervention in historical heritage, such as the Tàpies Foundation in Barcelona (Spain), and the Art Gallery in Wuhan (China). Both illustrate the analogies in the approach to different CONTEXTS through the lenses of material culture, as an indispensable tool to face the global challenges of heritage and contemporary architecture today.

Shanghai, July 8, 2018

[Plácido González]:
For a long time, heritage was a very constrained idea, implicitly conveying resistance to change. Now we propose to shift the focus and show heritage as a creative practice that is embedded in contemporary architecture. The first question is about this: What do you consider to be the greatest potential of heritage for the production of architecture today?

[IA + RS]:
We would refer first to where the production of contemporary architecture is now, comparing it with two kinds of paintings: still life paintings, and self portraits. If something has changed in the last decade in the world of academia and in the world of practice, it is the way we have moved from the self-portrait to the still life. The way the media treated architecture and the star-architect system was all about the extraordinary, the bizarre, the production of objects that could surprise everyone. The only way to get a work of architecture on the cover of a magazine was to make it very bizarre, to produce an almost impossible architecture that would immediately awaken people's interest, and particularly among those who are not experts. This has created a generation of architects repeating themselves with the same gestures; no matter where they were working, what the program was, the context, the scale, the culture, etc.: this is what we called self-portraits.

The idea of the still life, as an analogy between the world of painting and architecture, means that architects are trying now to put everything together and work with the disciplines that were once divided by modernist Taylorism: landscape, architecture, urban design, urban planning and other related practices. Taken to real life, students in different schools lived together, but they never merged these disciplines nor were able to understand the potential of interconnecting them. For this reason, we think that working with the organic and the inorganic; joining the scale of the landscape with the fabric of architecture; and trying to optimize the result in terms of quality of the public space and of the interior space has become more and more an issue.

Another important question is how new technologies are helping us understand the relationships between these apparently different ways to treat the territory and the city. With this we are not referring necessarily to parametricism, which is still the prevailing image that comes to mind when we talk about new technologies in architecture: we think thermodynamics offer much more interesting and rich opportunities beyond parametricism because they show interaction, which is everything: it is about dynamism, about how one thing goes from here to there, passing through different states. This is a key point to understand where we are now: we are very much focusing on interactions and much less on self-portraits; and on the translation of this idea to practice and to academia.

Secondly, we need to refer to the recovery of methodologies that were almost forgotten in the discipline. Among them, a key one is to behave like a documentary maker. The idea of documentary work is incredibly interesting for us, and has become more and more important in the world of contemporary artistic practices, among them literature: Emmanuel Carrere's novel *Limonov* is a good example. But if you think about cinema, we would have the films of Wim Wenders, or Werner Herzog with his *Cave of Forgotten Dreams* about the caves of Lascaux... Bruno Latour's work in the field of ideas is also quite important to understand and contextualize what the concept of the documentary can mean. Obviously, and referring to architecture, we have a hero of modernism like Cedric Price, or Rem Koolhaas (who we consider his heir in many respects). They are both perfect examples of how documenting is now at the core of new approaches to design. The next question is: what to document? In our tradition, documenting has been performed focusing mostly on two topics: context and program. The documenting of the context was a very rudimentary, almost simplistic approach: perhaps formal, perhaps atmospheric like Álvaro Siza sitting at the café in a European square, wandering with his pencil in a poetical way: we all know and love those sketches. Beyond this, we think the concept of material culture has become absolutely relevant for anyone trying to document whatever has a trajectory in time. A concept that comes from archaeology; it relies on techniques that allow you, using very few, minimal facts—a piece of ceramics, a bone, two or three stones at the foundations of a building—to reconstruct the everyday life of a civilization thousands of years ago.

We cannot achieve such precision, but the idea of approaching the context and the places where we act through the study of the material culture, means a huge difference in the way we treat tradition and modernity. In light of this, the recurrent idea, which was so frequent in the past, of an architect randomly buying some postcards in a foreign context and using some local three-centimetre ornamental patterns to enlarge them and turn them into the floor plan of a 200-metre-high skyscraper becomes immediately ridiculous and almost insulting for the local people living in this context. Instead, material culture focuses on matter; material culture is pure materialism, it means conceptually, ontologically, to believe that matter and our behaviour are closely related. The things that are at hand: this table, these glasses, this watch, this paper, in a way limit the way we can think, or the things we can think about. So this is materialism strictly.

In this panorama of what "documentary making" and material culture mean, we find again the contribution from thermodynamics to refer to the question of program: for many years we thought that analysis and synthesis were two discrete moments, impossible to connect at all but through purely poetic ways. We remember Aldo Rossi and Giorgio Grassi treating these topics from a structuralist perspective, in a very serious way, yet unable to connect these two moments. Thermodynamics may provide us the key, for example in the way we think about phase-change materials; those which in certain conditions dissipate enormous amounts of energy at the same time as they crystallize, interacting with the context in a very different way. Taken to our discussion, the material culture of a place is a boiling system where we would find the climate, the culture, the economy, the ecology, their evolution in time; up to a point where they crystallize and create a new state where all this information is embedded.

Therefore, heritage is important to the contemporary production of architecture, because there is no project, no design, that doesn't respond to some kind of heritage: it can be intellectual, physical, historic, typological, material; or put them all together. Going to the painting example, thinking in terms of still life, you cannot forget all these things, you cannot avoid these notions. It doesn't matter if you are working with a pre-existing building or an empty plot, for the relevant elements of the material culture are already there, in a very similar state, and this is the point. This is what makes me understand that heritage is no longer a marginal aspect in the activity of the architects, but can be more and more relevant to understand the connections with history, with material culture, and to what extent our practice in the present is constructing the material culture of our time.

[Plácido González]:
Another very interesting idea that you mentioned is that of the references. We would like to go into the ones you use to build the conceptual framework of your projects, and particularly those coming from modernism, and how maybe the most interesting chapter of the conflictive relationship between modernity and tradition is how modernity has also itself become a tradition. You have written and spoken in lectures and texts about the possible continuity of the modern project, beyond its postmodern depiction as a wasteful, environmentally unfriendly stage in the history of architecture. In what sense do you consider your production is continuing the grounds and values of the modern project today?

[IA + RS]:
Modernism is really relevant as part of our tradition in the context in which we grew up and part of our system of thinking. That is very clear. On the one hand, we agree that in many cases, modernity has demonstrated a negative outcome in terms of environmental and societal terms: there were many failures in the utopian approach of the first modernists, which are now obvious to everyone. And

on the other hand, we cannot forget that modernity is the only tradition we have to confront in terms of the new scales, the new programs, the new speed of construction, the new infrastructural impact of architecture and urban planning in the territory today. Maybe the Inca civilization, or the Romans, could serve as a highly poetic reference for the extent of today's challenges, but basically, the education that modernity gives us is the only operative one that we have. So in this sense, the tradition cannot be deemed completely positive nor completely negative: whoever chooses one over the other is really blind to the most common sense and concept of reality. This is one thing.

We have always exemplified the use of material culture with the lenses of our discipline through the direct study of two representative spaces for living: the house and the palace, compared at two different peak moments that are representative of their development in terms of modernity. In academic terms and from our experience teaching in different schools, this information becomes astonishingly important, giving you a whole dimension of how the material culture evolves, but also what remains from it; about how for example the thermodynamic issues that relate to climate have been solved in different stages of evolution. Attention to the two residential typologies of the house and the palace thus informs us about the simplest ideas that will always be useful; that have resulted from a huge experience of trial and error, creating the most efficient responses and model forms of organization with the most basic resources, almost without economic means.

An important conclusion that we extract from this also applies to the relationship between modernity and tradition; that is, that we have become 'orphans' of these relationships: we can only use their experience in terms of acknowledging the intelligence of the responses and admitting the impossibility of continuing with any of them. So you learn from the experience, but you cannot use it in direct terms. This can be interpreted either as a disgrace or as a blessing, and we would go for the latter option: we think it is a fantastic opportunity for a new architecture, one able to construct a new idea of architecture learning from these experiences, incorporating our means, our technologies, and our capacities today to create new responses.

For example, the scale of the old, traditional houses in Seville cannot be of great interest to the urban densities of China or even of Spain itself today, due to the speed of production in a global context, yet they are still relevant. At the same time, we are conscious that bringing the glass prisms of modernism to the south of Spain cannot be useful anymore, while on the other hand, they are undeniably beautiful, and we may acknowledge that they were created with the purpose of understanding the new possibilities of a relationship between the interior and the landscape, for instance. So in a way, we can admire them, we can understand them, and then the question arises: what can we do with them? How can we create the house, the palace of today? This is, in our opinion, the most important question that needs to be addressed in relation to the material culture and these two traditions. For us, they are equivalent and they enter into dialogue; they fight, and the fight is really productive, but not in terms of manipulating their contradictions directly. They stay there, but you have to rethink everything.

[Plácido González]:
Does this idea of being 'orphaned' become more intense when practicing in a context like China? What are the tools, in which sense does the approach differ depending on the context?

[IA + RS]:
Our minds always comes to China when talking about scale and speed. We don't know the exact proportion of square metres under construction in China and the rest of the world, but we think it may be very close to 50%. This has attracted us to work in this culture, because of its historic significance: there was a moment when Europe played a leading role, then America, and later East Asia, in particular China. Therefore, it is a natural consequence that the best architecture has been produced first in Europe, later in the United States and in Latin America, and now it is the time for important architecture to emerge in China. We have a great interest in working under very different conditions compared to what the modernists found when they developed their theories. It is an excellent place to observe, experiment and test if these ideas about material culture and their related methodologies can become relevant; if the idea of thermodynamics can help to construct a new way to think about architecture and the discipline in general terms; and ultimately, to contribute to the natural, final aim of architecture, which is a social service to create better conditions of life. That's very clear. So for us it is a great opportunity to be contributing and collaborating in this hyper project which is the new China: a much more interesting context than any other nowadays.

Referring to your question, we don't feel that we are behaving in a different way. Obviously the scales are different, but the methodology that we referred to before comes partly from academia, partly from our intellectual interest in different aspects of reality, and partly from our experience in practice in Spain, Latin America and China. So in different proportions, these contexts have contributed to give precision to and clarify these ideas, which three years ago were still under development. Maybe back then we lacked the possibility to develop a more systematic intellectual construction with them. We think this is a relevant aspect, but not contradictory, nor completely surprising, which results from the obvious acknowledgement about how the scale of the programs and the production speeds are changing.

Material culture gained in significance for us when we started to work on international projects. Take for example Latin America, where despite the fact they share Spanish as a language, the context is similar, but not exactly the same in the end. You have to develop a deeper insight to find similarities and differences and slowly establish this dialogue, this way to get closer to the territory and to the place through the study of material culture. Having constructed this method based on our experience developing projects abroad, we now proceed to use it in the places that we supposedly know, in order to discover them and to know them better, to understand them, before starting to think about the project. At that initial moment there would be no sketch, there would be nothing yet, but we would allow ourselves some time and distance to develop this conversation about the place.

[Plácido González]:

This relates to the estrangement from the past that David Lowenthal spoke about when he said that the past is a foreign country, no matter if it is the past of your own city or your own family. We understand this as a symptom of change, from the universalist approach of modernism to the current sensitivity towards a place as a key enabling the ubiquitous presence of globalization. We think about it when seeing, for example, the renovation that you have recently completed in Wuhan of a historic building from the 1920s, and the ways through which the interpretation of historic architecture can avoid falling into nostalgia. This is important in China as well as internationally, due to the role that heritage plays in the production of a collective identity, and which is frequently producing idealized visions of the past, which once defined should never be touched. This could be compared to current discussions in Europe around the idea of 'frugality', which you depicted years ago in your text 'Bartleby, the architect' and his 'I would rather not' motto, as part of a creative attitude. We would like to know if such an idea is still valid as a reference when dealing with a heritage project here in China.

[IA + RS]:

Before we went to Wuhan, you know that we had the opportunity to renovate another industrial building years ago for the Tàpies Foundation in Barcelona, with a similar scale and almost identical situation. It was in fact the first industrial building built in the Eixample, the city extension of Barcelona designed by Cerdá in the second half of the 19th century, which responded to an idea of combining non-polluting industries, such as printing companies, with the residential environment of the blocks.

Both the projects in Barcelona and in Wuhan tell us many interesting things. The first one that we have learnt these years after being more and more involved in rehabilitation projects at both architectural and urban scales, is to seriously question the idea of not touching and intervening in heritage buildings, which when we were students we considered the smartest approach. By this, we refer to the use of techniques to render interventions invisible, freezing the fabric in time, which was characteristic of the Italian school in those days, acting like doctors and denying any kind of creativity. We think that this is the most wrong-headed approach ever, the most banal in terms of cultural construction. We prefer those historicists of the 19th century who recreated, and who by recreating, were enjoying their creativity contributing with beautiful eclecticism to the built environment that you can enjoy in so many cities of Europe today.

Having said that, the idea of intervening in a historic building has different values in different contexts, and so it is the case in China. It is important to understand that whatever you do will be a moment in the course of culture and of the discipline, as well as its relationship with time and entropy. So it will reflect how at a certain moment, we act according to what is more important, incorporating the social and cultural and political considerations that we may find in history and projecting them into the future.

For example, in the Tàpies Foundation in Barcelona, the building had experienced a previous hyper post-modernist intervention, designed by a very good architect. I always recall that when I was student I visited this post-modernist intervention in the Tàpies foundation because I thought it was a very interesting work, and I liked it. Then when I returned twenty-five years later to work on the same building, I couldn't believe how much the architect had added to it incorrectly. But at the same time, it was clear that what had been done back then was wholly invalid three decades later; it was a masquerade, exactly the opposite to what the building demanded today. Tàpies' idea was to respond to the wisdom and the idea of the place, recovering the atmosphere of the printing industry that was originally there. So what we had to do was basically to clean the house, to take out all the stuff that was completely unused and to give the character back to the beautiful structure, which was basically an American loft transferred to Barcelona, exposing its cast iron elements, recovering the skylights with beautiful natural light that had been closed off, recovering the original thick wood pavement, changing completely the colours, everything. So the atmosphere changed radically. It was great because Tàpies had the opportunity to see the result before he passed away, and in the opening day he told us: 'I'm so grateful, I have been waiting for twenty-five years to see this building as it is now', which is the best compliment we have ever received from a client.

And then we move to Wuhan, to what used to be a religious bookshop and publishing company in the former British Concession. Over the years, it had almost been destroyed: every room was subdivided and occupied by different families, so now it is incredible to compare what we saw the first day we arrived to the site, and what we have now there. Initially it was impossible to know the name of the architect, but through the government we identified an architect from that time who used a similar repertoire in the city and to whom the building could be attributed, and based on that hypothesis we started to establish analogies, and so on. We had to document what we had, so that we could take decisions on the basis of these assumptions, which despite not being hundred percent certain, nevertheless seemed to be the most reasonable.

At the outset, considering the extent of the damage and the plans for the building to become an art gallery with a bookshop, we thought that we could be less restrained than in Barcelona; that we would have the opportunity to design a kind of more open interior, applying a more modernist category to understand the space. But the position of the client was radical: they really wanted to recreate, in the literal sense of the term, a history that was almost invisible in the physical reality of the building. And they made incredible research into, for example, interior design: 99% of the building was damaged, but where they could find a frame of a door which was probably original because it was well decorated, or one stick left from a fragment of a railing... and from these elements, the whole appearance could be recreated anew. We also had to reconstruct the load-bearing walls, which was a difficult task because of accessibility requirements like elevators, fire regulation elements like an additional stair, etc.

It was a difficult combination of factors, but they were doing great work following the idea of recovering a bookshop, which helps you think of the extent of the challenge, about many of the similarities through which the project attempted to go back to the origins, but at the same time, to incorporate major exceptions such as the kind of books that would be brought back into the building: no longer religious books, but art books. We are happy with the results because it is a service for the community, and after years of destruction of heritage in China, we think this question needs to be addressed with extreme care. Besides some decorative intrusions we don't agree with, but which were reduced to a minimal extent, this is what they were doing: a very dedicated attempt to give a valid response through systematic research into what the building looked like originally, and furthermore, considering the role that it plays in the community. In a way, these two projects help us to understand the powers currently in play in the construction of the city. You have to understand what they mean and to elaborate them; not only from a structural perspective, but particularly in its cultural context. If you want to contribute you have to understand what is interesting for architecture, and how to push for it and make it real. But comparing the two interventions, despite being very different, at the same time we think they are providing a very similar service to society.

[Note: This is an edited version of an interview published in August 2018 in the website of the journal Built Heritage (https://www.built-heritage.net/abalos-sentkiewicz-interview)]

CaixaForum Museum in Atarazanas Reales. Seville, Spain. 2009

The project integrates the Caixaforum museum in Las Atarazanas—a building that originated in the 12th century as a shipyard—making it stand out more within its urban surroundings, enhancing the experience of its interiors and its unique views of the cityscape, by applying the following interventions:

- Creating a northern entrance with a public portico behind one of the city's former gates, the Postigo del Aceite, bringing the museum closer to the monumental Cathedral and Giralda (and providing plenty of space for the queues of visitors).
- Concentrating Caixaforum's ground-floor exhibition area around a wide walkway that respects the original spatial structure.
- Restoring the original (river) level in Bay 7, creating a public information point for visitors to learn about the history of Las Atarazanas.
- Creating an observation deck overlooking the Torre del Oro, the Guadalquivir River, the Cathedral and the Giralda, revealing the historical connections between these surroundings and Las Atarazanas. This area includes a cafeteria and restaurant.
- Producing new facings and volumes with industrial shipbuilding techniques, giving Las Atarazanas a new vitality befitting its history.

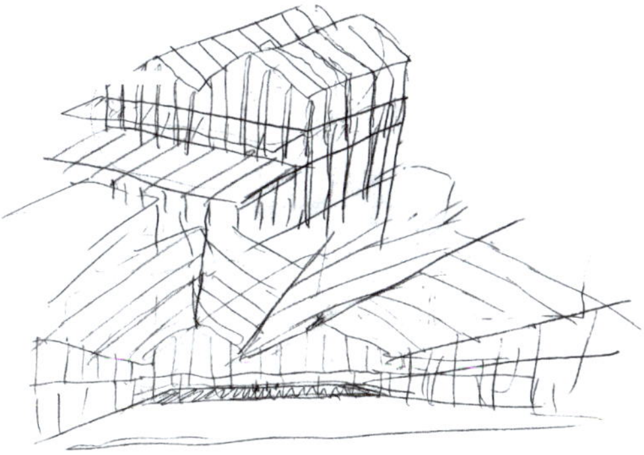

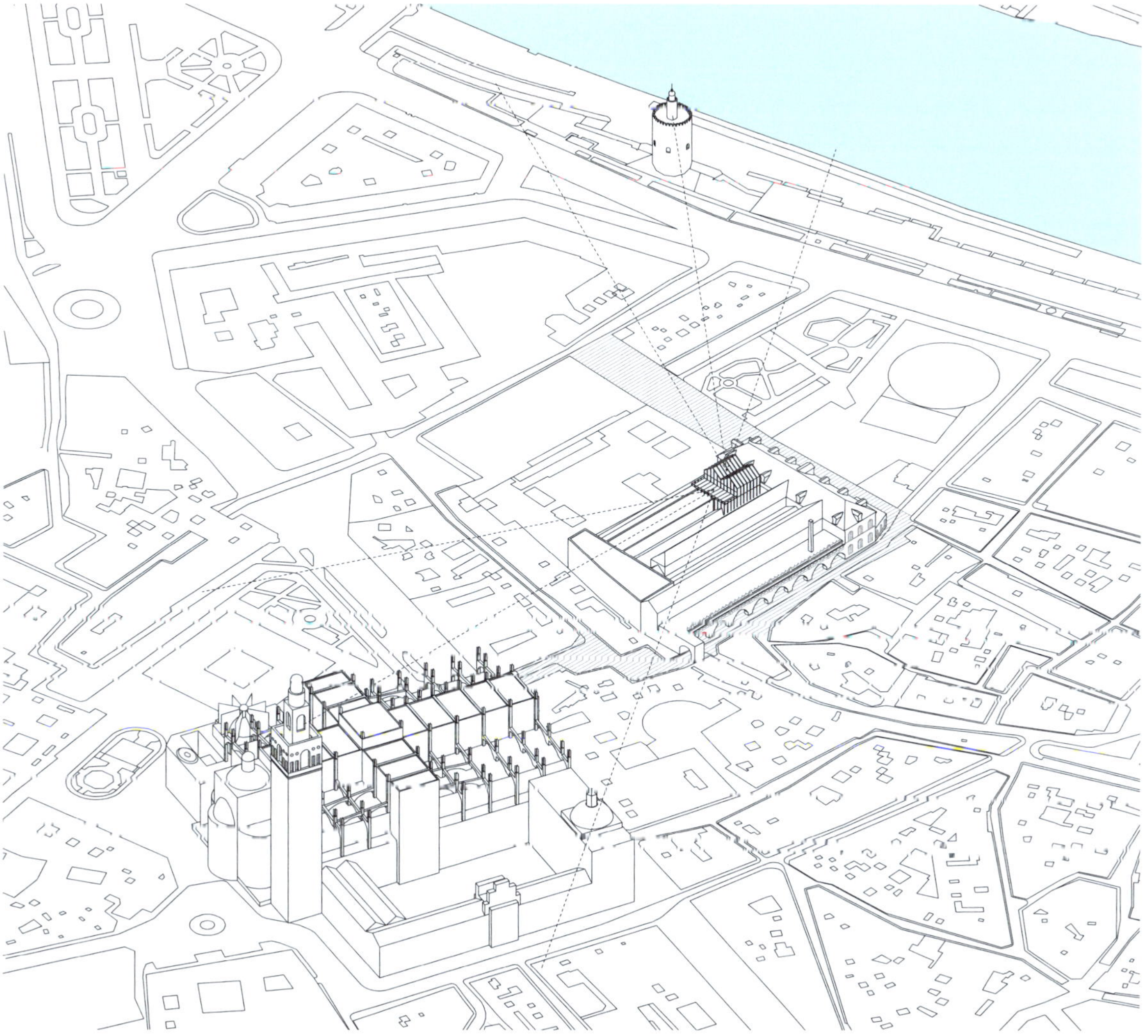

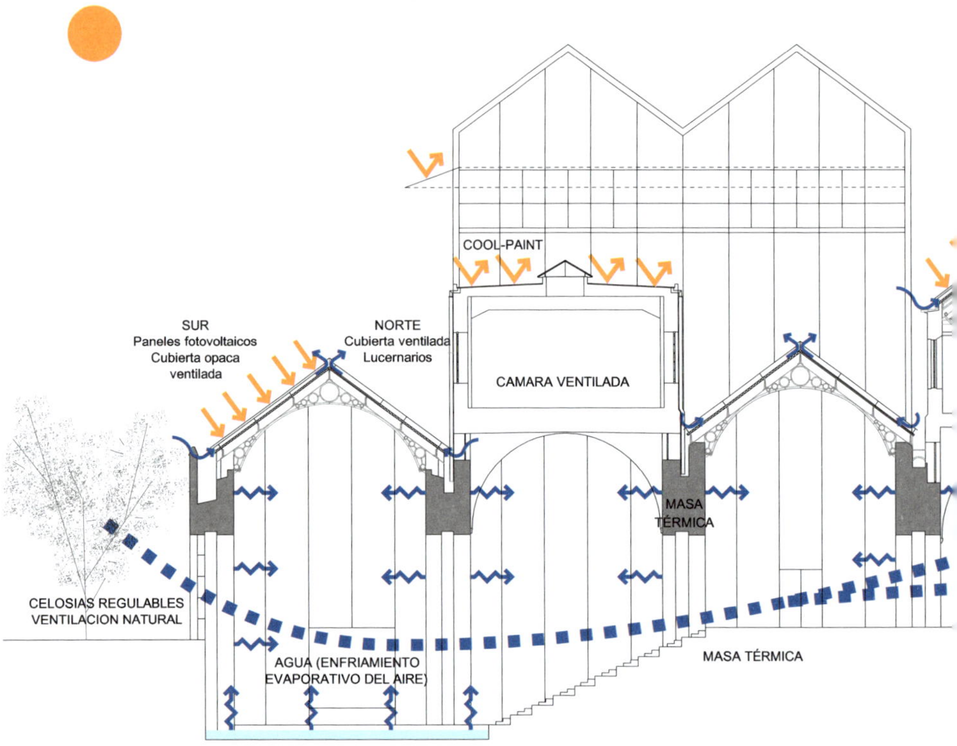
COOL-PAINT
SUR
Paneles fotovoltaicos
Cubierta opaca
ventilada
NORTE
Cubierta ventilada
Lucernarios
CAMARA VENTILADA
MASA
TÉRMICA
CELOSIAS REGULABLES
VENTILACION NATURAL
AGUA (ENFRIAMIENTO
EVAPORATIVO DEL AIRE)
MASA TÉRMICA

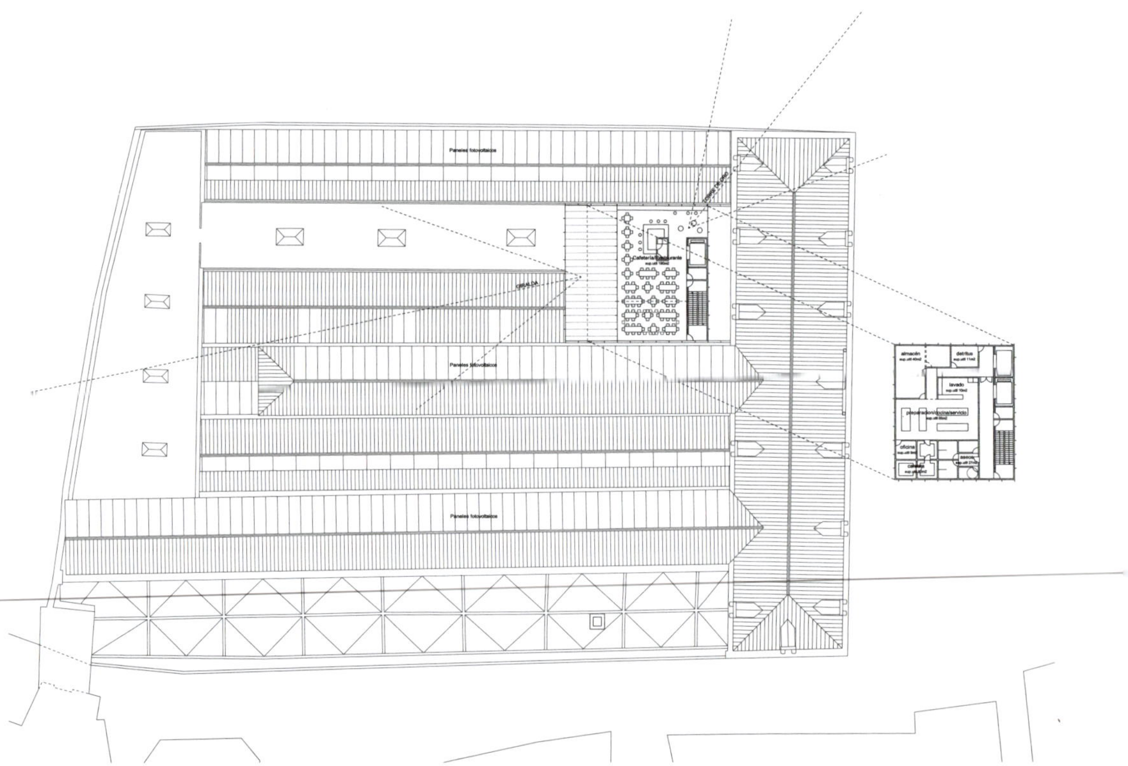
Paneles fotovoltaicos
almacén
detritus
lavado
preparacion/cocina/servicio
oficina

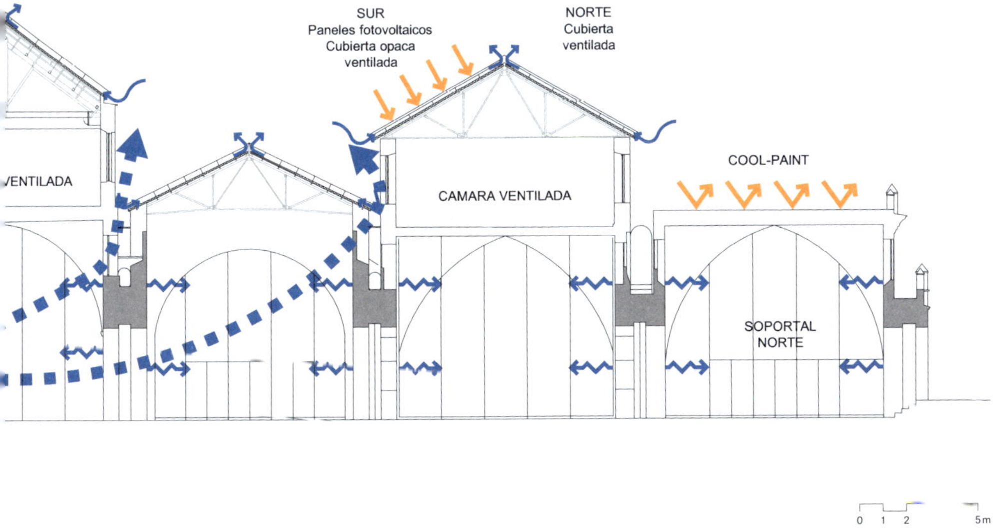
SUR
Paneles fotovoltaicos
Cubierta opaca
ventilada
NORTE
Cubierta
ventilada
COOL-PAINT
CAMARA VENTILADA
SOPORTAL
NORTE
0 1 2 5m

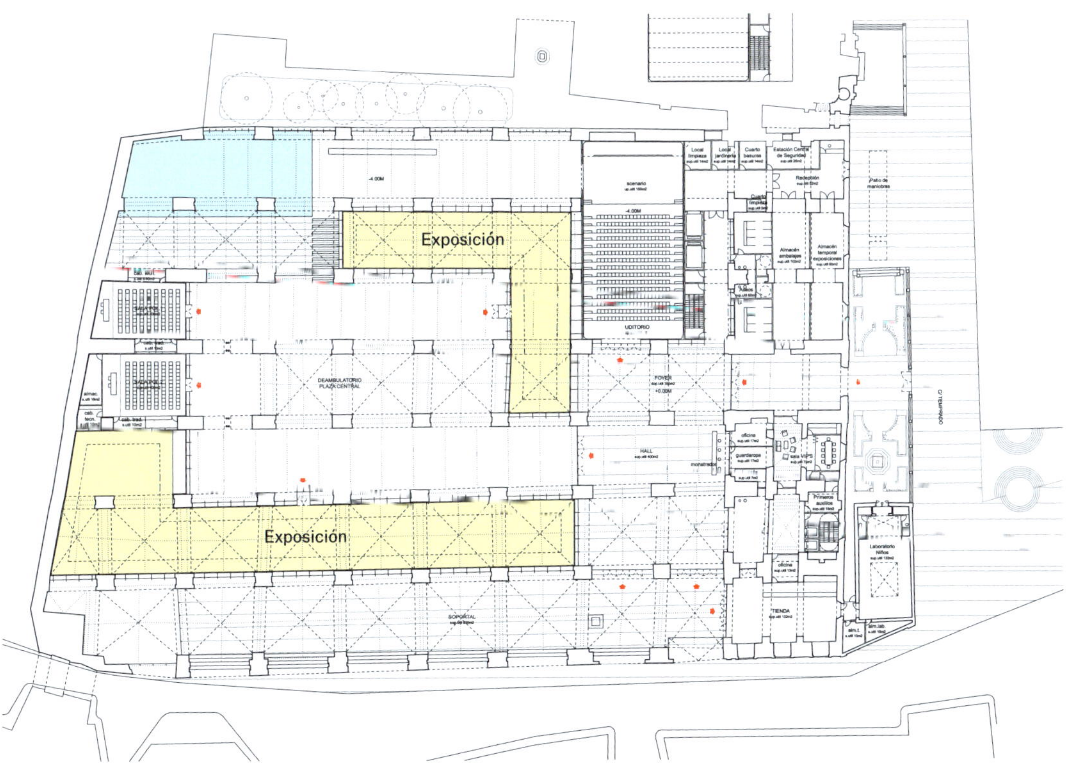
Exposición
Exposición

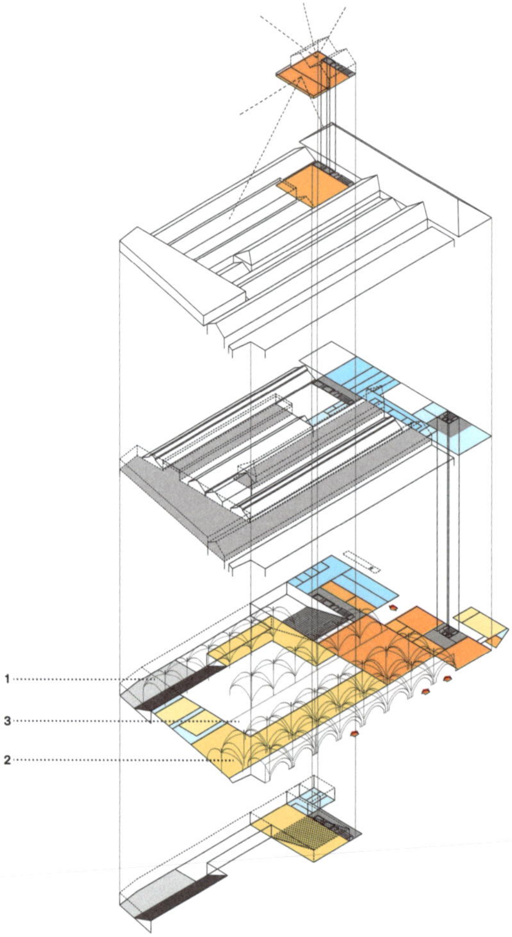

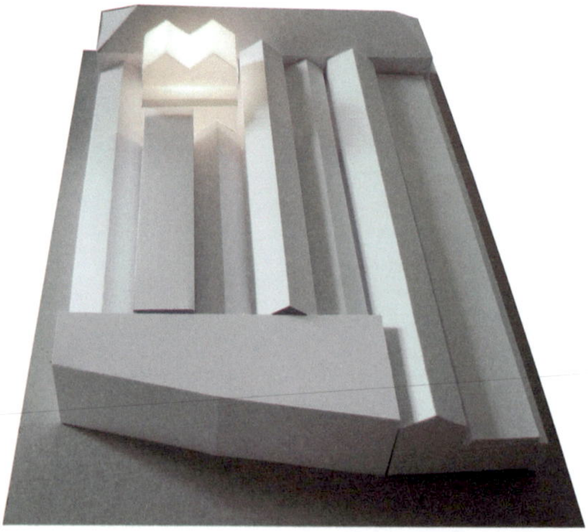

1. Recovering the original water level

2. Exhibition galleries

3. Central bays with pipeclay paving

Antoni Tàpies Foundation. Barcelona, Spain. 2007-2010

In renovating the Antoni Tàpies Foundation, our primary intention was to open up this historic building to the public with new galleries, archives and learning spaces, concentrating the offices into a new, three-floor pavilion to the rear of the plot and with an exit onto the city block. But the Antoni Tàpies Foundation is also keen to help consolidate a new generation of museums that double up as centres of cultural production, hence the multi-use spaces adapted to a wide range of artistic practices, to the need for a thermodynamic balance, to the appraisal of a legacy, and to neutralize the spatial ambiance to intensify the experience for visitors, who can visualise the entire programme underpinning cultural production and the modernist building itself as an integral part of the exhibition space. Environmentally, the extension substantially improves the original building's natural lighting and form factor, containing it in a single volume that reduces energy exchange, with a design that has increased its area without altering the existing climate control systems.

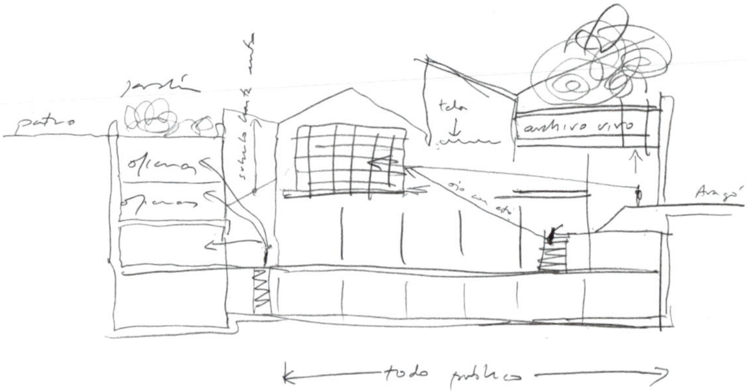

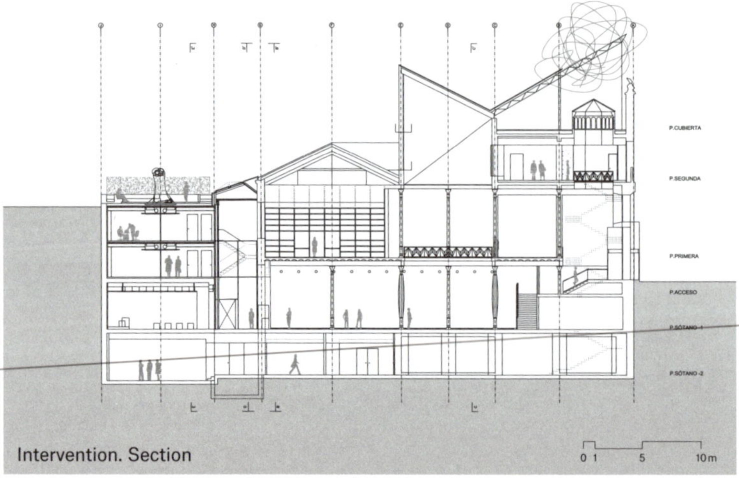

Intervention. Section

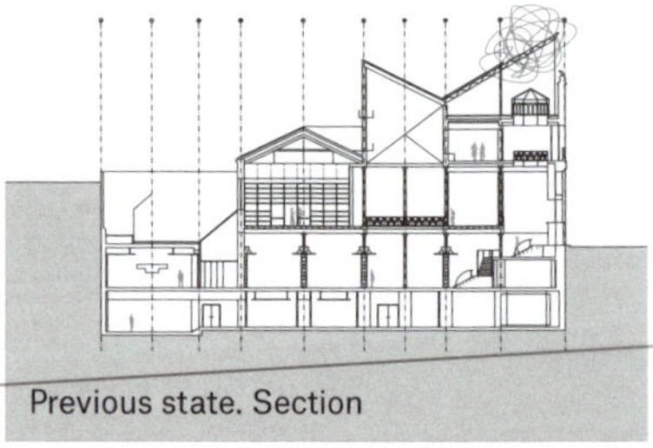
Previous state. Section

FUNDACIÓ ANTONI TÀPIES

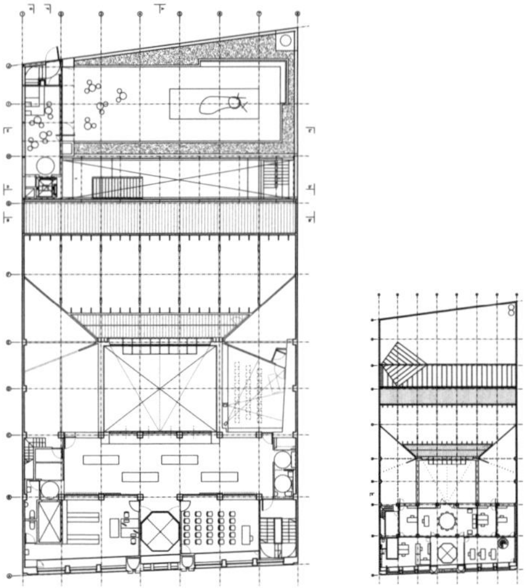

Level 2

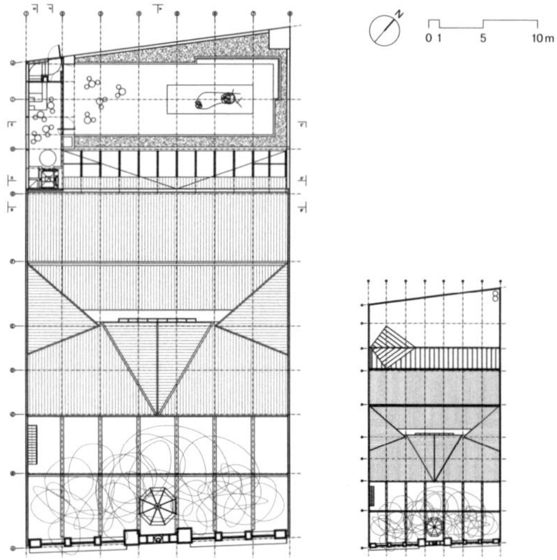

Roof plan

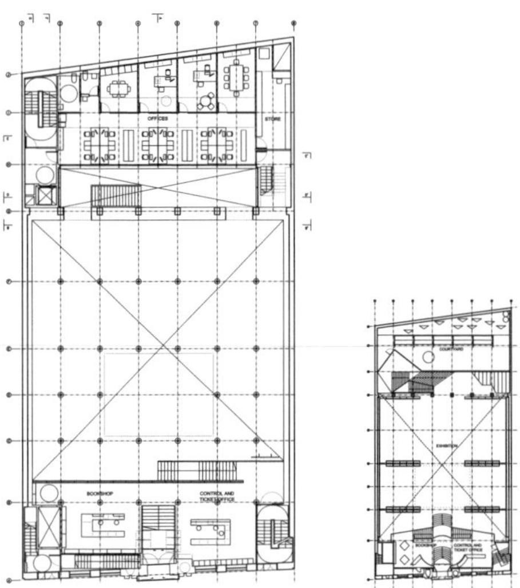

Ground floor plan

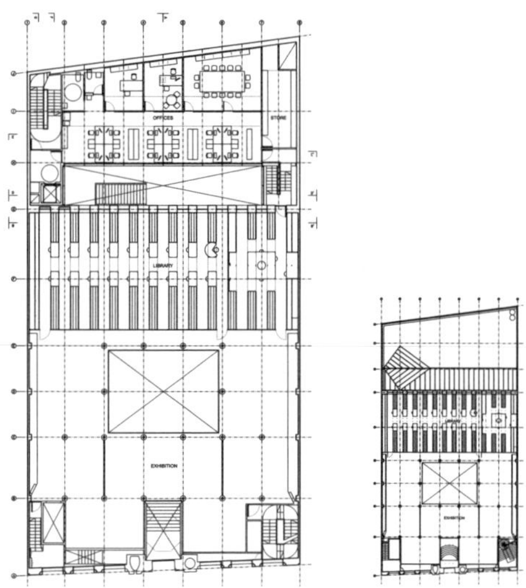

Level 1

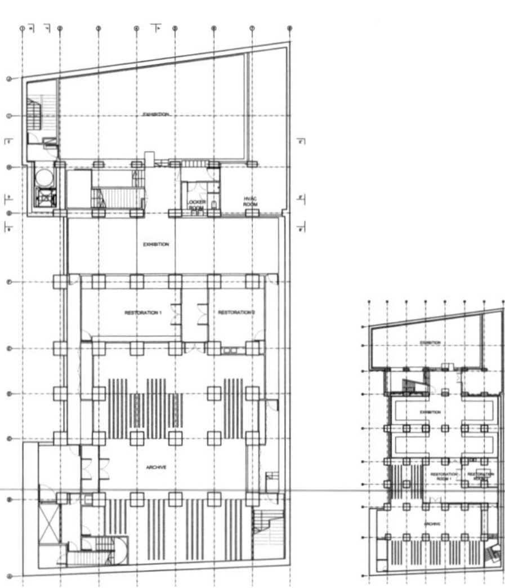

Level -2

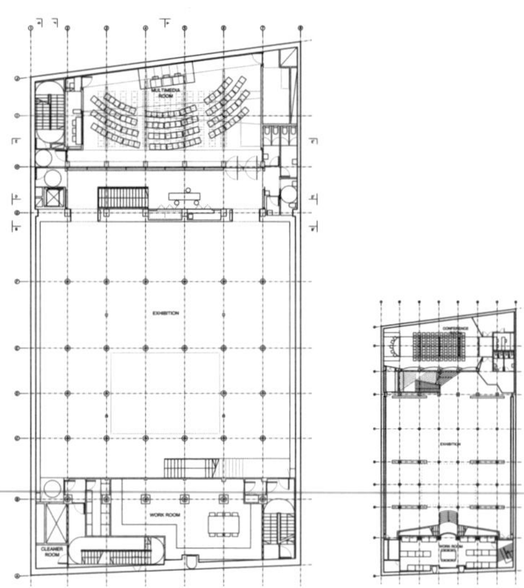

Level -1

Antoni Tàpies.
llocs de l'art

Espai
C

City Museum and Art Gallery. Wuhan, China. 2016-2017

The restored building belonged to the Chinese headquarters of the Religious Tract Society, an English publisher of religious books. Built in 1911 by R. E. Hemmings, it had an interesting, monumental gallery along its main façade, open on the second and third floors, with a corniche underneath arches at each end of the main, triple-height frontage. The building, subject of a systematic study by UDg Lianchuang Internacional, was derelict and even used as substandard accommodation. As a result, only a few of the ornamental features inside had survived the ravages of time to provide clues for the interior restoration. A fourth floor, a later addition, was practically in ruins, and some parts of the structure had disappeared completely. The architectural design focused on a meticulous restoration of the original building's exterior; out of necessity, a looser interpretation was required for the interiors to be repurposed as an art gallery as the first phase in the regeneration of a large residential British Concession district developed along the Wuhan / Quingdao Road. A small rooftop pavilion and garden was added for special events and inaugurations at the museum.

安全通道

Restoration of Residential Building on Calle Barquillo. Madrid, Spain. 2009

Adapting residential heritage buildings to new lifestyles requires an understanding of how to connect urban memories to today's idea of "a good life"—one apparently removed from the past yet which forever reverts to it, albeit in a different way. With this project we sought to set up a dialogue between the summation of rooms whose use is defined by personal items and a typical 19th-century wall structure, replacing the irrelevance of the exterior landscape by building an interior one based on spatial concatenation, use of light and reflections. This adapted the house to a programme suitable for single occupants, couples or families—or all of them at once—while preserving its architectural form. The pre-existing decorative elements are integrated into the layout of living rooms and objects, introducing a temporal dimension that coexists with contemporary use.

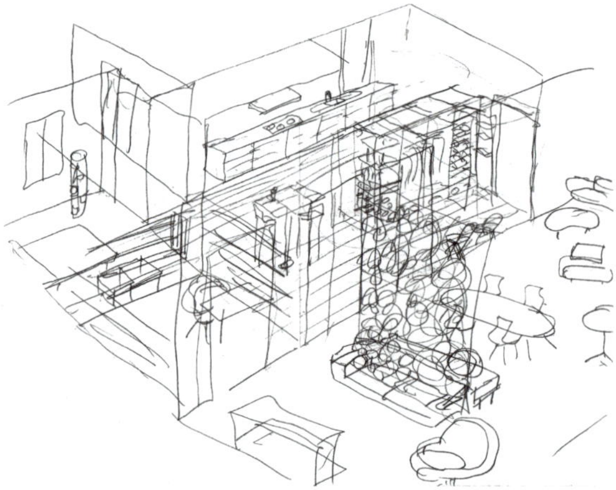

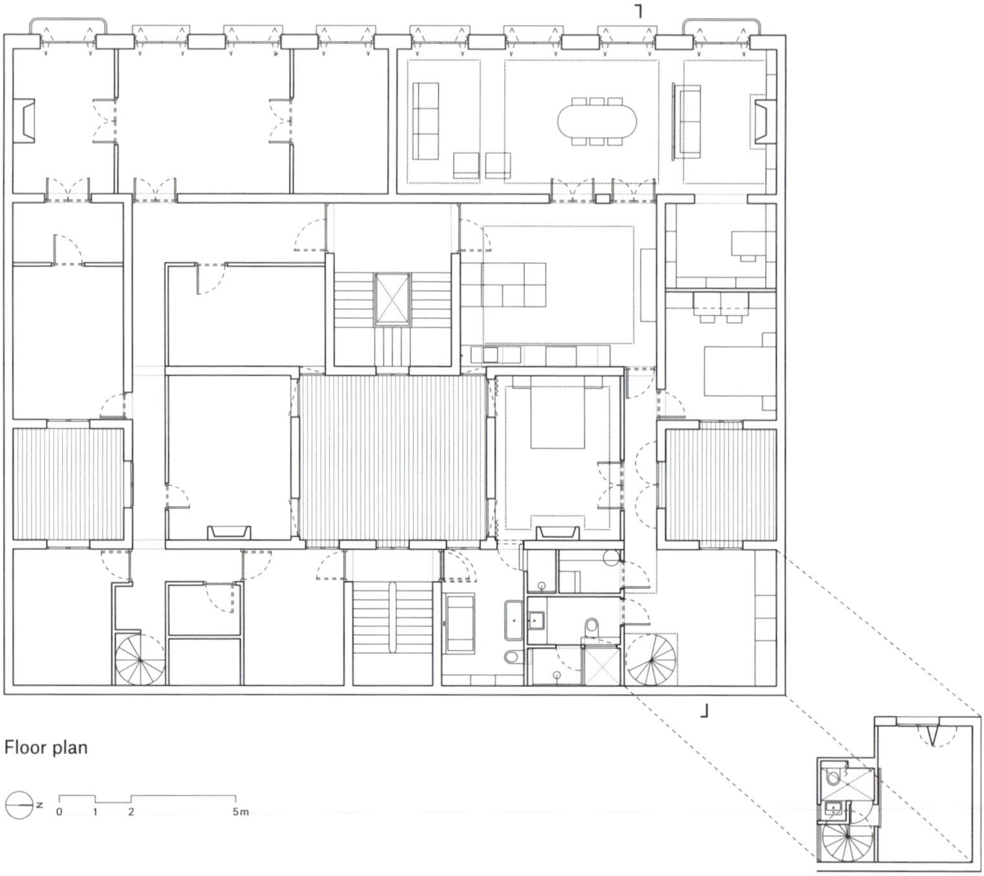

Floor plan

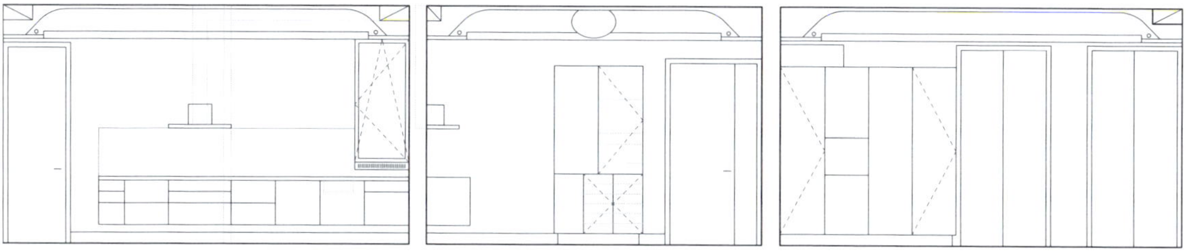

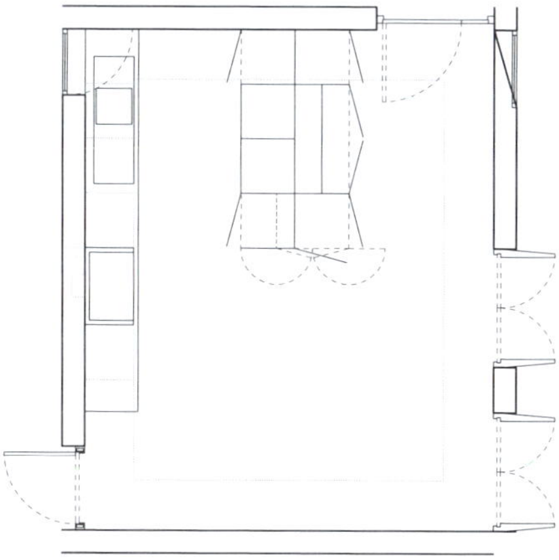

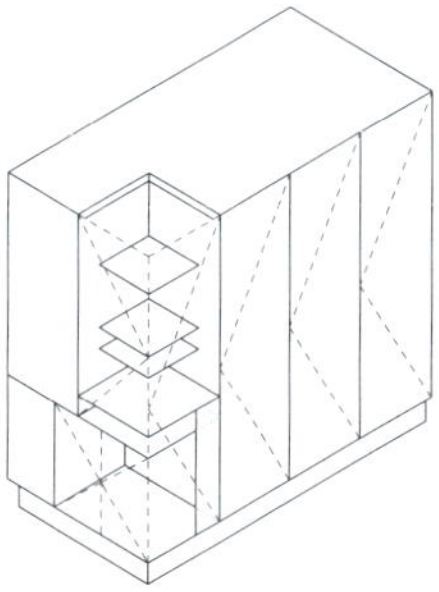

Kitchen detail

RICHARD AVEDON

Atelier Albert Oehlen. Bülher, Switzerland. 2007–2009

This small construction on a steeply sloping site almost permanently covered in snow takes the shape of a white prism encrusted in the hill toward the north and juts out over the landscape toward the south. It houses a diaphanous atelier and a semi-basement used for storage. A picture window connects the atelier and the landscape, while natural light enters through two skylights. The main volume and skylights are cut away in triangular form on the slope, giving the building its distinctive appearance. With its industrial finishes, volumes and white colour scheme, the project makes an effort to blend in with the nearby residential buildings and the snowy landscape of the Saint-Gallen district. In terms of its environmental credentials, the built structure and its underground area strive to be as compact as possible. The south-facing openings (with smart blinds that can be given specific orientations) capture the sunlight and provide the best possible lighting conditions for the work space. Heating is provided exclusively by geothermal technology, supported by a highly inert construction system: a concrete structure in the underground areas, and wood laminates elsewhere, using particle boards with recycled paper and salt insulation, all covered with industrial panels outside, a green roof as a continuation of the slope and zinc clad skylights.

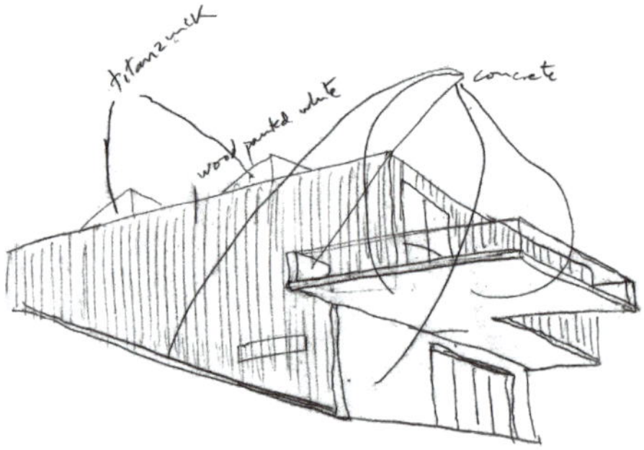

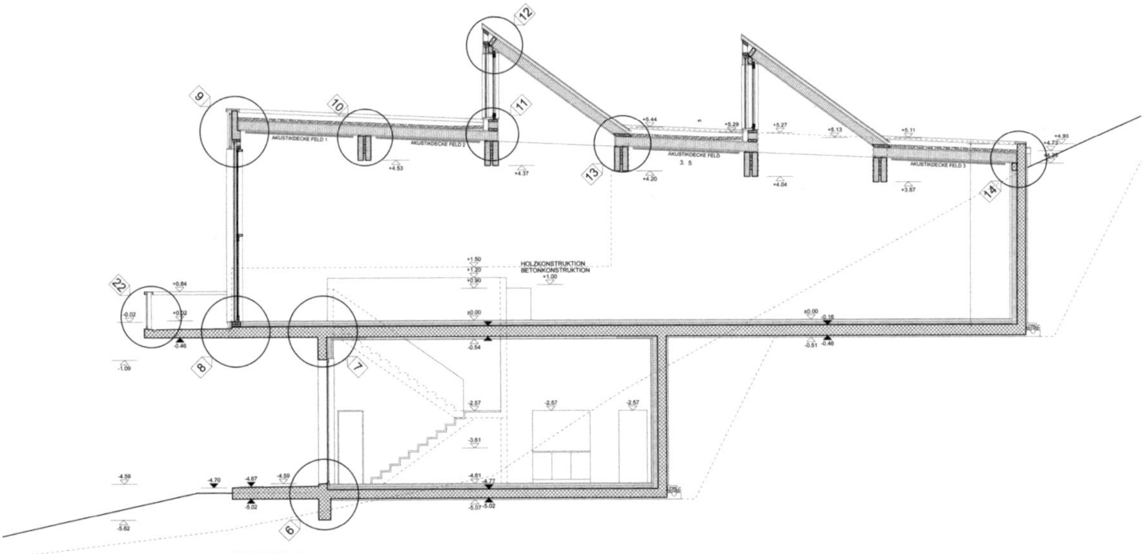
HOLZKONSTRUKTION
BETONKONSTRUKTION
AKUSTIKDECKE FELD 1
AKUSTIKDECKE FELD 2
AKUSTIKDECKE FELD 3

SCHNITT A-A

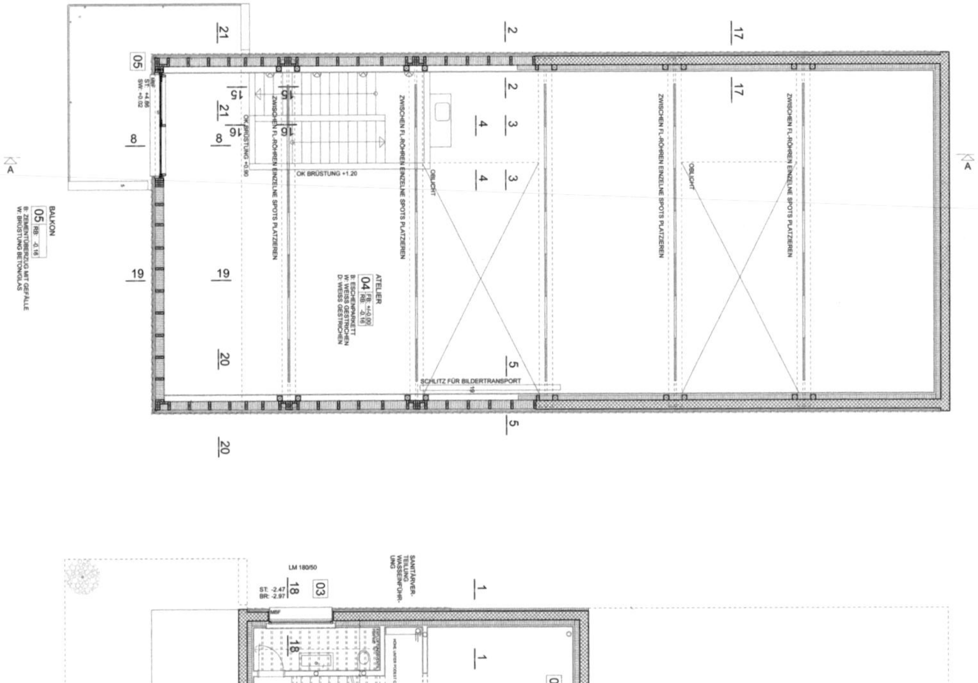
ATELIER
BALKON
OK BRÜSTUNG +1.20
OK BRÜSTUNG +0.90
ZWISCHEN FL-RÖHREN EINZELNE SPOTS PLATZIEREN
OBLICHT
SCHLITZ FÜR BILDERTRANSPORT

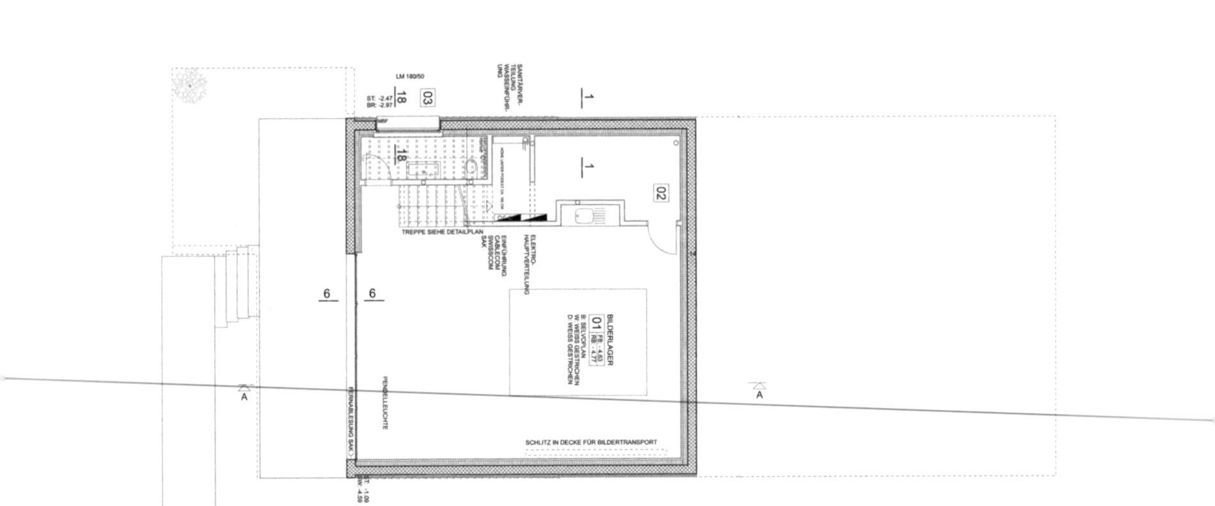
BILDERLAGER
TREPPE SIEHE DETAILPLAN
SCHLITZ IN DECKE FÜR BILDERTRANSPORT
PENDELLEUCHTE
LM 180/50

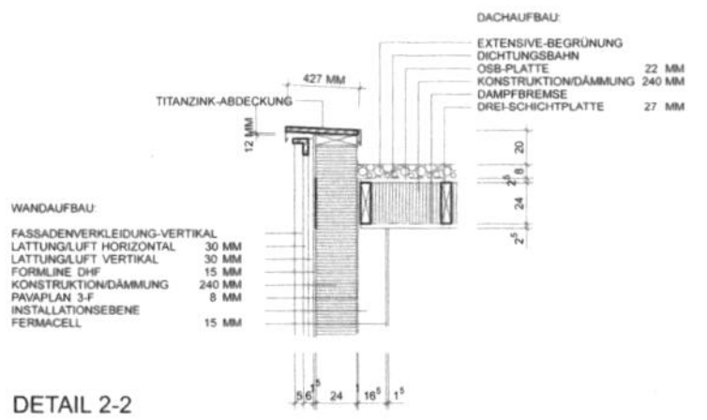

DETAIL 2-2

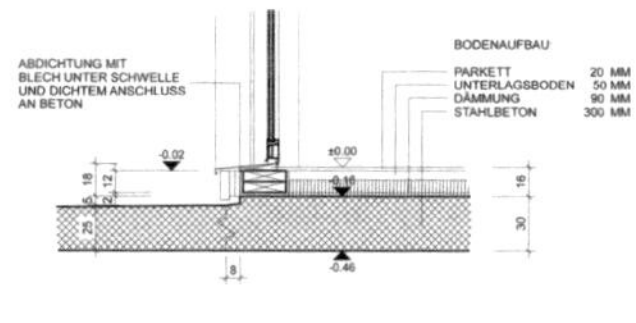

DETAIL 8-8

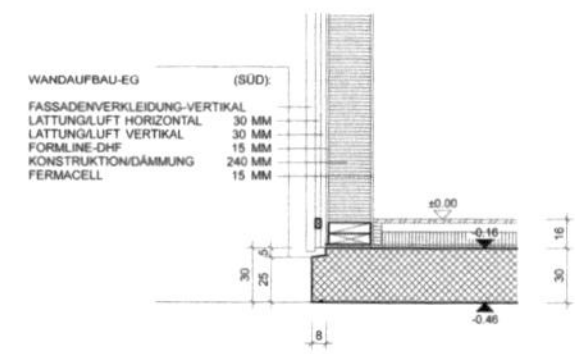

DETAIL 19-19

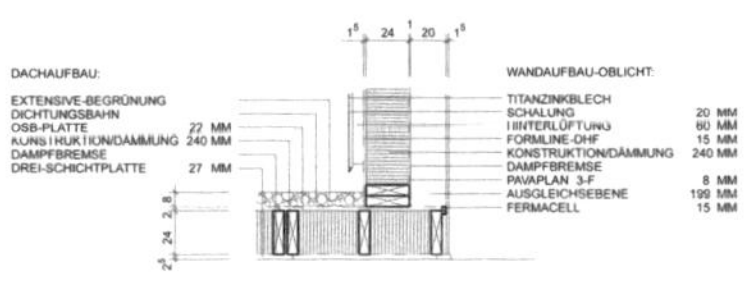

DETAIL 3-3

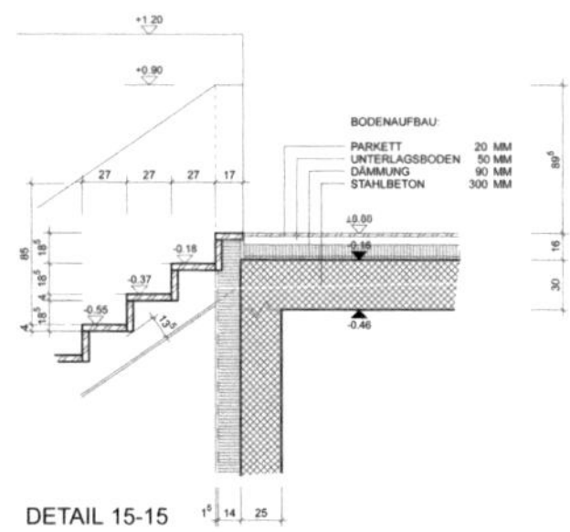

DETAIL 15-15

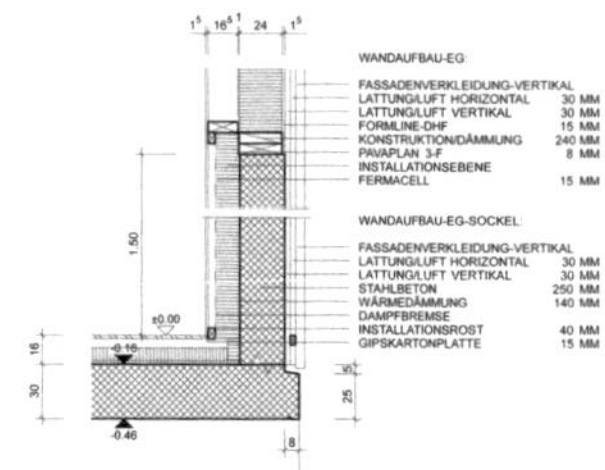

DETAIL 20-20

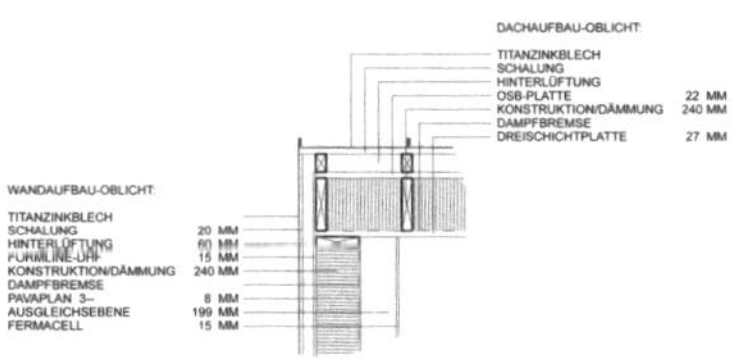

DETAIL 4-4

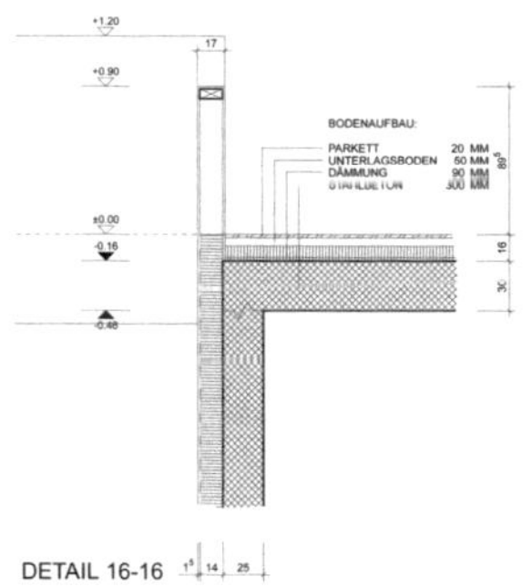

DETAIL 16-16

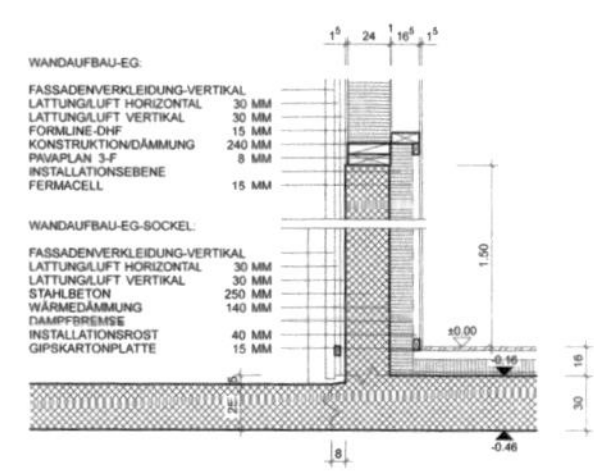

DETAIL 21-21

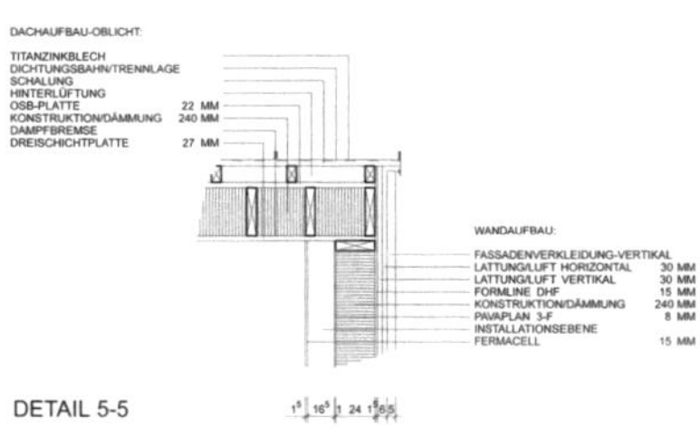

DETAIL 5-5

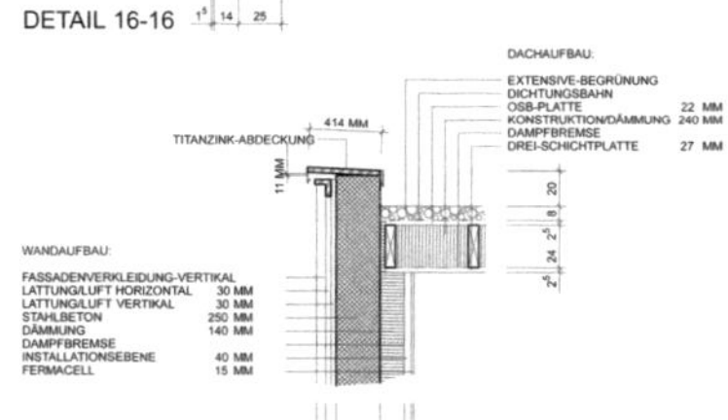

DETAIL 17-17

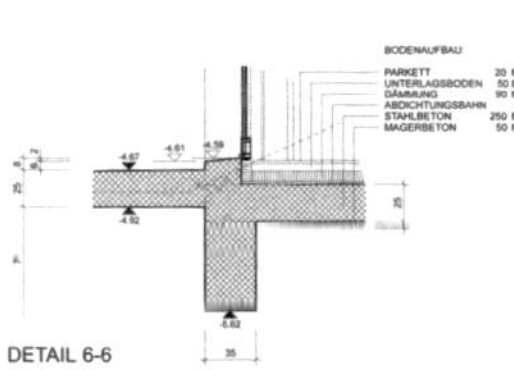

DETAIL 6-6

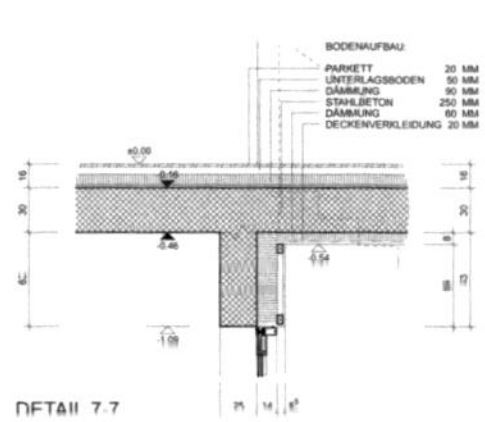

DETAIL 7-7

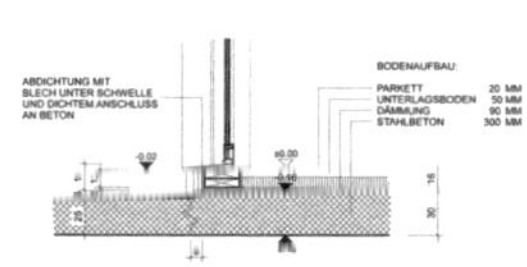

DETAIL 8-8

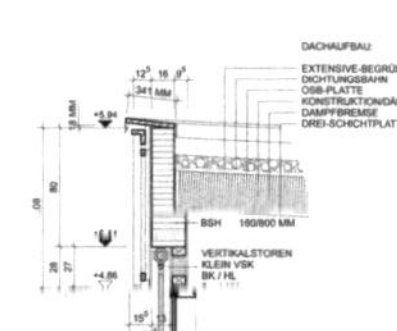

DETAIL 9-9

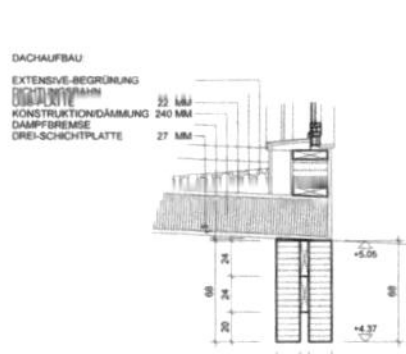

DETAIL 11-11

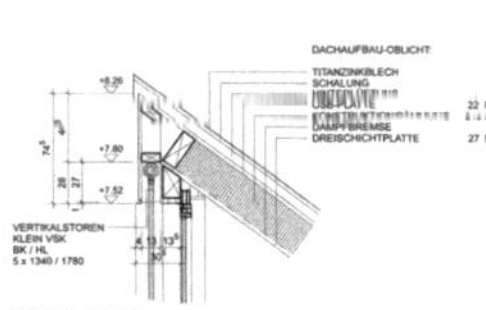

DETAIL 12-12

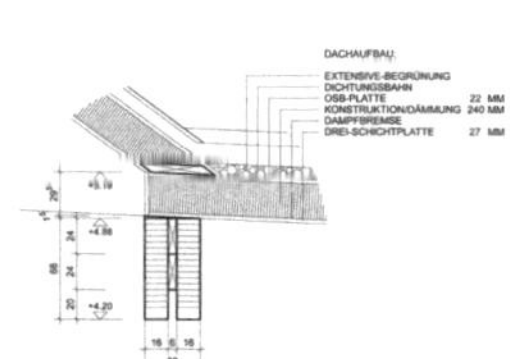

DETAIL 13-13

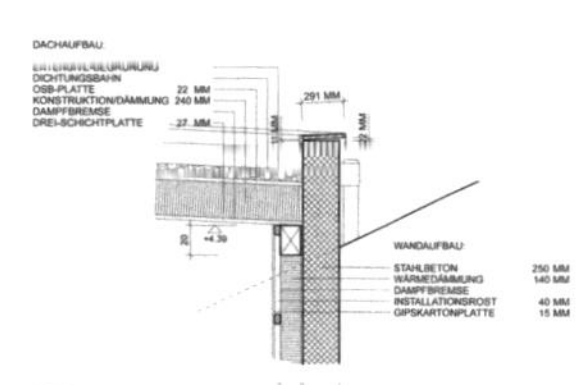

DETAIL 14-14

Co-living Aranberri. Itziar, Guipúzcoa, Spain. 2006-2014

Situated halfway up a slope on the border between an industrial and a natural landscape, four residences for the members of a single family form a group. The construction's placement was chosen to avail of views over the garden, mountains, and sea. The orientation also makes best use of solar gain and ventilation, while protecting the privacy of occupants. Organized as a co-living arrangement, it is the first built experience that has seen a diverse family group establish a residential complex where the living spaces are intermingled both with productive spaces (agricultural on the one hand and artistic on the other) and with spaces for exchange and socializing. The project was developed through a self-construction process in which the future inhabitants were actively involved in distributing roles according to their preferences, training and experience.

0 1 2
5m

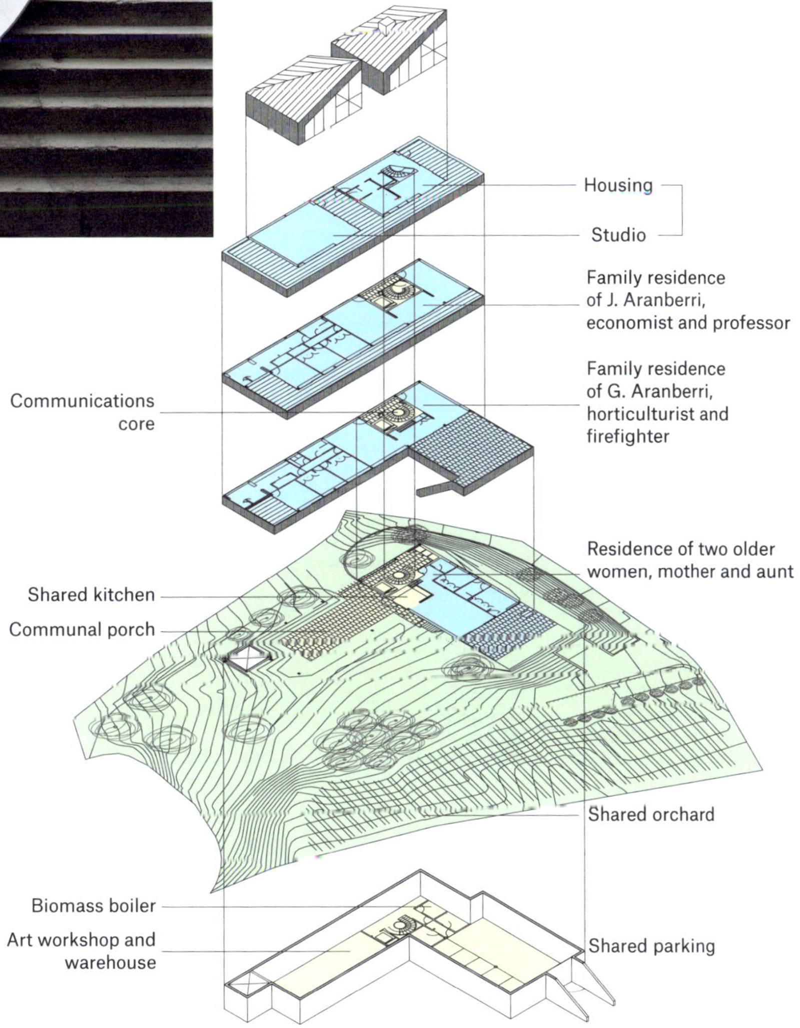
Housing
Studio
Family residence of J. Aranberri, economist and professor
Family residence of G. Aranberri, horticulturist and firefighter
Communications core
Residence of two older women, mother and aunt
Shared kitchen
Communal porch
Shared orchard
Biomass boiler
Art workshop and warehouse
Shared parking

Seniors' Residence and Day Centre. Los Llanos de Aridane, Island of La Palma, Spain. 2020-

For seniors who require care, we have proposed a model of spatial organization distinct to that usually found in 'old people's homes' and inspired by the fragmentation of residential units around a shared space, a strategy typical of the Carthusian monks. The project is located on the island of Palma and comprises eight pavilions surrounding a shared cloister and garden. Each pavilion is home to a small number of residents, helping to avoid the epidemiological issues linked with large-scale residences, a problem of particular resonance today. In addition, the sloping site enables all the medical and maintenance services required to be located beneath this complex, while the pavilion roofs provide terraces and shared spaces overlooking the sea, the sunset and the outline of the nearby National Park, while enjoying the gentle climate and breezes of this delightful location.

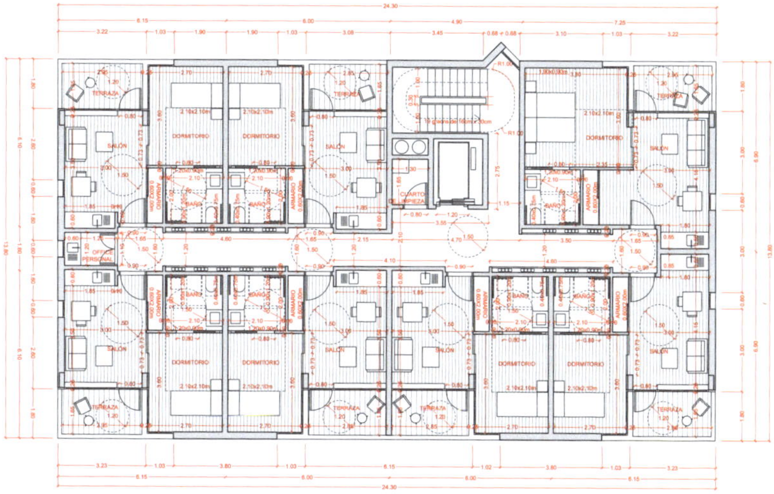

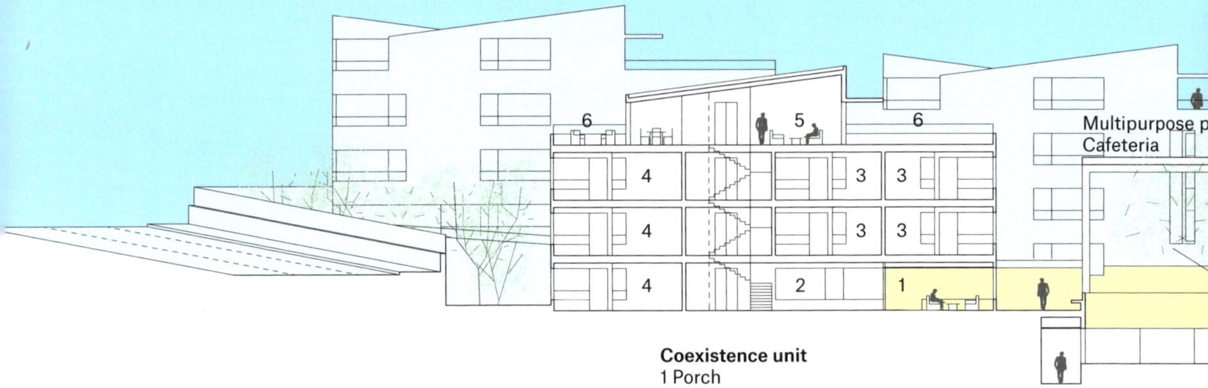

Coexistence unit
1 Porch
2 Lobby
3 Single housing
4 Double housing
5 Common area: dining room, kitchen, living
6 Terrace

DAY CENTER:
CD1 Porch
CD2 Lobby
CD3 Director's office + reception / meeting room
CD4 Dinning room
CD5 Multipurpose room
CD6 Multipurpose care office
CD7 Rehabilitation therapy room
CD8 Nursing room
CD9 Geriatric bath
CD10 Toilets

SERVICE AREAS:
1 Parking for staff and visitors
2 Staff area:
2A Changing rooms and staff toilets
2B Maintenance staff room
2C Office for staff per plant (in UC plants)
3 Logistics area:
3A General kitchen
3B Garbage room
3C Laundry service
3D Dirty room
4 Storage:
4A General material warehouse
4B Storage of personal belongings
4C Facilities area
5 Health personnel area:
5A Medical office
5B Nursing room
5C Staff office
5D Medicine room
Administrative area:
6 Lobby
7 Management and offices
8 Meeting room
9 Reception of relatives
10 Toilets
11 UC connection

COMMON AREAS:
Multipurpose room + multipurpose care office (included in CD5 and CD6 Day Center)
Rehabilitation therapy room (included in CD7 Day Center and ground floor)
12 Chapel
13 Farewell room

Basement floor plan

Staff area Kitchens Dinning Day Center access

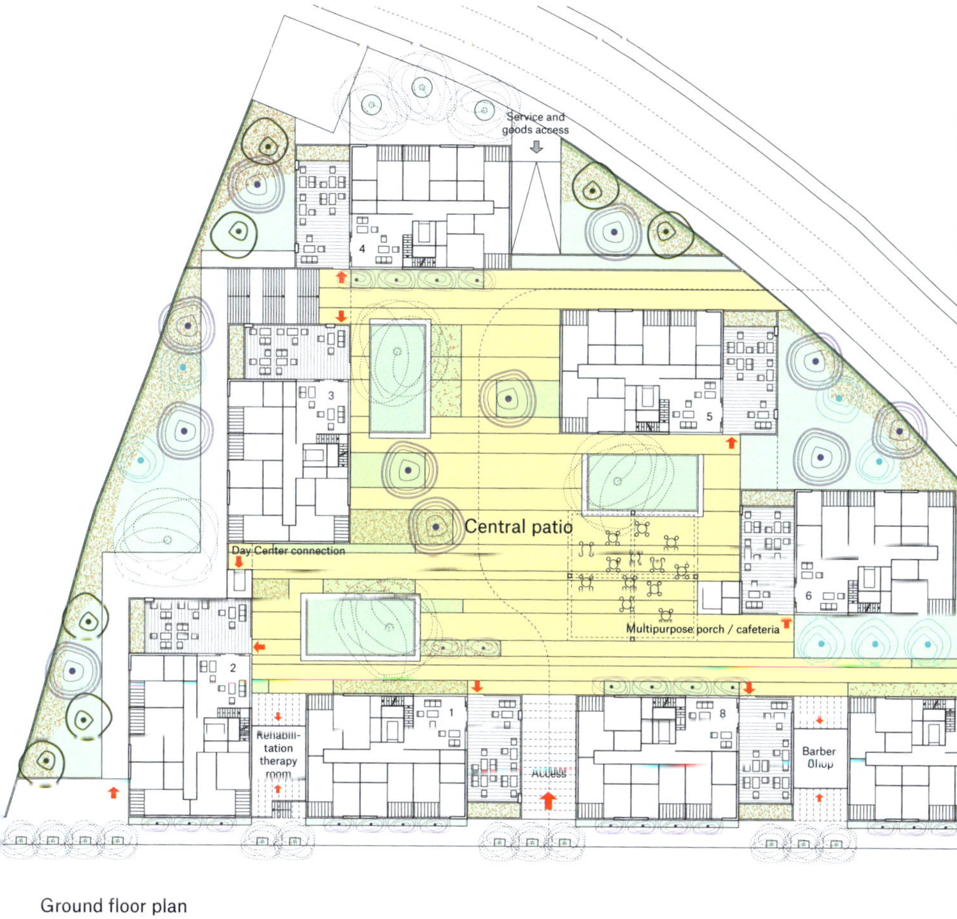

Ground floor plan

Coexistence unit

1 Porch
2 Lobby
3 Single Housing
4 Doube Housing
5 Staff Office
6 Cleaning room

Coexistence unit

Common areas
1 Kitchen
2 Dinning room
3 Living
4 Toilets
5 Cleaning room
6 Terrace

Attic floor plan

Instead of the garish option of assigning a different color to each façade, the choice was made to identify each pavilion by means of ornamental, floral and geometric motifs on the balcony roofs and canopies, color printed using photographic processes on tile. Eight patterns were designed, one for each residential unit, so that each block can be quickly identified by the color and motif, helping to improve the spatial orientation of the residents.

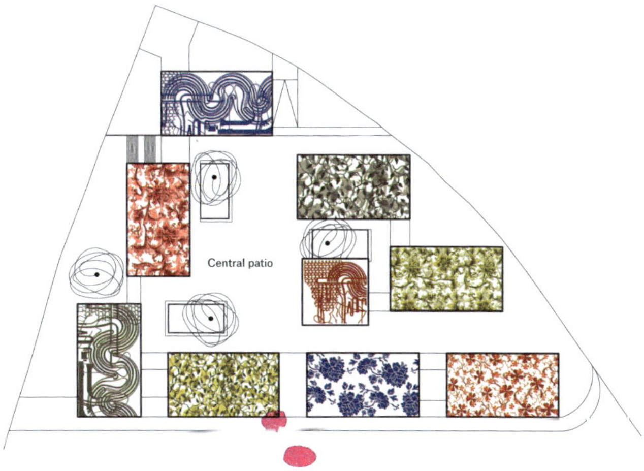

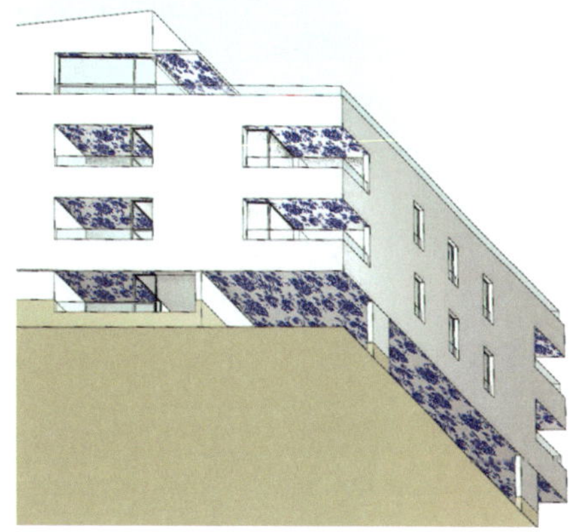

Spanish Cultural Centre. Buenos Aires, Argentina. 2011

The premise of this project is to provide universal access to every space—turning a desirable norm into a spatial concept informing the entire design. Therefore, the Palacio Buschiazzo inverts its main entrance to face the large central courtyard with its new stone-paved esplanade, framing this layout while the porticoed complex and new Interpretation Centre are ranged around a space with gardened areas and trees, freeing up room and creating a sense of greater space.

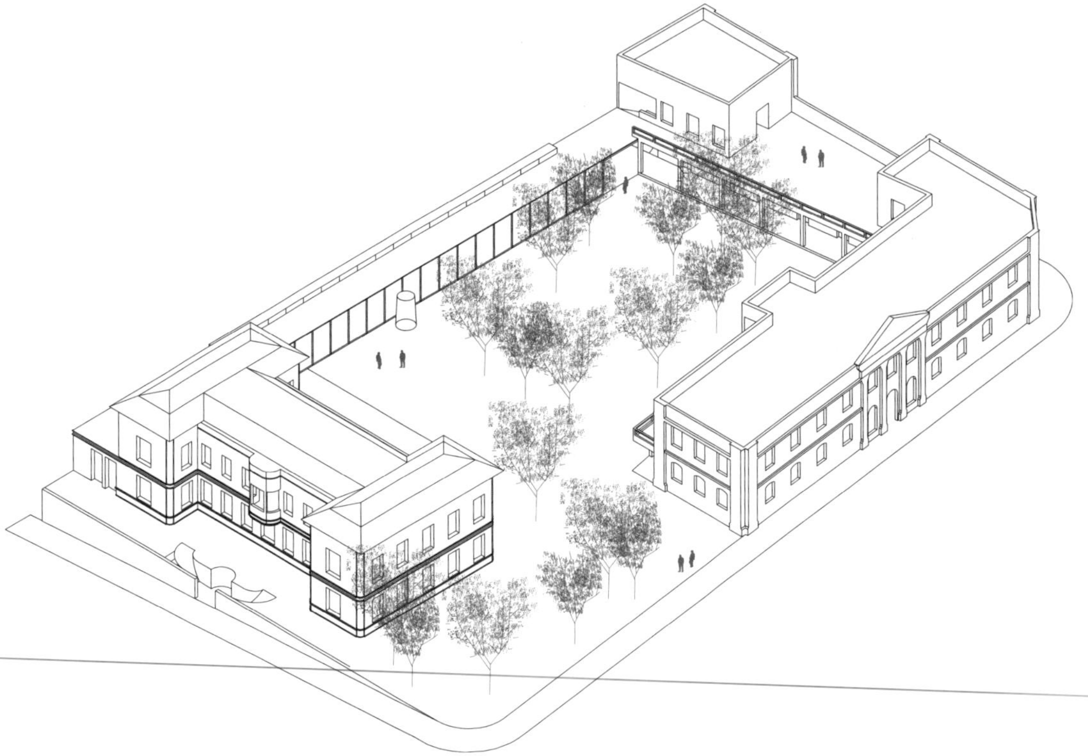

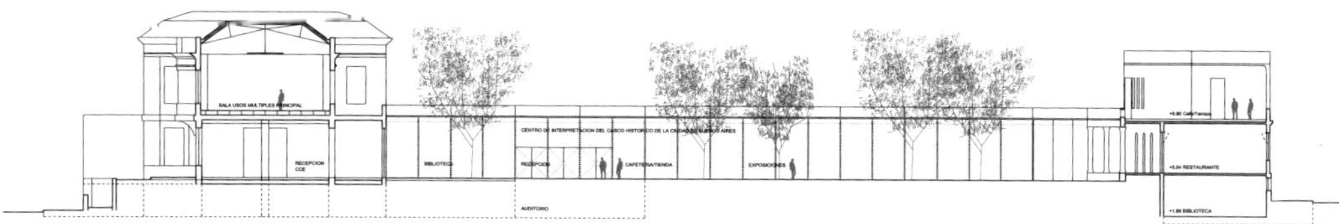

2

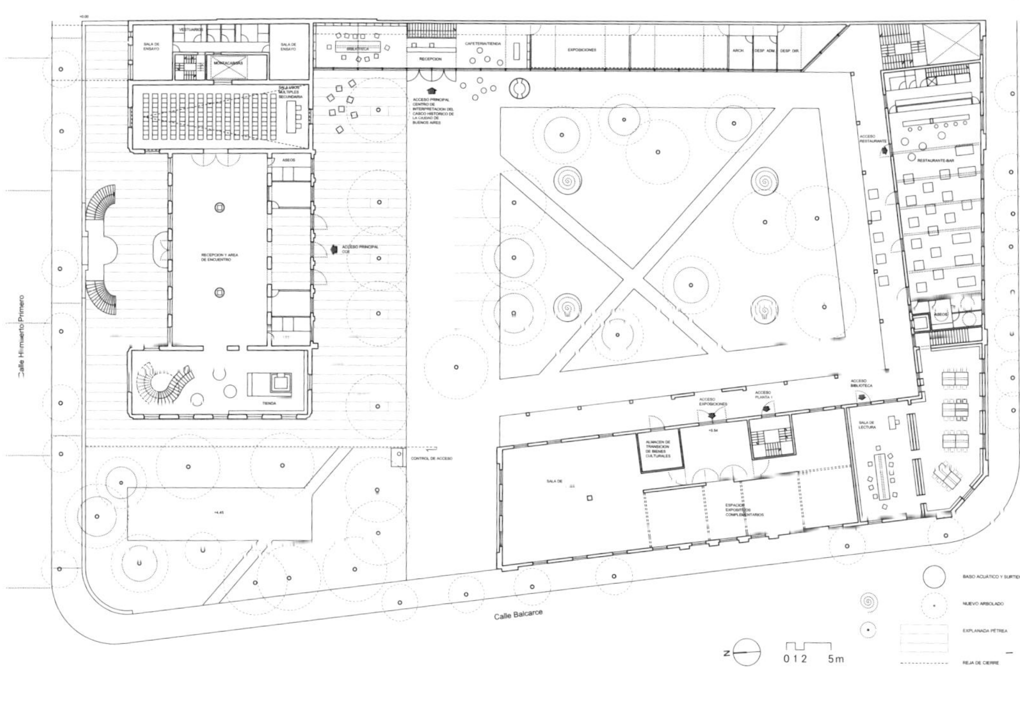

Integrating the High-Speed Train (TAV) Line in Atotxa Station. Donostia-San Sebastián, Guipúzcoa, Spain. 2018

This building complex is identified with one of the most traditional yet also contemporary Basque musical instruments: the *txalaparta*, a set of wooden planks arranged on benches. This form of percussion had virtually disappeared a few decades ago, but is now enjoying a resurgence as a unique instrument included in sophisticated musical compositions, including by Steve Reich. A *txalaparta* on an urban scale also has sculptural qualities, a unique and original object placed at the foot of the Tabakalera building to resonate with the institute and its artistic and cultural mission. This provides an elegantly simple solution that adapts to the site's restrictions, overcomes the difficulties of placing the TAV station in Donostia, and achieves the utmost sustainability by creating a new public space on top of the station.

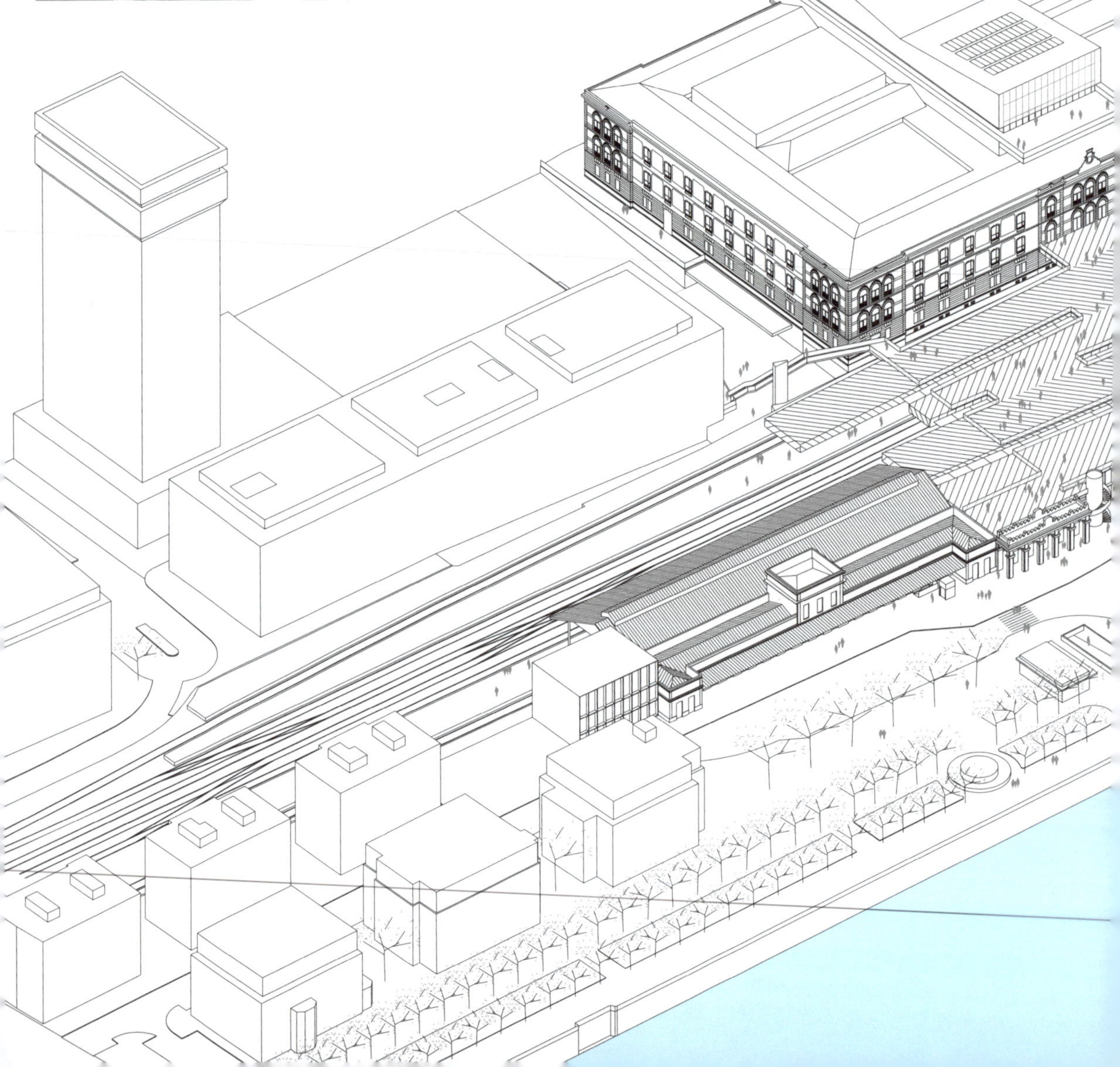

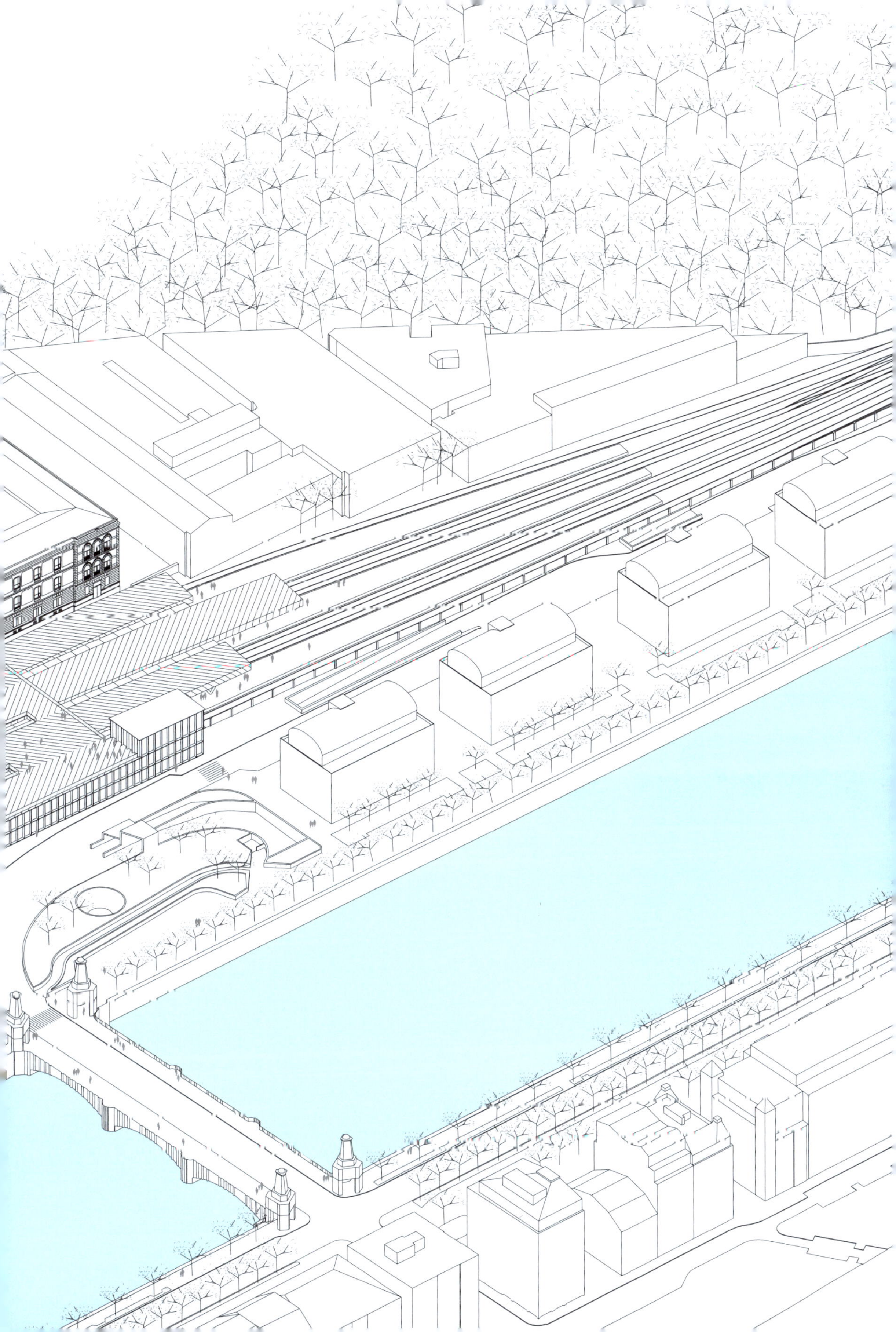

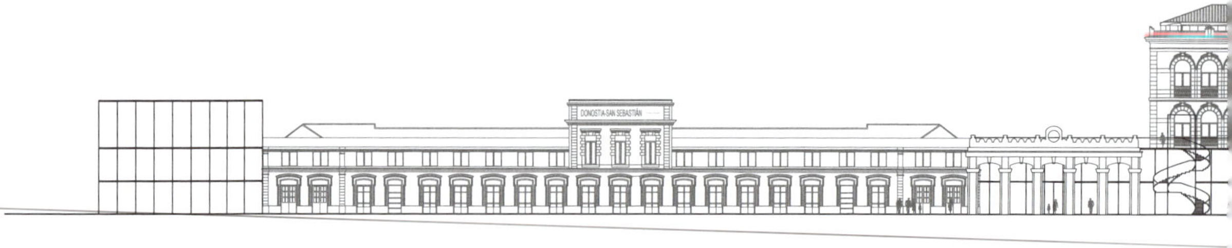
DONOSTIA-SAN SEBASTIÁN

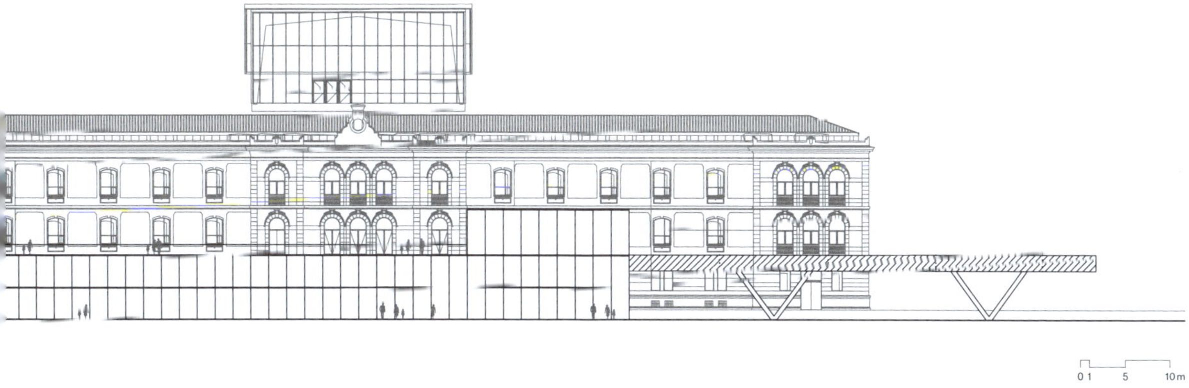
0 1 5 10m

Urban Design in Quart de Poblet. Valencia, Spain. 2018-

Based on the already-approved partial urban development plan, this design creates a neighbourhood that includes 861 residential units, shops and facilities. A series of small, robustly urban blocks are planned for the outer perimeter, contrasting with the interior frontages open to broad, internal green spaces. This dual approach not only responds to the homes' typologies, with living rooms facing the inner garden, but also to the aspiration to create a new urban area with a neighbourhood feel, with rows of shops and a scale that is full of vitality and offers people a sense of familiarity. We wanted to give the blocks a texture, volume and material quality that resonates with the richness of the city's 19th and 20th-century developments. By steering clear of a formal definition to the façades, we avoided an excessively geometric and minimalist radicalism, better suited to other contexts. For this project it seemed more appropriate to create a "softer", joined-up feel; we used some accents and curves to break away from an overly uniform look that would go against the neighbourhood feel we were seeking to create. We used four interlinked, staggered towers around the unique block opposite the Huerta del Molí d'Animeta park, a cultural heritage site. This design ensures maximum exposure to sunlight and open space in regard to the neighbouring volumes, and produces an active and iconic frontage by the park.

The housing units' typologies are organized around a central, prefabricated nucleus, with bedrooms facing the urbanised area and the living rooms and kitchen overlooking the block's interior. This layout minimizes circulations, optimizes cross-ventilation, allows for an en-suite master bedroom and the living room facing the garden, avoiding the feel of a "tube house". The home's space offers great flexibility with its open-plan design and with its single fixed point being the service nucleus and wet rooms.

Apartment Type 1A
2 bedrooms

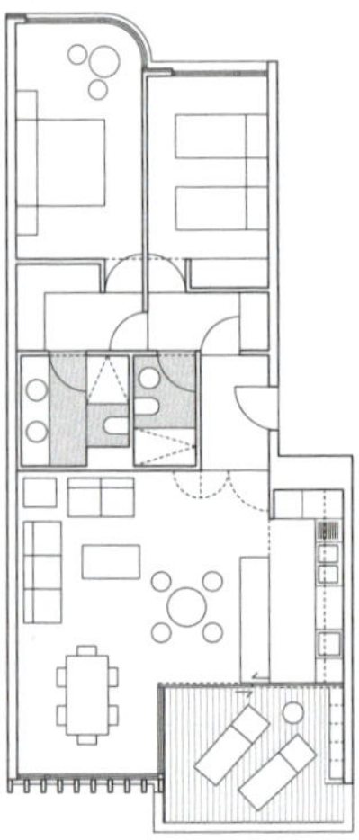

Apartment Type 2A
3 bedrooms

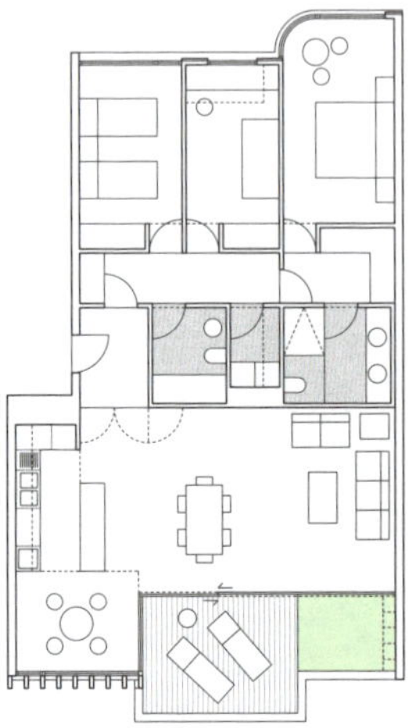

Variations

1.B

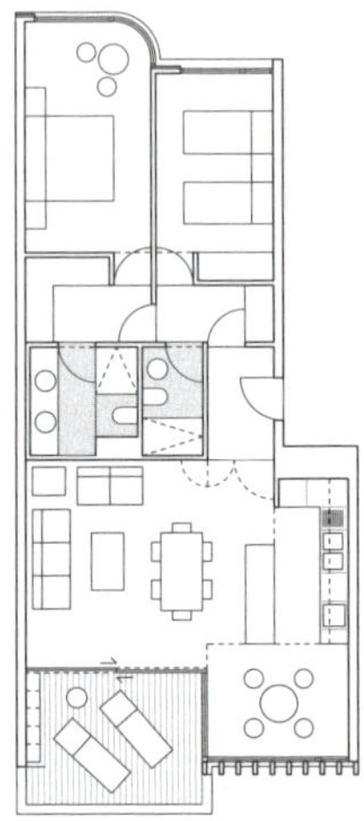

2.B

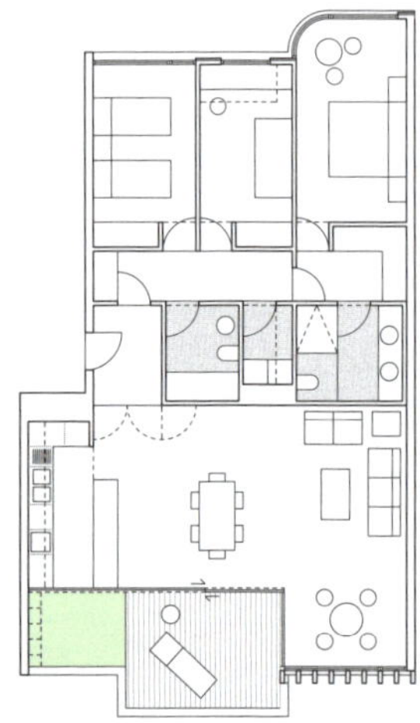

1.C

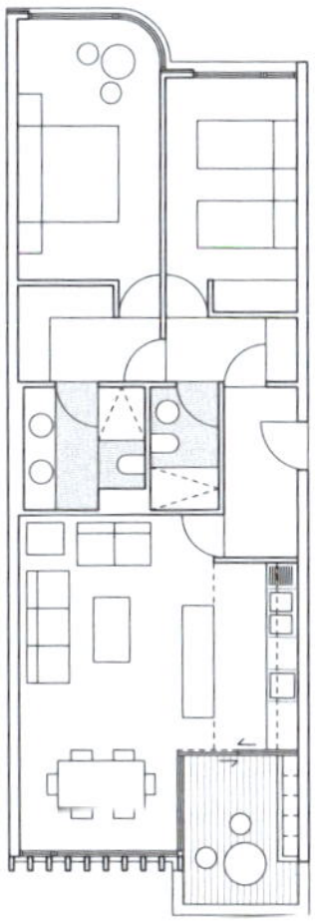

2.C 4 bedrooms

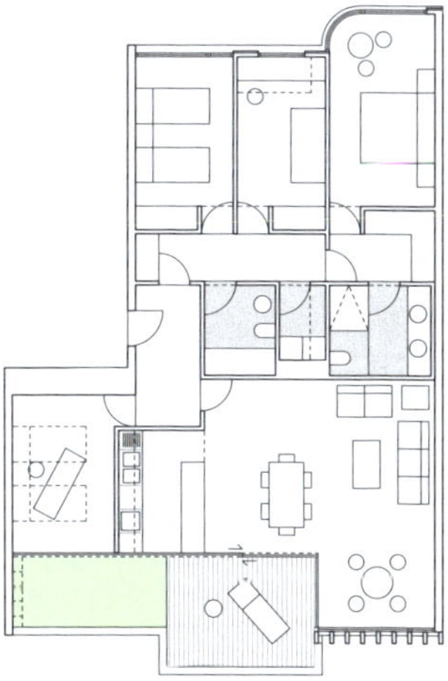

2.D 4 bedrooms

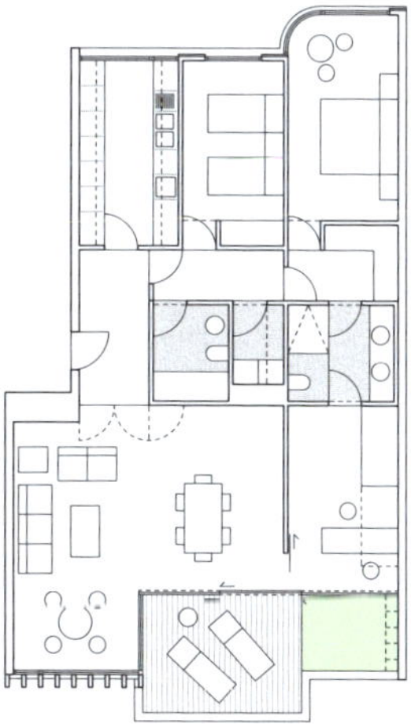

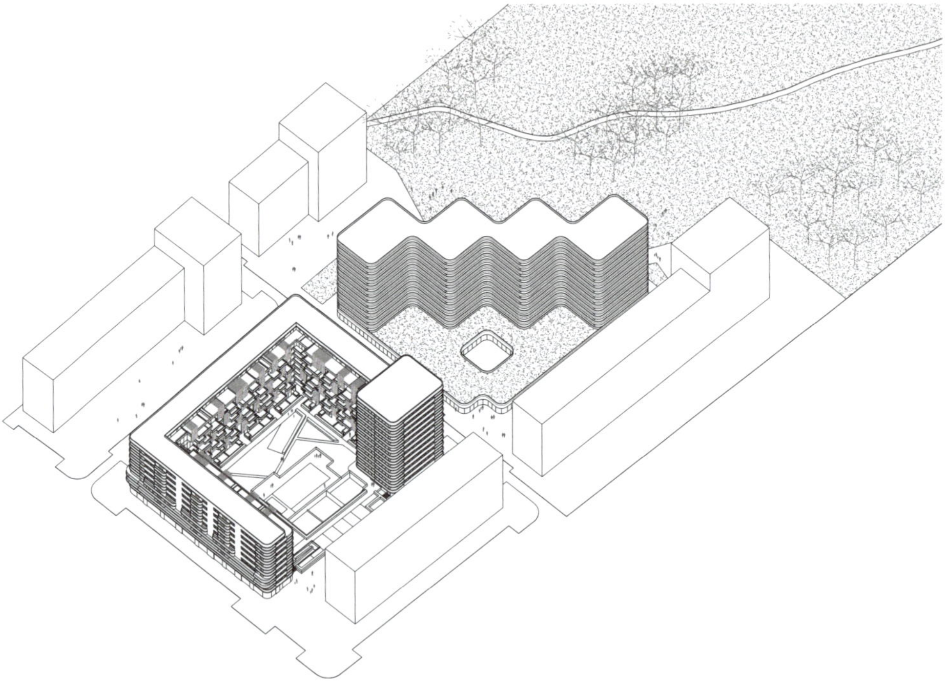

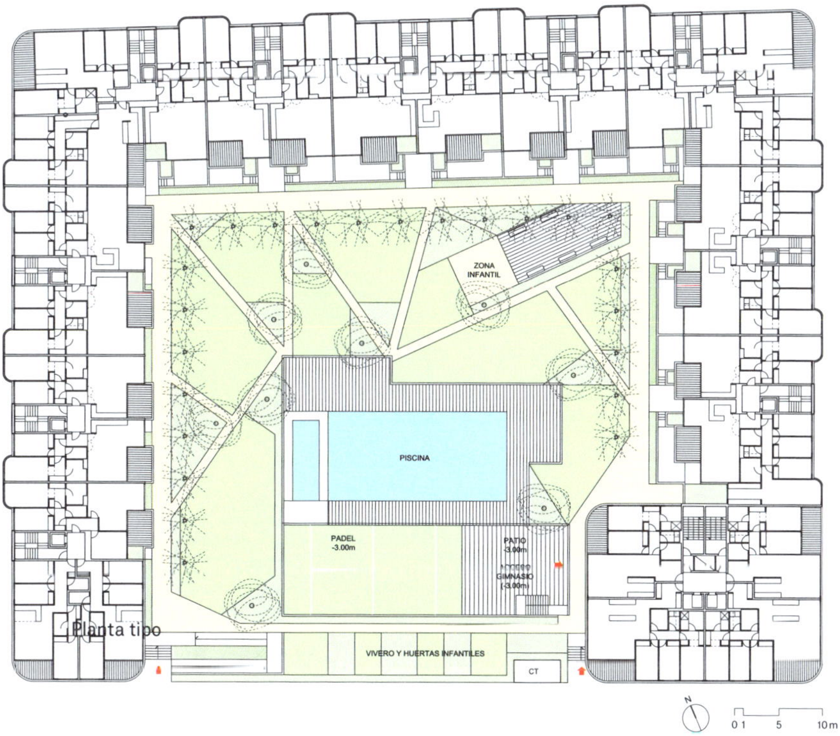
ZONA INFANTIL
PISCINA
PADEL -3.00m
PATIO -3.00m
GIMNASIO (-3.00m)
Planta tipo
VIVERO Y HUERTAS INFANTILES
CT
N
0 1 5 10 m

Solar Tower. Sociópolis, Valencia, Spain. 2008-2012

The Solar Tower rises up as a hybrid—half Banco de Bilbao, half Torres Blancas—both by Sáenz de Oíza in Madrid, both wonderful yet radically different. The project merges them to signal a shift away from the social housing of recurring, anonymous iconographies; instead, it explores the possibilities of a tower that narrows at the top, multiplying exterior and interior spaces with their own identity. The use of a reflective cladding and a curvilinear geometry that becomes more accentuated as it rises creates a series of reflections that naturally lifts the gaze upward toward the pinnacle of this high-rise building, in line with a thoroughly tried-and-tested model in the American city, modelled so often on the Giralda Tower. The Solar Tower received Valencia's highest energy-rating certificate.

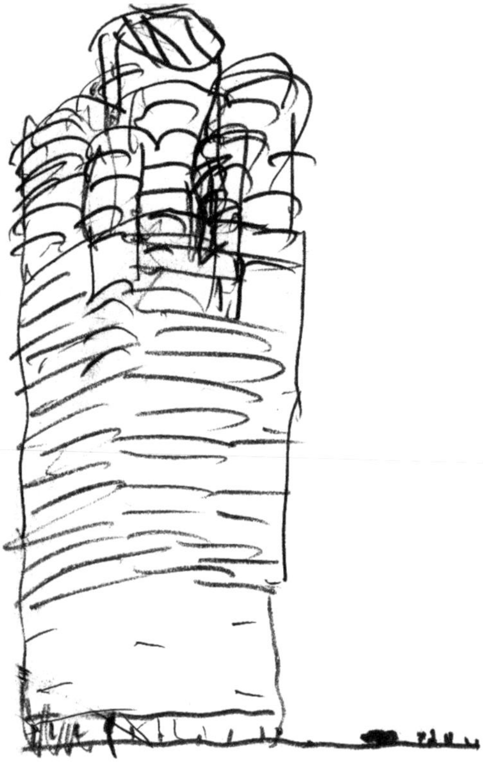

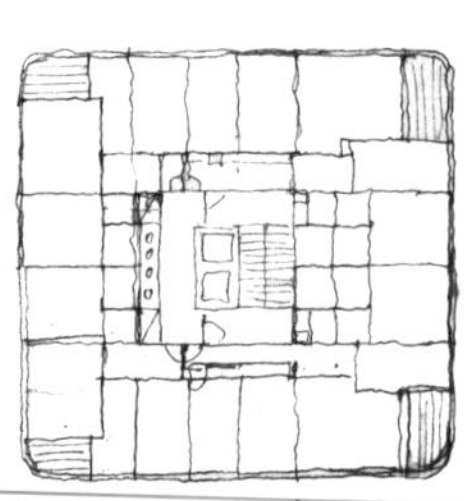

Banco de Bilbao / Torres Blancas. Francisco Javier Sáenz de Oíza

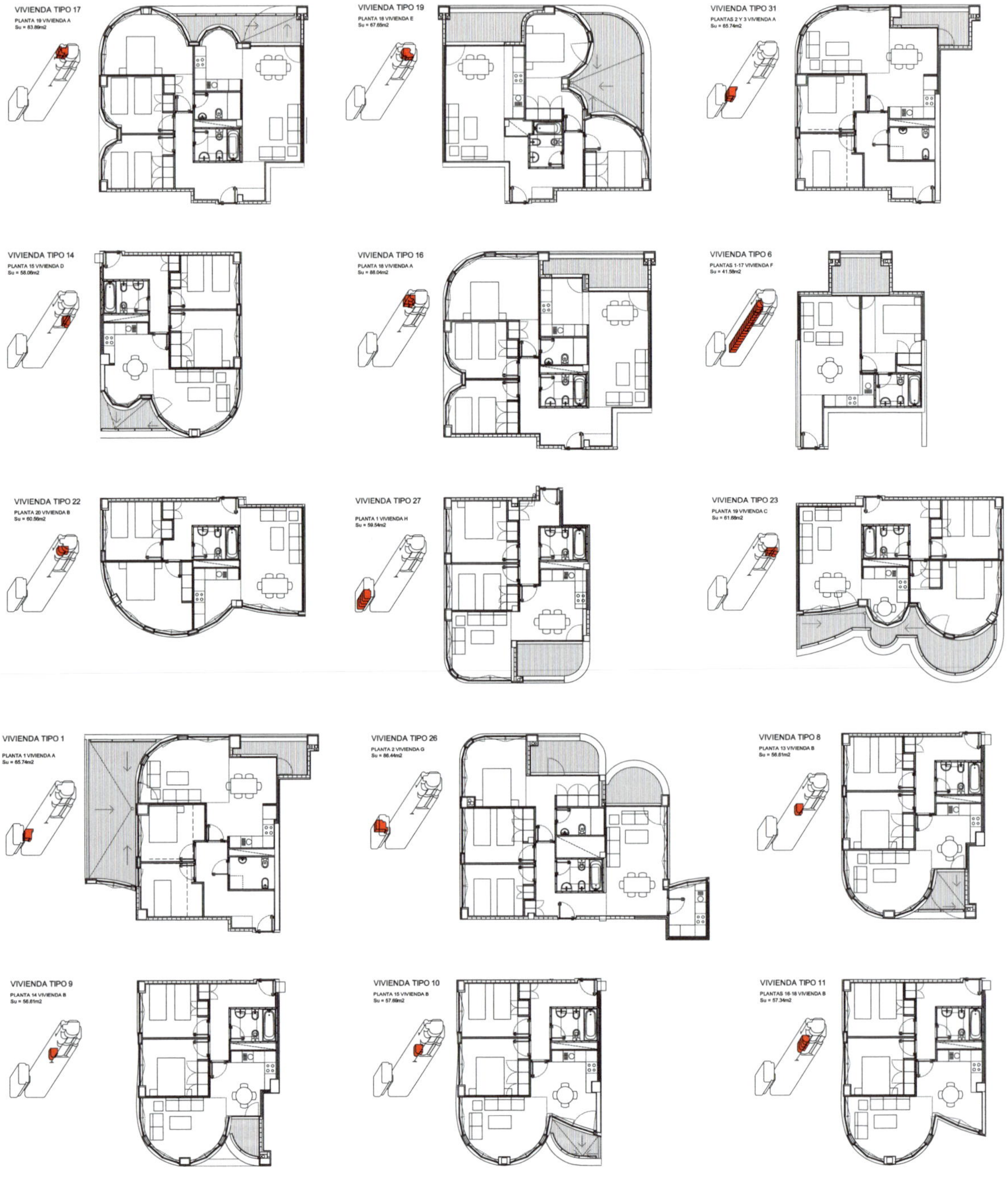

Typical dwellings. Floor plans and location in the tower

VIVIENDA TIPO 4

PLANTAS 1-12 VIVIENDA B
Su = 58.50m2

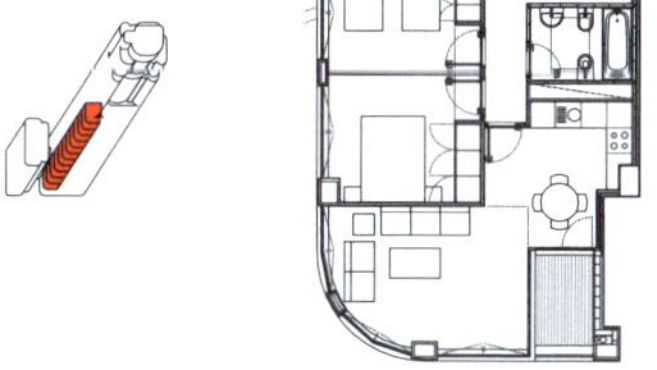

VIVIENDA TIPO 13

PLANTAS 16-18 VIVIENDA C
Su = 44.91m2

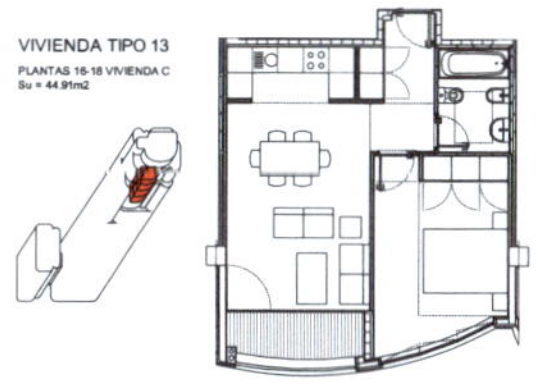

VIVIENDA TIPO 5

PLANTAS 1-14 VIVIENDA D
Su = 58.50m2

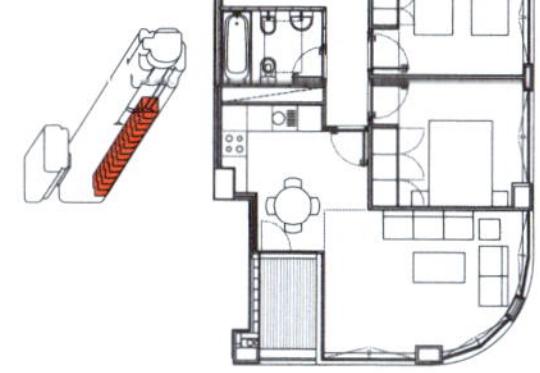

VIVIENDA TIPO 18

PLANTA 20 VIVIENDA A
Su = 83.99m2

VIVIENDA TIPO 29

PLANTA 3 VIVIENDA G
Su = 58.31m2

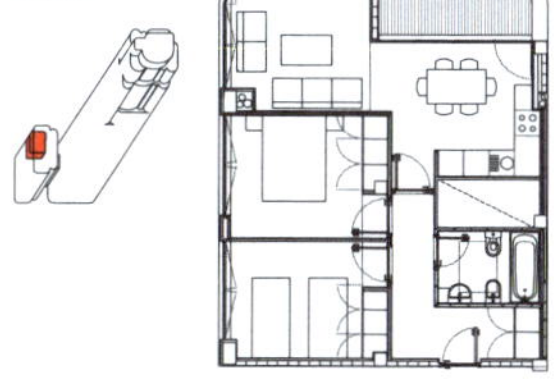

VIVIENDA TIPO 3

PLANTAS 1-17 VIVIENDA E
Su = 65.74m2

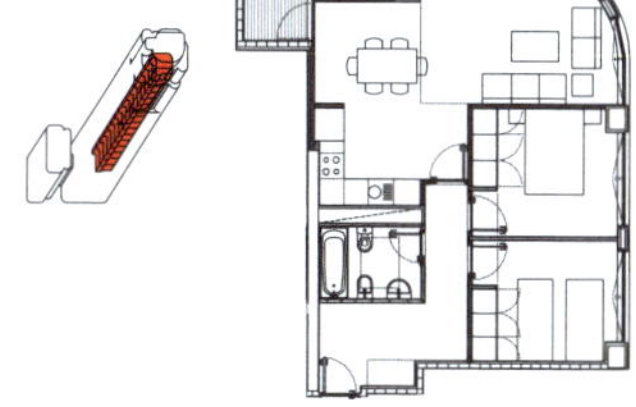

VIVIENDA TIPO 2

Su = 65.74m2

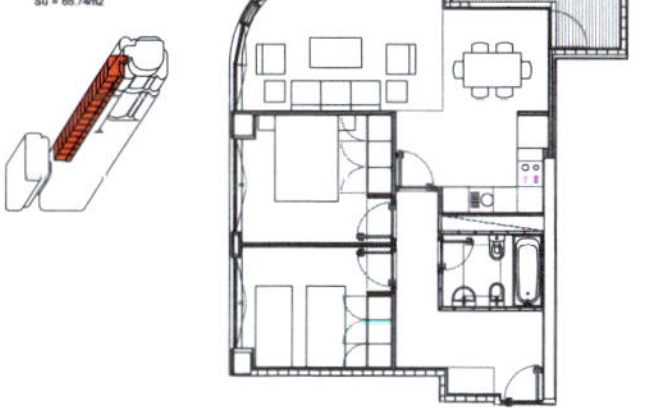

VIVIENDA TIPO 7

Su = 60.00m2

VIVIENDA TIPO 15

PLANTAS 16-18 VIVIENDA D
Su = 57.92m2

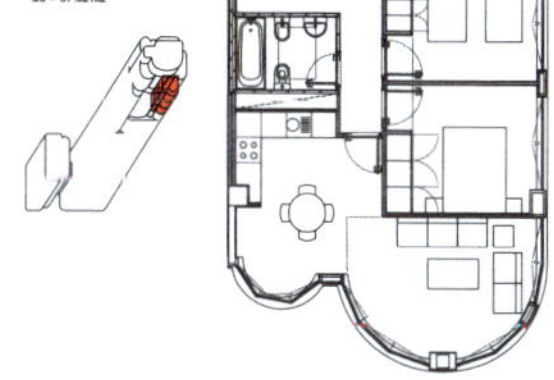

VIVIENDA TIPO 21

PLANTA 19 VIVIENDA B
Su = 60.56m2

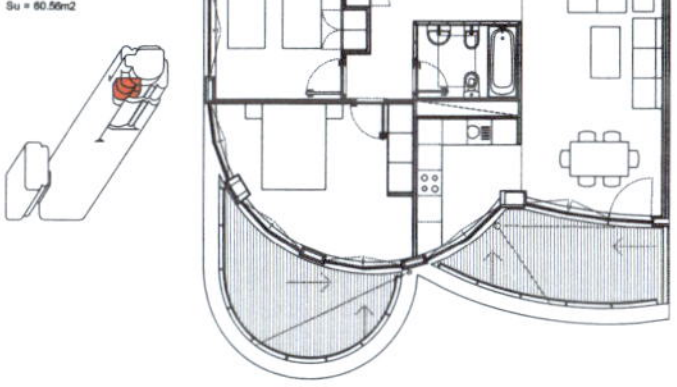

VIVIENDA TIPO 12

PLANTA 15 VIVIENDA C
Su = 48.22m2

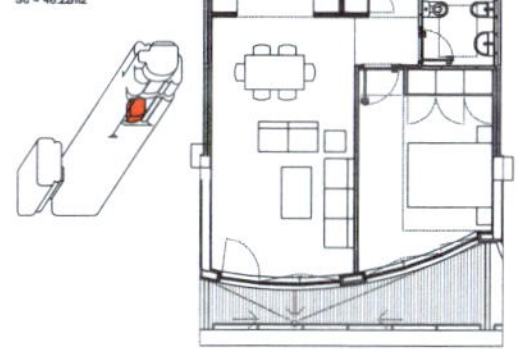

VIVIENDA TIPO 24

PLANTA 20 VIVIENDA C
Su = 61.68m2

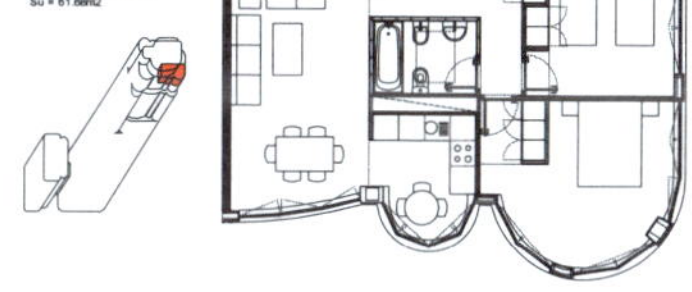

VIVIENDA TIPO 30

PLANTA 3 VIVIENDA I
Su = 50.12m2

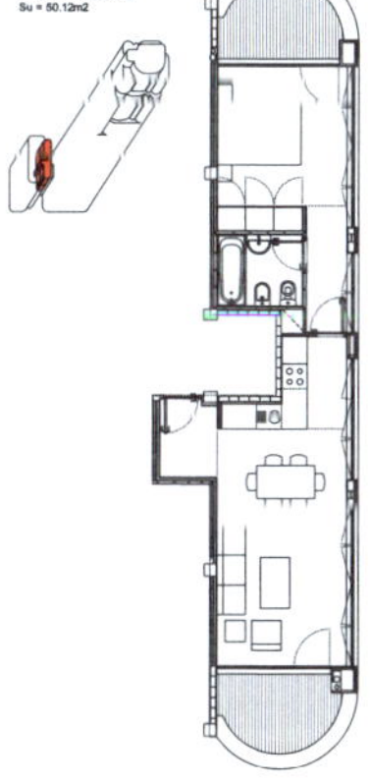

VIVIENDA TIPO 28

PLANTA 1 VIVIENDA I
Su = 46.13m2

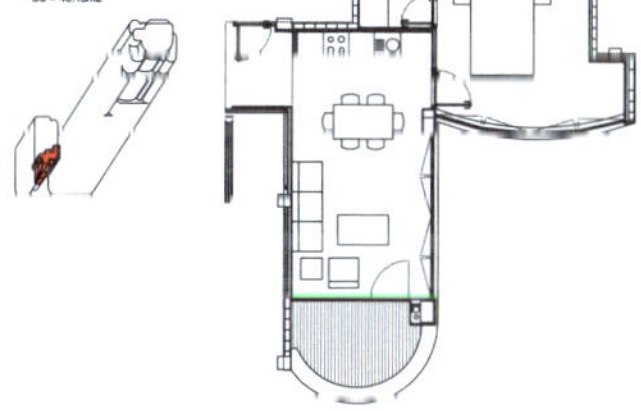

VIVIENDA TIPO 20

PLANTAS 19-20 VIVIENDA D
Su = 67.29m2

0 1 2 5m

New District Citizen Square and Productivity Promotion Centre. Hangzhou Bay, China. 2017

The New District Citizen Square and Productivity Promotion Centre is a building complex that concentrates the public services of Hangzhou Bay's urban district. With its pre-defined volumes and programmes, the design focuses on creating a contemporary language that can integrate the richness of the local landscape with the opportunities for energy efficiency. It is designed around a large, central green space with facilities, and this area connects the various buildings, programmes and levels. Built on a human scale, its softly curving contours welcome residents, intensifying the perception of the landscape and enhancing natural ventilation. The series of overlapping public spaces at the building's different heights was chosen for the development of the final project.

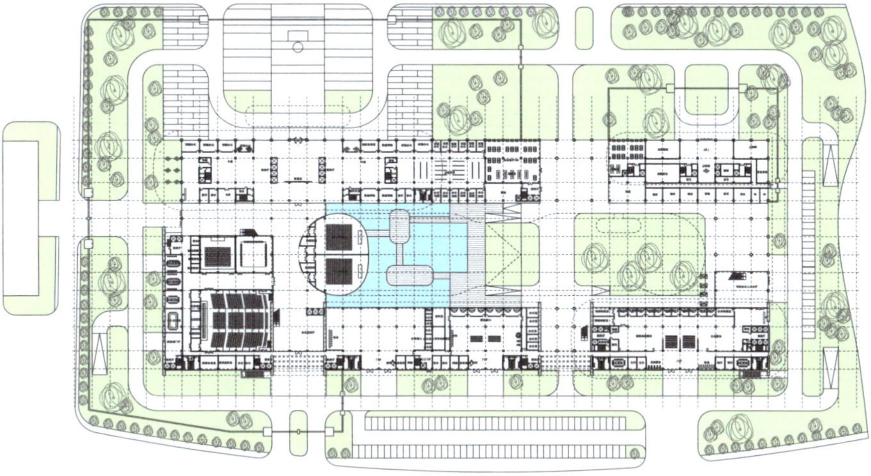

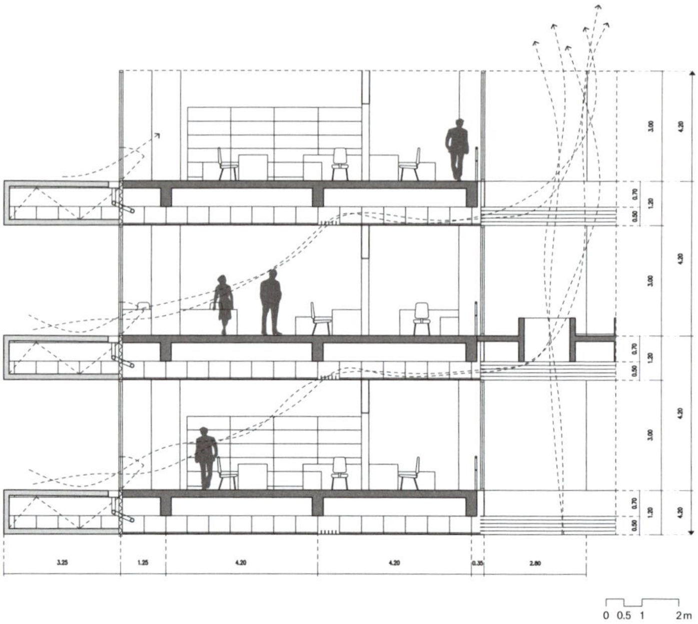

Princeton Carpark. Princeton University, New Jersey, US. 2007-2009

This project is one component of a major adaptation to the vehicular access to the Princeton University campus. It is also part of a broader landscaping initiative and project for the University's environmental, sports and laboratory facilities. The need for a large carpark (the second-largest volume in the whole complex, after the stadium) and the interest in giving this infrastructure a specific character are present in the three decisions defining the project: its curved corners are not only well-suited for car use and blend in with the shape of the stadium, but they also provide orientation and shape to a type of infrastructure normally lacking such qualities; it also includes small alternative programmes (offices, bus station, gymnasium) needed to add vitality and security to this area; the ornamental surroundings clearly signal the proximity of the beautiful Princeton campus. After it was approved, the project was brought to a halt after one of the university's eminent professors said that he did not want to spend his final days watching the fluorescent lights of a carpark from his bed.

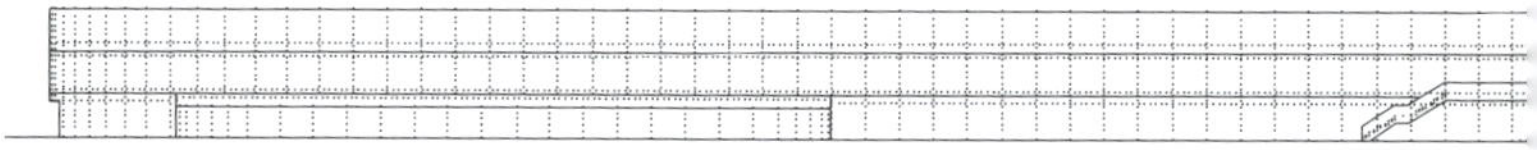

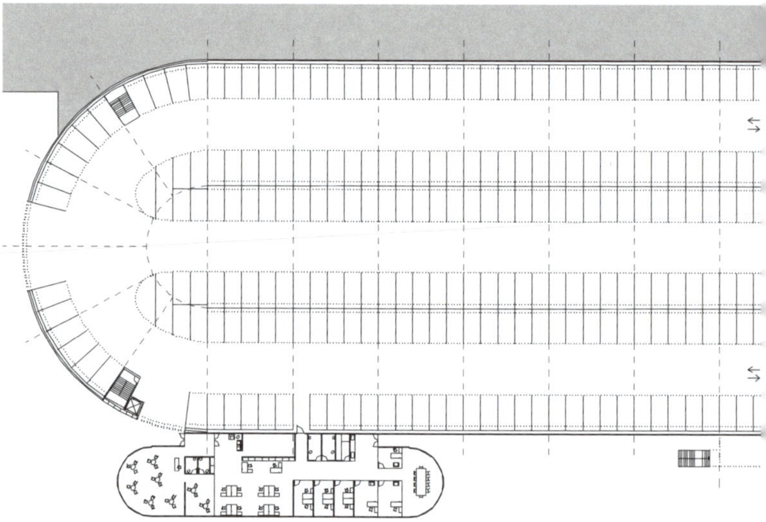

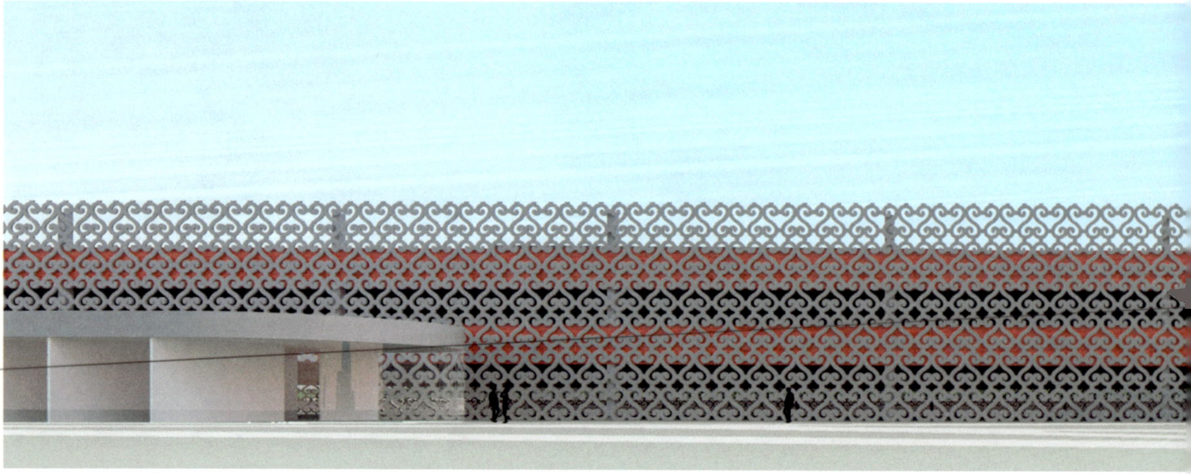

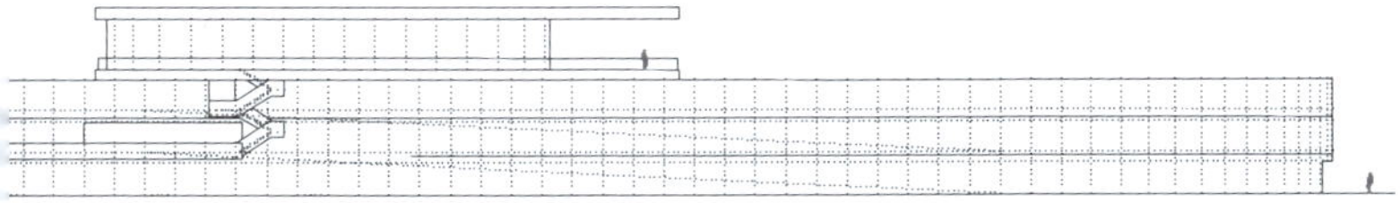

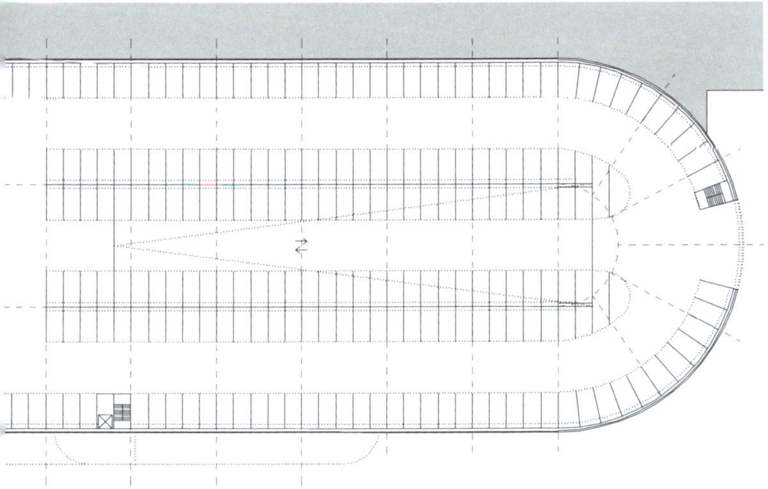

The Flying Spine. Walkway in the Zhang Jia Bang Park. Pudong, Shanghai, China. 2016-

The competition called for submissions to develop a zig-zagging route to explore the large park under construction in Zhang Jia Bang, passing over and under the intervening infrastructure and creating an unobstructed route for walkers, bicyclists, joggers, etc. We chose a fishbone structure whose elements never require double curvature and also result in a recognisable shape, inspiring its name: The Flying Spine. Spanning a total length of 5.5 kilometres, elevated along approximately half of its length, this route also includes pavilions for taking a rest or exercising, observation decks, areas offering shelter from the sun and rain, and washrooms, all built with the same construction system as the bridge itself and ending up at a final pavilion for rest and contemplation at the park's large scenic and recreational lake.

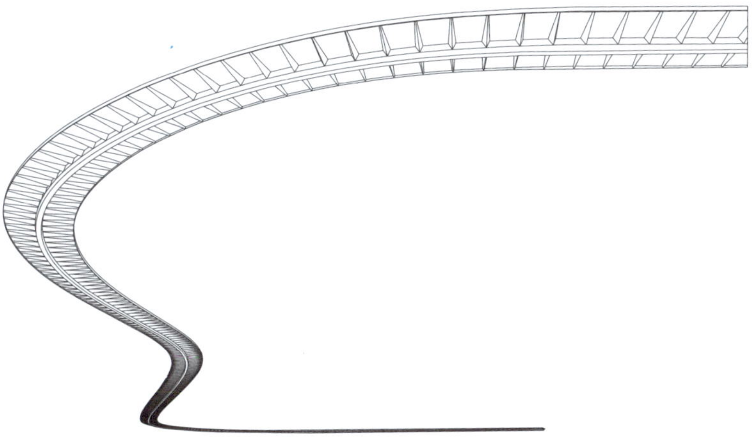

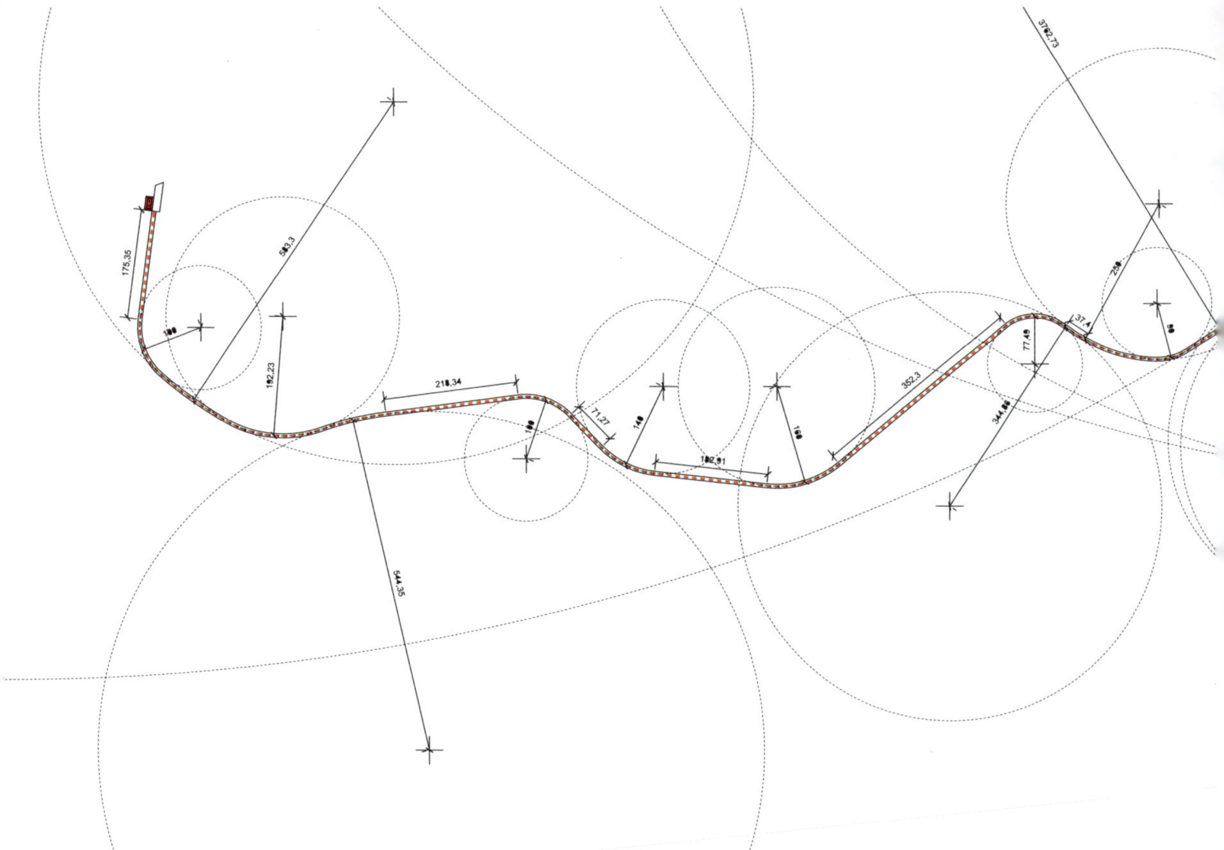

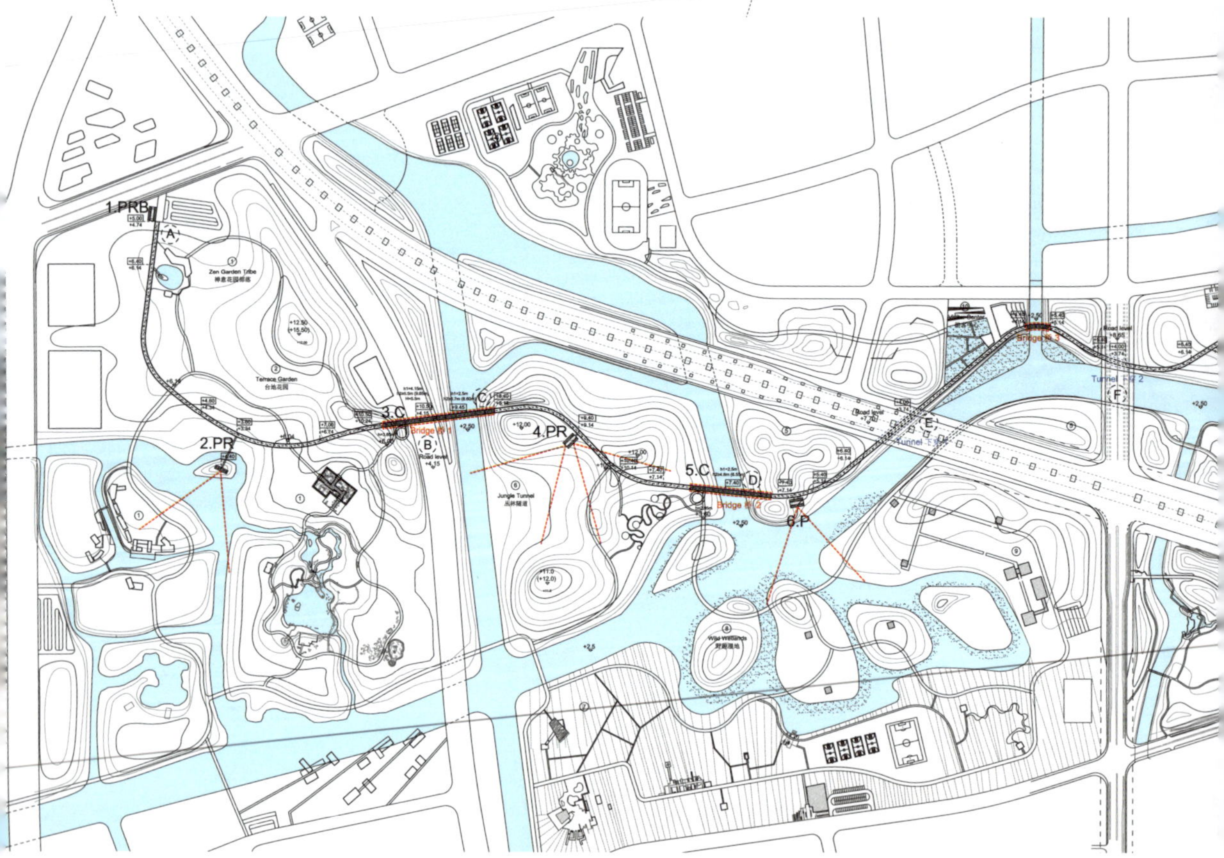

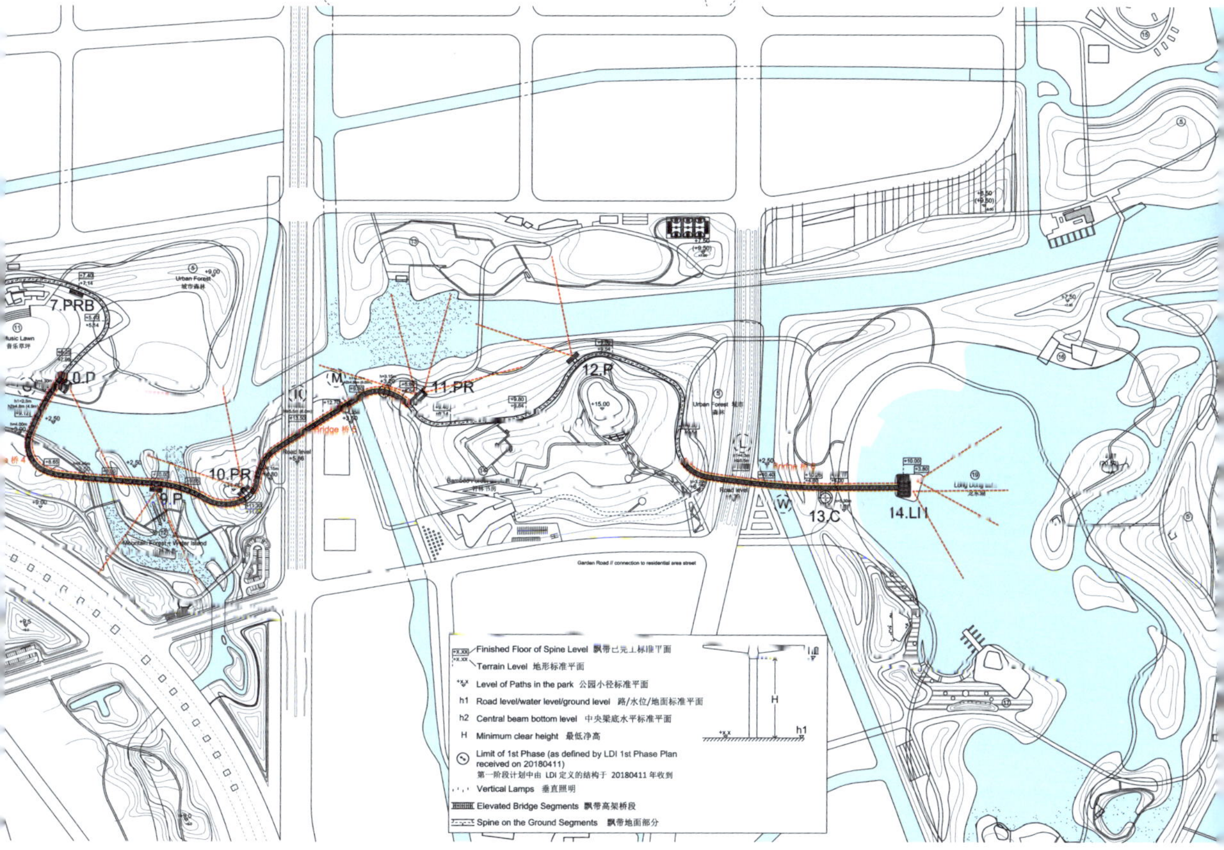
7.PRB
8.0.D
9.P
10.PR
11.PR
12.P
13.C
14.LI1
Music Lawn
Urban Forest
Bamboo Forest
Garden Road // connection to residential area street
Finished Floor of Spine Level 飘带已完工标准平面
Terrain Level 地形标准平面
Level of Paths in the park 公园小径标准平面
h1 Road level/water level/ground level 路/水位/地面标准平面
h2 Central beam bottom level 中央梁底水平标准平面
H Minimum clear height 最低净高
Limit of 1st Phase (as defined by LDI 1st Phase Plan received on 20180411)
第一阶段计划中由 LDI 定义的结构于 20180411 年收到
Vertical Lamps 垂直照明
Elevated Bridge Segments 飘带高架桥段
Spine on the Ground Segments 飘带地面部分

Shanghai Grand Opera House. Shanghai, China. 2017

Until now there has been no opera house in the world with an architecture able to express the emotion that opera produces in a person: the perfect symbiosis of an instinctive sentiment that emanates from our organic, earth-bound selves, with a unique feeling of spiritual soaring or floating. Buildings based on historical models or trite metaphors alluding to musical instruments are no longer valid. We want to express, as abstractly and concisely as possible, the contrast between earthy passion and spiritual levitation that makes opera the most intense cultural and emotional experience that art can produce. The Shanghai Grand Opera House is not designed like any model or any banal figurative expression. By contrast, it will require and generate a commitment analogous to listening to an opera, seeking to resonate with its experience transferred into the physical language of architecture.

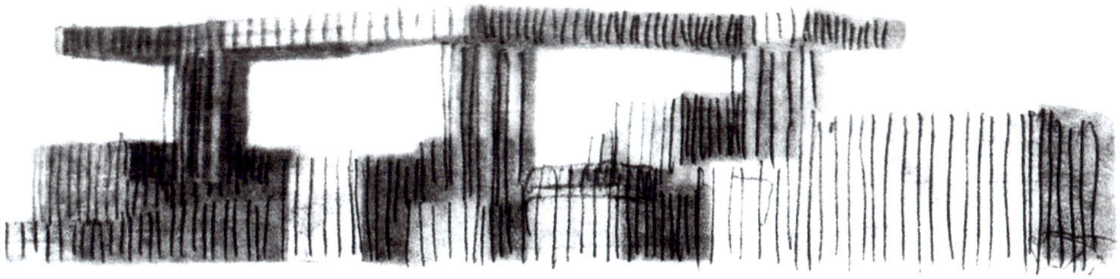

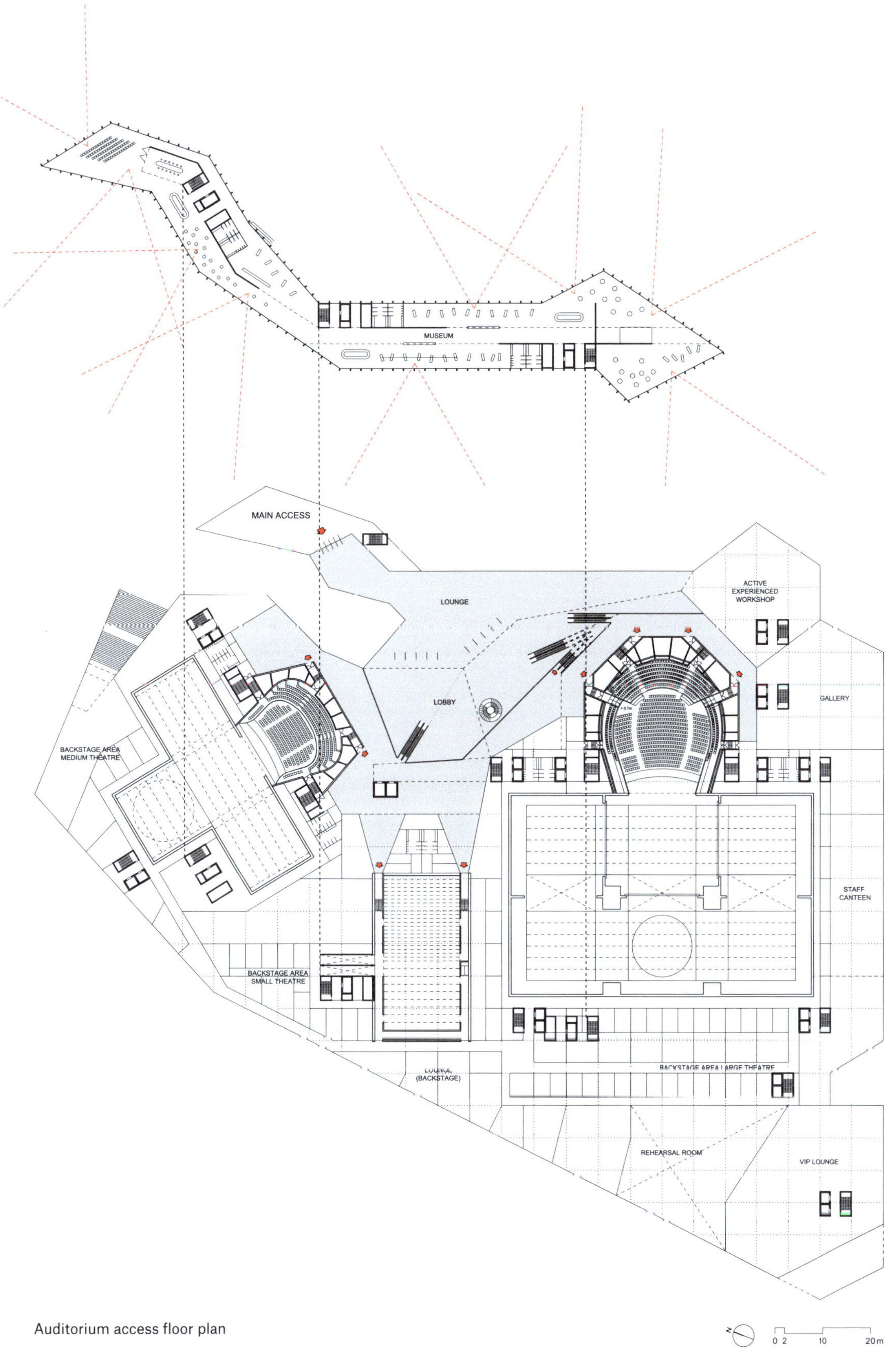

Auditorium access floor plan

The question of how we understand thermodynamics in our projects comes up frequently, since we know that it is often not immediately apparent in our work (at least for those who, when they hear "thermodynamics" immediately see arrows, colours, diagrams and soft forms). We acknowledge that we are proud that this is not the case even though we have spoken, written and taught extensively on this subject. We have varied, concise and complementary answers that clarify this issue, so let us turn directly to them:

1. *We are pragmatic, not visionaries.* Many circumstances, including the calibration of client needs according to environmental sensitivity or the available budget, force us to modulate our parameters and choose the most pertinent strategies in each case. The important thing is to always insert a thermodynamic agenda, however small it may be, because once infiltrated, the commitment increases exponentially in almost all cases.

2. *We never talk about thermodynamics but rather about architecture, thermodynamics, and beauty all at once.* By adopting this point of view, we align ourselves with centu ries and centuries of the discipline—in both its vernacular versions (all vernacular architecture is the progeny of material culture, resources, and thermal performativity) and its more cultivated versions (see Vitruvius or *The Four Elements of Architecture* of Gottfried Semper, for example).

3. *We are not ingenuous.* We are interested in qualitative knowledge as long as it has a presence in the form, matter, and flow (exchange of energy and fluids between the building and its environment). Form is also about orientation and relationships with public space. Matter does not consist of "finishes" but rather mass, corrugation, inertia, organization, material culture. Ventilation is also part of health, quality, and pleasure. Detailing these connections provides essential information prior to initiating the design. This information consolidates what is important and prevents serious initial mistakes that are always difficult to correct once an architectural idea expressed by an initial sketch misguidedly seduces us. These concerns are our primary data and are used as minimal filters for the imagination at the outset of the project. Only in this way is thermodynamics viable in design.

4. *We eschew orthodoxy.* We recognize issues, possibilities, opportunities, imagination, references. creation. Just as there are good experts, and it is desirable to have them—for example on structural issues—it is good to start early with the experts in thermodynamics. But it is also good to know that practically identical forms and organizations serve to solve very different climate programs and situations, and optimally in both cases. That is to say, there is no function-form determinism related to the principles of thermodynamic design, rather collections of formal operations that can be applied here and there. Experts not only quantify and correct the shortcomings of initial qualitative assumptions, at their best they are creative and provide wonderful ideas, inventions, references and suggestions.

5. *There is no perfect metric for measuring the sustainability or energy efficiency of buildings.* Super-sealed closed refrigerator/*Passivhaus* buildings, for example, seems to us a farcical methodology in climates with long periods of temperate weather. We use the principles of *Passivhauss* when the demand for stability of the hygrothermal parameters in the interior are high, for example, in biological or pharmaceutical laboratories, in data centers, or in museums—all typologies that require year-round interior climatic stability regardless of the outdoor climate.

6. *We use rules of thumb*, namely Willis Carrier's psychrometric climate charts, especially the current and more elaborate ones such as the charts from UC Berkeley that have recommendations for expanding comfort areas through external and internal passive resources. They also quantify the relative contribution of each recommended strategy. Learning to read these psychrometric tables takes only a few hours. As another form of common sense, we also study vernacular architecture and the long evolution of a place's material culture. We document examples of both historic and modern local houses and grander palaces. We take nothing in particular from this study; instead we discern more general principles and practices. Ultimately we make three psychrometric graphs: of the external climate; of the building considered as an inert mass (that is, without any type of conditioning); and, finally, of the passive or active conditioning systems. This simple method allows us to rapidly learn to develop an intuition similar to the one that architects have already developed with regard to structural aspects—we know for instance about the specificity and intricacy of shear, moments, inertia, elastic limits; yet in design we use simple rules to pre-size structural elements. And so it goes with thermodynamics. There are, after all, two manifestations of energy in buildings of a very similar nature: thermal energy and mechanical energy that are practically subject to the same variables in their formulas.

7. *The lexicon matters. Form / Matter / Flow is our mantra.* Once internalized, it helps us to forget and retain knowledge at the same time: like when we forget the rules of driving when sitting behind the wheel, even while their naturalization within us guides our behaviour. If we talk about architecture, beauty, and thermodynamics as designers, we not only need the support of experts but also a more disciplinary reflection on the cultural/professional purposes of architecture in their capacity to incorporate thermodynamic criteria into design processes. For example, consider hybrid programs and their potential utility for creating nested and interconnected layers of interchange. In such hybrids, it may be interesting to maintain a certain material dualism, combining areas with materials of great thermal inertia—which serve as energy storage—with materials that exhibit much more rapid or even instantaneous responses to ambient climate changes. What we seek to convey is this: to reach a new idea of thermodynamic beauty it is necessary to think what thermodynamic consciousness implies in pragmatic, material, and formal terms, and to pass through certain degrees of ugliness. You can ask those who queue up to contemplate Picasso's *Les Demoiselles d'Avignon* at the MoMA (New York), where the ugliness of three prostitutes is raised to the iconographic category of Three Graces, giving a completely new dimension to the art of the 20th century. (Despite many believing, blindly, that only beauty prevails in *Les Demoiselles d'Avignon*, ugliness and beauty preside at the same time—and that is its great artistic value).

8. *We should be cultivating a new primitivism* with a certain empathy toward monstrous hybrids and thereby eliminating the big constructive lie of the modern building that Carrier universalized: that buildings should reduce their volume to a minimum air, because you have to weatherize it mechanically—lower the volume, lower the maintenance cost. Likewise, the lie that thermal insulation is a panacea that solves all the energetic problems of architecture. The method of determining the insulation required in the façades and the roof can now be considered technologically prehistoric: it does not take into account the climatic variation in time, as in day and night, not to mention the variation of the hygrothermal parameters in the different seasons. It does not count the passage of clouds, the orientation and movement of air, the shade of the trees, unstable cross ventilation of air, or the more stable natural buoyancy ventilation of air. Actually, R-values and psychrometrics, which are the primary weapon of the mechanical engineer that sizes the air conditioning systems, do not evaluate something as essential in the perception of the climate as direct exposure to solar radiation. The insulation apparatus is therefore, as a technological and calculation model, a pseudo-scientific lie that remains unchallenged exclusively because of industrial interests and the acquiescent momentum of architectural pedagogies. Today, we know much more and we have more sophisticated means of measuring changes over time, the effect of mass or porosity, the distribution of inertia, and we can even design *ad hoc* materials, which can be modelled for certain conditions.

The new primitivism is based on the absolute simplification and at the same time the absolute sophistication in the use of each material, in the single leaf or double leaf wall, capable of having a controlled performativity adapted to the climate, to the use, to the changing conditions, to the evaluation of comfort throughout the different seasons, and depending on the thermodynamic balances that you want to obtain in each case. This idea of a radical simplification—precisely through an ability to design the performativity of buildings with matter and air—is the key to thinking about a new generation, not only of buildings but of architects capable of modulating the metabolism of what they design with elementary criteria and advanced parametric tools. Do not deceive us anymore: the "refrigerator" building is an American model of the past aimed at repurposing the military industry of World War II and transferring it to serve civil construction. This was done in tandem with selling insulating materials that isolate us from public life and from the city. We better think now beyond past models of unnatural and anti-biological building. That paradigm is responsible for much of the environmental failure of the industrial civilization we have inherited. Buildings, whatever their form, orientation, program, materiality, occupation, are thermal machines exposed to an external climate and an internal metabolism; subject to changing conditions, to internal and external flows of accumulation and dissipation of energy with conditions of better or worse air quality (chemical and acoustic pollution), and that essentially inhabit a relatively stable environment, as they are not mobile. They are inanimate entities subjected to the animate conditions of life. Everything we do that contradicts this very simple formulation is doomed to perpetuate the problems inherited from modern buildings. (And surely we must insist that air conditioning is not, *per se*, an enemy; it was a great invention, one more in the process of learning to manipulate physical-building medium exchanges).

9. *Ergo, the need to rethink architecture thermodynamically does not end in buildings.* Sustainability, as understood in current environmental assessment systems, often converts streets and public spaces into thermodynamic dumpsters where supposedly sustainable or intelligent buildings pour all their toxic waste. We have returned to the medieval *Gardyloo*! —albeit a gaseous version rather than a liquid one. It is therefore essential to avoid the modern division between three disciplines—architecture, urbanism, and landscape—that in fact always interact as a single whole. Whether or not we are blind to this reality, architecture, landscape, and urbanism manage energy resources and metabolic work in an necessarily coordinated way, because they share the same space-energy-material medium. Let us never be fooled by those who destroy collective life in favor of the isolated comfort of private buildings.

10. *In question too, in the end, is the pedagogy of the architectural discipline in its current profoundly modernist/*

Taylorist configuration, wherein architects are trained to integrate technical knowledge of structural mechanics at the expense of more fundamental thermodynamic criteria. This precludes progress and intellectual advancement regarding contemporary architecture, but also understanding of historical ones, vernacular or otherwise, and how they mediate material culture. Architects need the authority of both the discipline of architecture and at the same time the mechanical and thermodynamic capacities of architecture. This places architecture in an extraordinary situation: that of needing to make a qualitative leap in the understanding of air, matter, time, metabolic cycles, and the ecological interrelation of the different constructive and urban subsystems. An extensive review of ourselves as architects—who we are, what we serve and what responsibilities we must take on—is necessary if we want to be a positive part of a freer and healthier society.

Technical knowledge is not the central problem in the evolution of architecture. Our collective reflection on the discipline and on its pedagogy should focus on the aesthetic and cultural implications of these technological changes and thus necessarily develop new design techniques in light of: emerging taxonomic knowledge, the construction of innovative protocols for project documentation, and how historiographical documentation and material culture are also essential steps toward an architecture with a new environmental quality. Some time ago we wrote: "Only if there is a true aesthetic dimension, if there is an idea of beauty implicit in thermodynamic conceptions, can they interest architecture in a non-circumstantial way and will it make sense to work step by step on them." To further elaborate on this, we refer to the great observation of Alejandro de la Sota: "Architecture is the air we breathe, albeit an air replete with smells, with learning, an air transformed by that same thing, by Architecture."

PLANTA Project for the Sorigué Foundation. Balaguer, Lérida, Spain. 2014–

The Planta project is on the same site as the Plana del Corb gravel processing plant, in a location that connects the quarry to the original topography. This makes it both a museum space for the Foundation's collection of contemporary art, and an observatory for the entropic process of time and human activity, connecting the experience of art to the world of ecology and manufacturing. The Planta project is also a 7,500 m^2 "thermal machine" built with materials extracted from the quarry based on a layout of form, matter and flow that passively regulates radiation, lighting and ventilation employing advanced thermodynamic concepts. This synthetic dimension, responding to programme (museum, observatory, thermal machine), performance and matter, seeks to connect different periods and local cultures by using local resources and iconographic elements to produce an artefact whose "new primitivism" clearly shows an interest in reappraising the value of time, history and entropy in today's world.

FLUJOS: Oliva. (1.500 camiones /año de Septiembre a Enero)

FLUJOS: Cereales . (1.500 camiones /año de Septiembre a Enero)

FLUJOS: Salida prefabricados. (350 camiones /año de)

FLUJOS: Salida material asfaltico. (5.500 camiones /año)

FLUJOS: Salida de aridos. (20.000 camiones /año)

FLUJOS: Extraviales. (2 camiones permanentes de 7.00h a 15.00 h)

MT

Olivares

Embalses

Caminos peatonales

PROGRAMA: Cultural

PROGRAMA: Industrial-Aridos

PROGRAMA: Industrial-prefabricados

PROGRAMA: Industrial-asfaltico

PROGRAMA: Agrario-Oliva

PROGRAMA: Agrario-Cebada

PROGRAMA: Oficinas

PROGRAMA: Investigación

PROGRAMA: Representación (área privada)

PROGRAMA: Graveras

PROGRAMA: Aparcamiento

PROGRAMA: Acopio material

Local climate: a semi-arid plain with extreme seasonal changes in temperature. Programme: a public building with a valuable collection of contemporary art. The building has two "users": people and the art collection, with differentiated requirements for thermal comfort. The annual climate and thermal comfort charts indicate that the site's yearly thermal stability (its geothermal conditions) is the ideal passive resource to bring the building into the comfort zone. The project's compact (cubic) shape, the mass of the material available on site (concrete) and its semi-embedded location between the level of the original ground and of the area already quarried by the machines, combine to minimise exchanges with the exterior: these are all actions related to form and matter of immediate thermodynamic effectiveness.

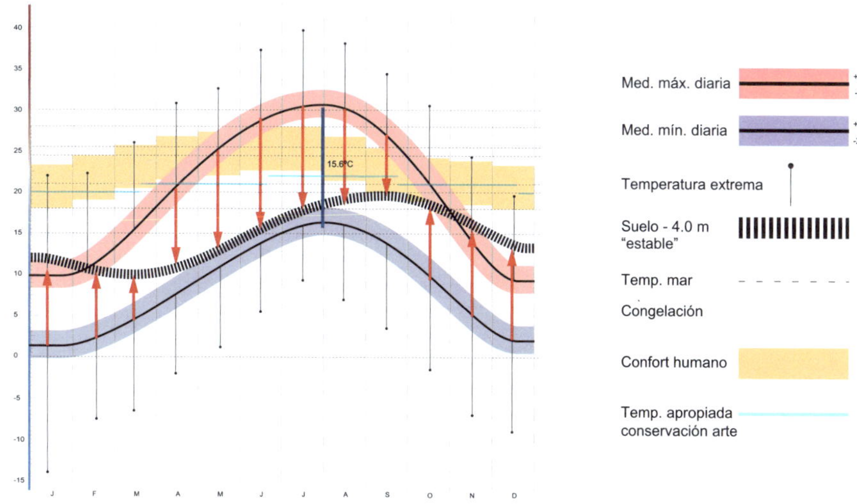

Saw-tooth openings in this basic volume allow natural light to enter the interiors from the north, creating a roof with south-facing photovoltaic panels to meet the electricity needs, complemented by solar water heating panels.

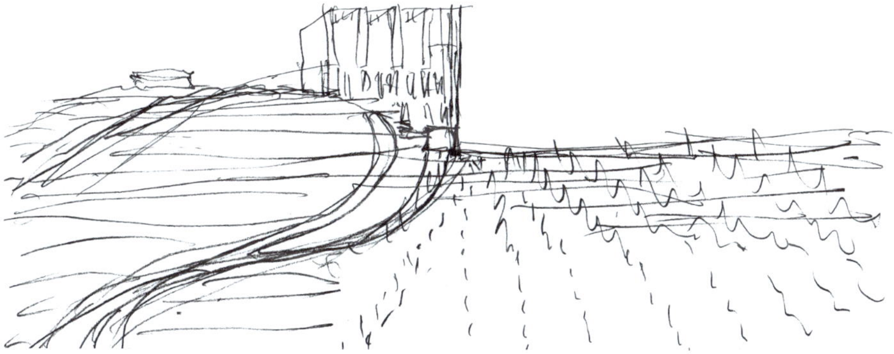

The weight reductions designed for the inner walls and slabs as a conduit for technical flows (air, water, electricity) dispenses with other interior finishes and use their mass as radiant and convective surfaces.

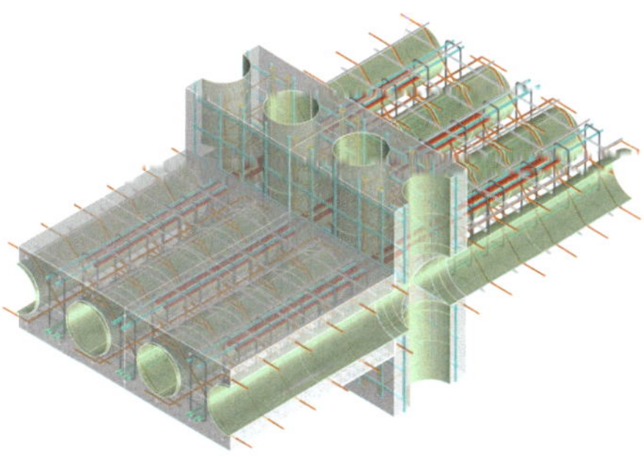

1. Exterior conditions

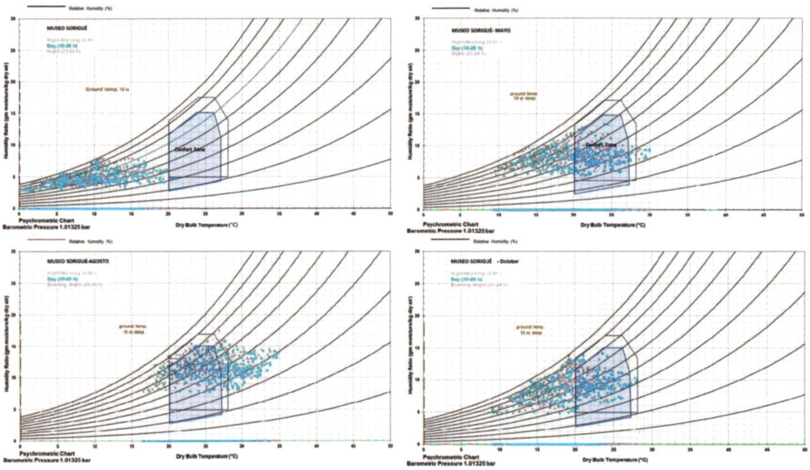

1. Exterior climate: the local climate is relatively cold and humid in the winter, and cold-to-warm during the other seasons, except during the summer months.

2. Basic design: form and matter

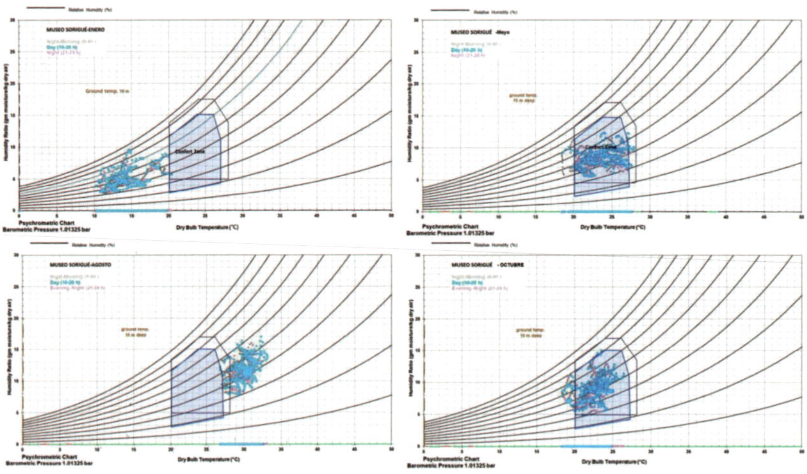

2. Interior climate: the building, considered as form and matter, inherently benefits from a decent level of interior comfort in spring and autumn, giving a certain symmetry to the slight discomfort in the summer and winter, which leads to the use of geothermal energy as a stabiliser.

3. Optimized design: passive systems

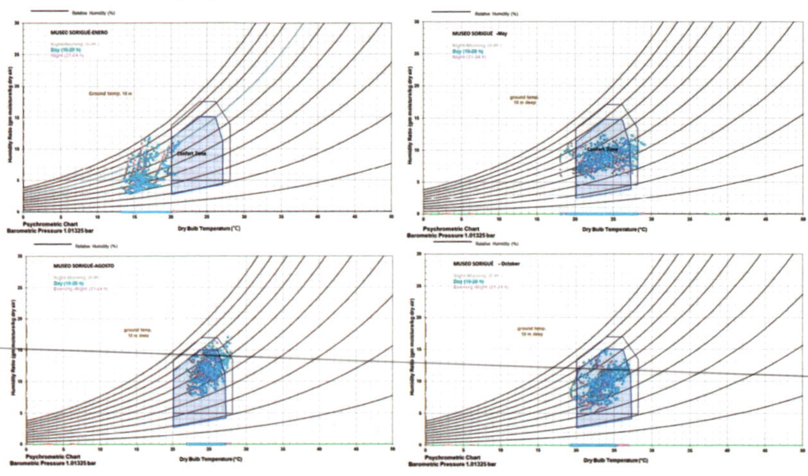

3. Temperate interior climate: Prefabricated Canadian wells at the gravel quarry placed underneath the building regulates and channels the air through the construction's walls and slabs, balancing thermal factors during the most extreme seasons.

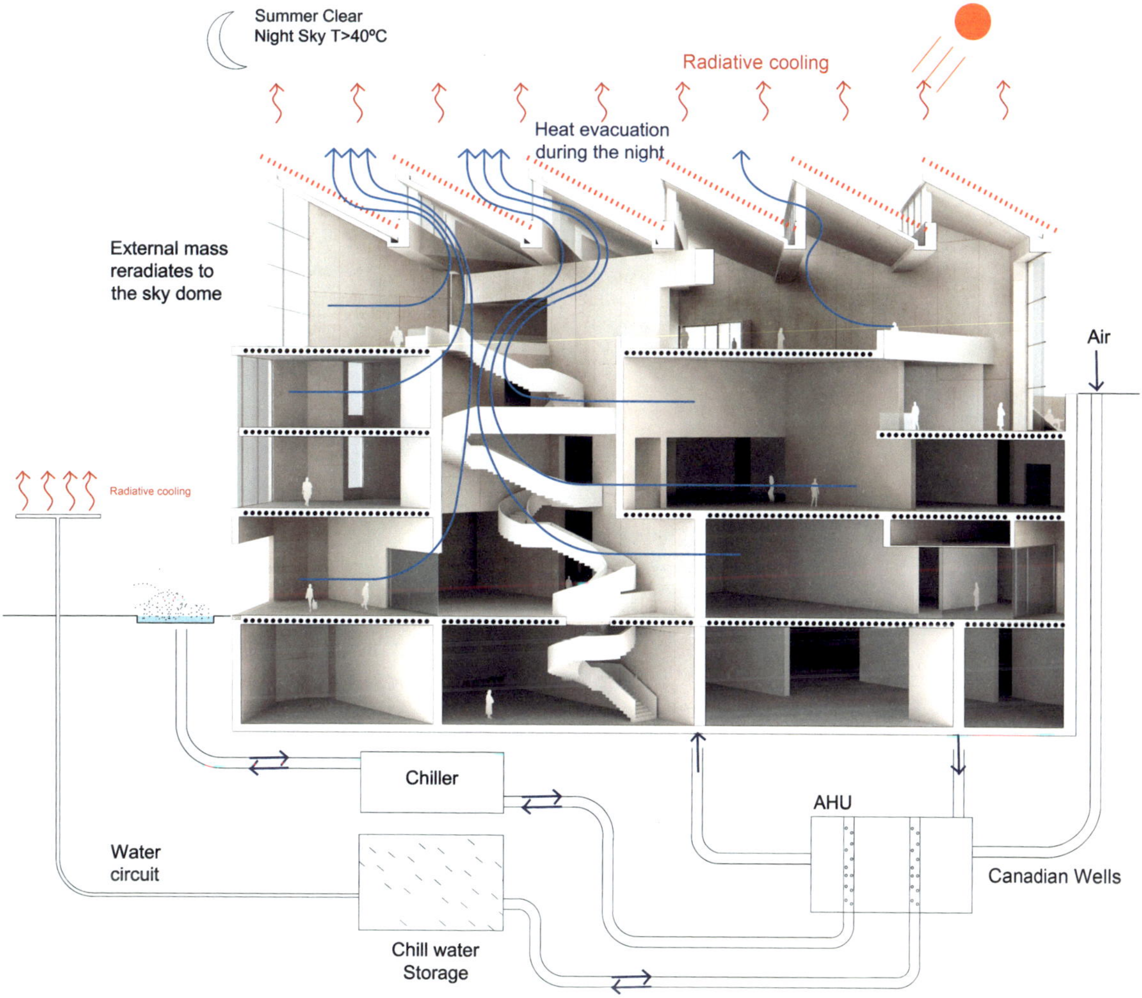
Summer Clear
Night Sky T>40ºC
Radiative cooling
Heat evacuation
during the night
External mass
reradiates to
the sky dome
Air
Radiative cooling
Chiller
AHU
Water
circuit
Canadian Wells
Chill water
Storage

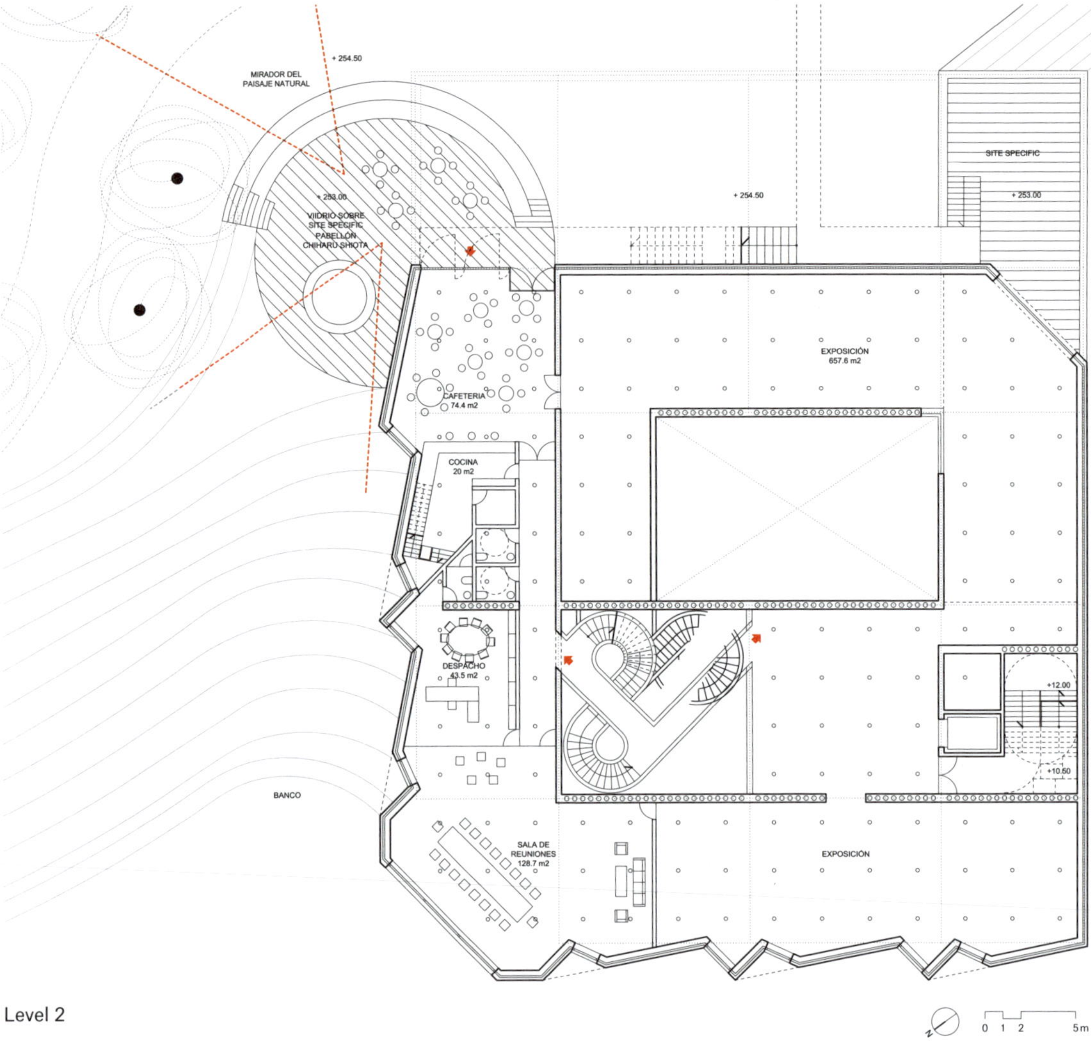
+ 254.50
MIRADOR DEL
PAISAJE NATURAL
+ 253.00
VIDRIO SOBRE
SITE SPECIFIC
PABELLÓN
CHIHARU SHIOTA
+ 254.50
SITE SPECIFIC
+ 253.00
EXPOSICIÓN
657.6 m2
CAFETERIA
74.4 m2
COCINA
20 m2
DESPACHO
43.5 m2
+12.00
+10.50
BANCO
SALA DE
REUNIONES
128.7 m2
EXPOSICIÓN
N
0 1 2 5m

Level 2

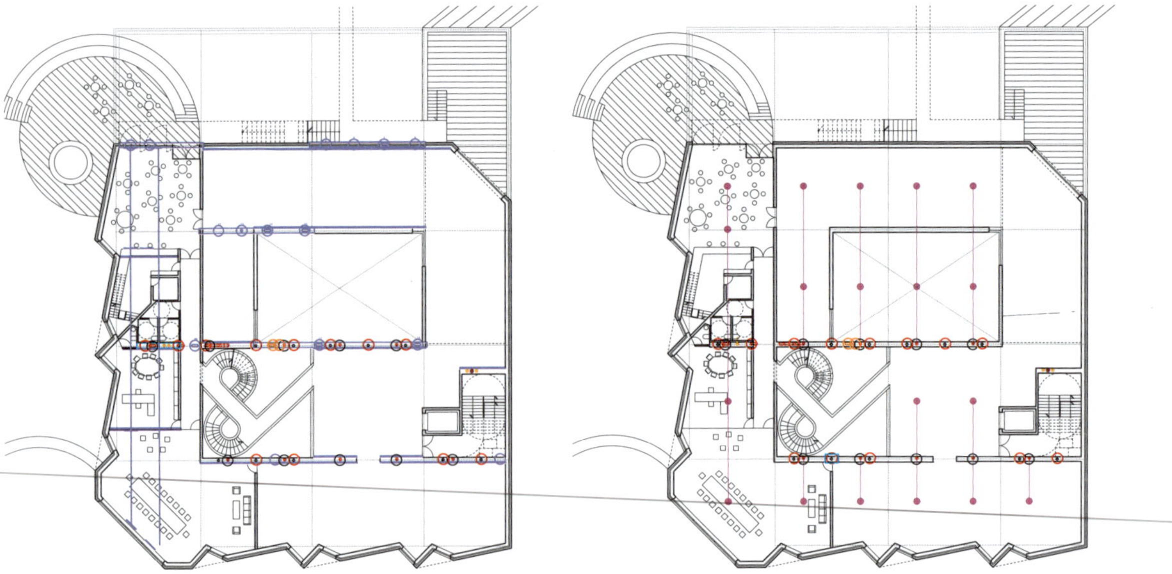

MEP

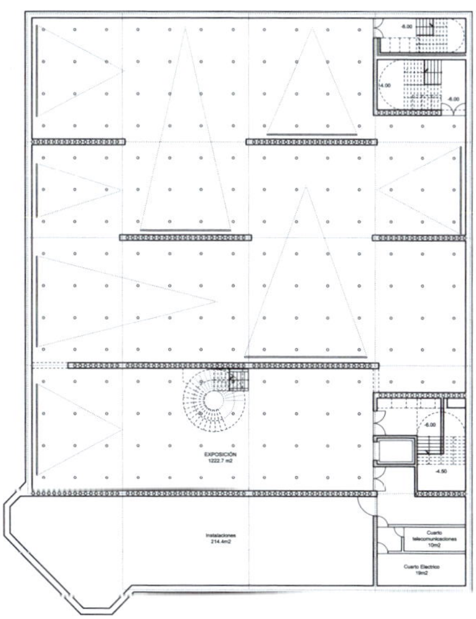

Basement floor plan

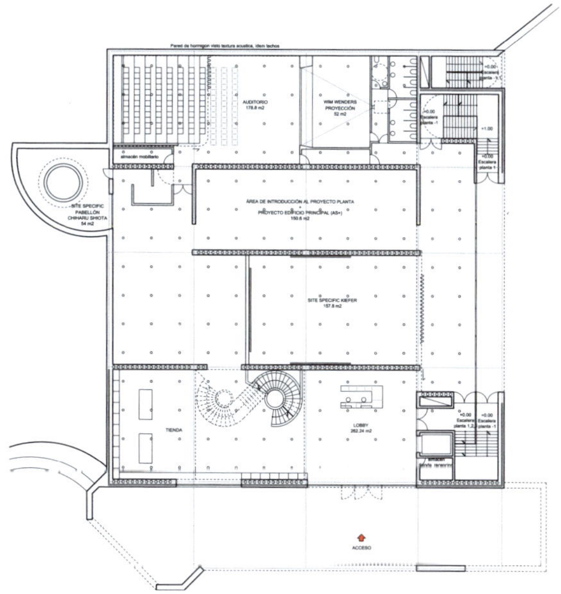

Ground floor plan

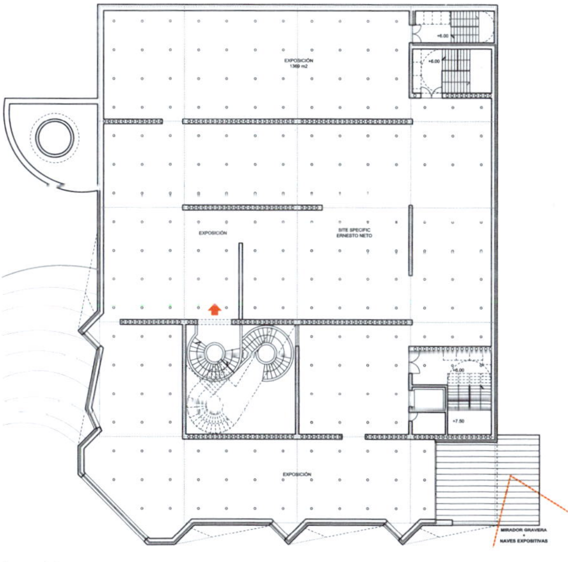

Level 1

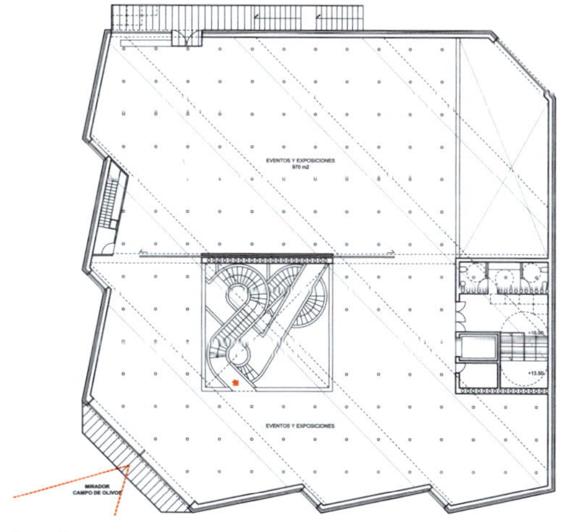

Level 3

NEW
PRIMITIVISM

Shanghai Museum East. Shanghai, China. 2016

The Shanghai Museum East consists of a solid, rectangular volume that opens up onto a large expanse of land around the Pudong Government Centre, the Science & Technology Museum and Shanghai's Century Square and Century Park. This is the extension of Shanghai Museum West, which has one of the world's finest collections of traditional Chinese art. The building's shape and material quality gives it a timeless feel, yet also one of complete openness thanks to the entrance portico that literally opens up the museum and its central courtyard to the city and its citizens. A sawtooth roof oriented to benefit from light from the north brings in natural light to most of the collection, while the southern face of the same roof design acts as a solar photovoltaic collector, offsetting the energy needs to ensure the right level of illumination and thermal comfort in the museum. The project's design reflects a traditional duality of Chinese philosophy, by consisting of void and mass, a construction as solid as rock yet fluid as air.

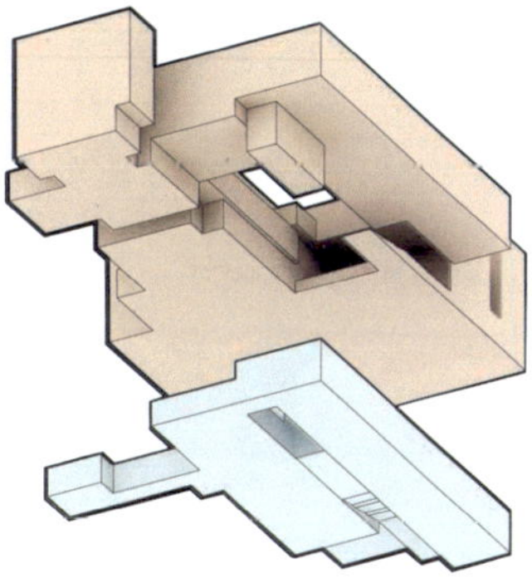

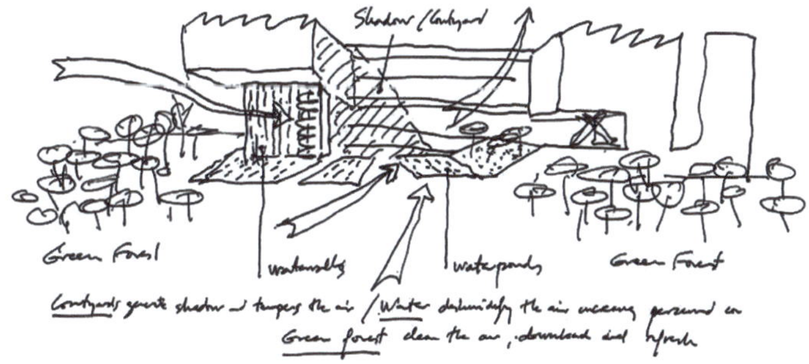
Shadow Courtyard
Green Forest
waterponds
Green Forest

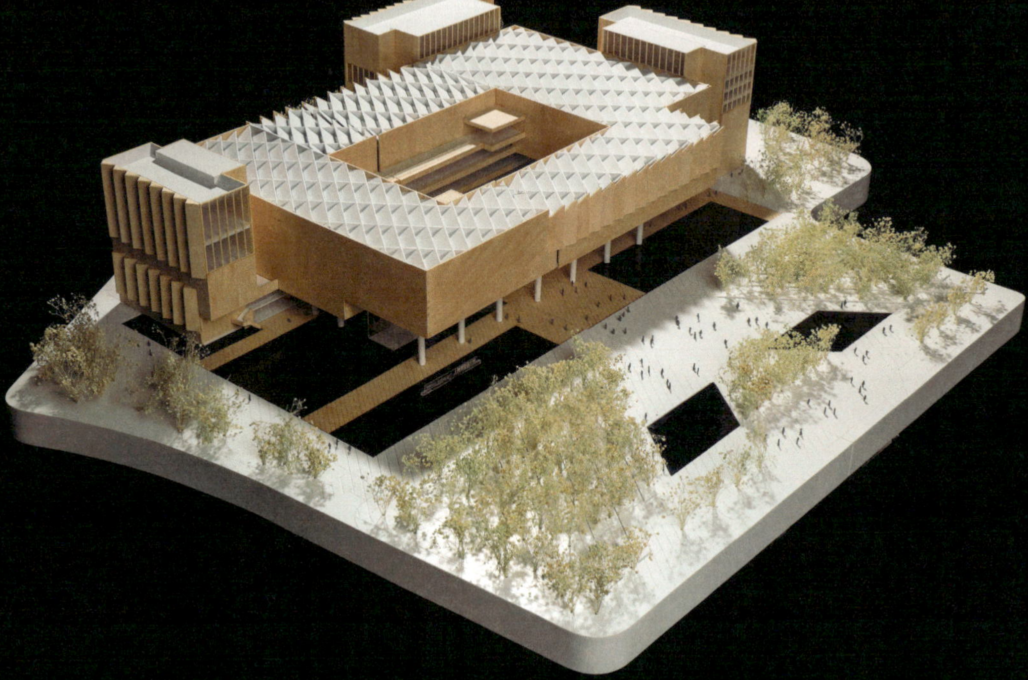

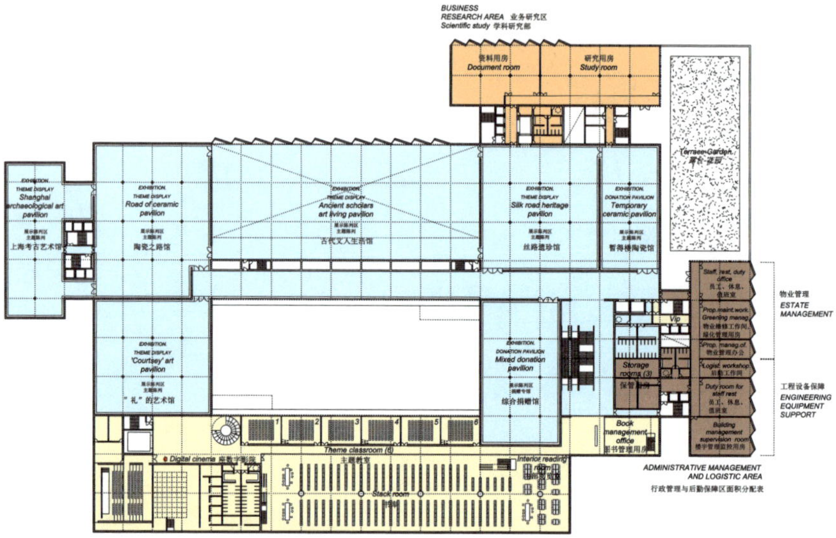
BUSINESS
RESEARCH AREA 业务研究区
Scientific study 学科研究部
资料用房
Document room
研究用房
Study room
Terrace Garden
Shanghai archaeological art pavilion
上海考古艺术馆
Road of ceramic pavilion
陶瓷之路馆
Ancient scholars art living pavilion
古代文人生活馆
Silk road heritage pavilion
丝路遗珍馆
Temporary ceramic pavilion
暂得楼陶瓷馆
'Courtsey' art pavilion
"礼"的艺术馆
Mixed donation pavilion
综合捐赠馆
Storage rooms (3)
保管用房
Vip
Book management office
图书管理用房
Digital cinema 数字影院
Theme classroom (6)
主题教室
Stack room
Interior reading room
物业管理
ESTATE MANAGEMENT
工程设备保障
ENGINEERING EQUIPMENT SUPPORT
ADMINISTRATIVE MANAGEMENT AND LOGISTIC AREA
行政管理与后勤保障区面积分配表

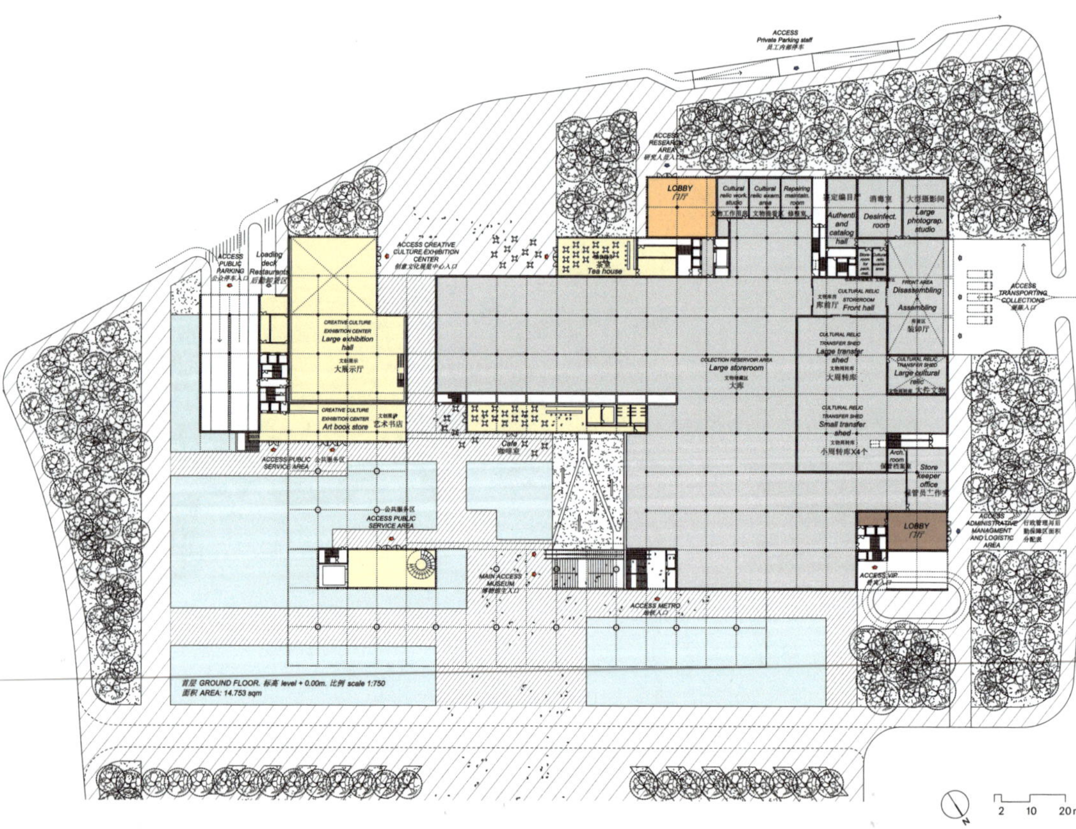
ACCESS
Private Parking staff
员工内部停车
LOBBY
门厅
Cultural relic work studio
Cultural relic exam area
Repairing maintain. room
Authenti and catalog hall
Desinfect. room
Large photograp. studio
ACCESS PUBLIC PARKING
Loading deck
Restaurants
ACCESS CREATIVE CULTURE EXHIBITION CENTER
创意文化展览中心入口
Tea house
CREATIVE CULTURE EXHIBITION CENTER
Large exhibition hall
大展示厅
COLLECTION RESERVOIR AREA
Large storeroom
大库
Front hall
Disassembling
Assembling
装卸厅
ACCESS TRANSPORTING COLLECTIONS
Large transfer shed
大周转库
Large cultural relic
Small transfer shed
小周转库X4个
Art book store
艺术书店
Cafe
咖啡室
ACCESS PUBLIC SERVICE AREA
公共服务区
Arch. room
Store keeper office
保管员工作室
LOBBY
门厅
ACCESS ADMINISTRATIVE MANAGMENT AND LOGISTIC AREA
ACCESS VIP
贵宾入口
MAIN ACCESS MUSEUM
博物馆主入口
ACCESS METRO
地铁入口
首层 GROUND FLOOR. 标高 level + 0.00m. 比例 scale 1:750
面积 AREA: 14.753 sqm
2 10 20 m

Interior. Spanish Pavilion at the XIV Mostra Internazionale di Architettura, La Biennale di Venezia.
Venice, Italy. 2014 / Zuazo Gallery, Arquerías de Nuevos Ministerios, Madrid. 2015

The theme chosen to celebrate 100 years of modern Spanish architecture is the prevalence of architectural control over interior space combining with the lessons learned from vernacular architecture with languages of modernity, characterising an environmental and atmospheric awareness that has survived in many forms over the course of the century and

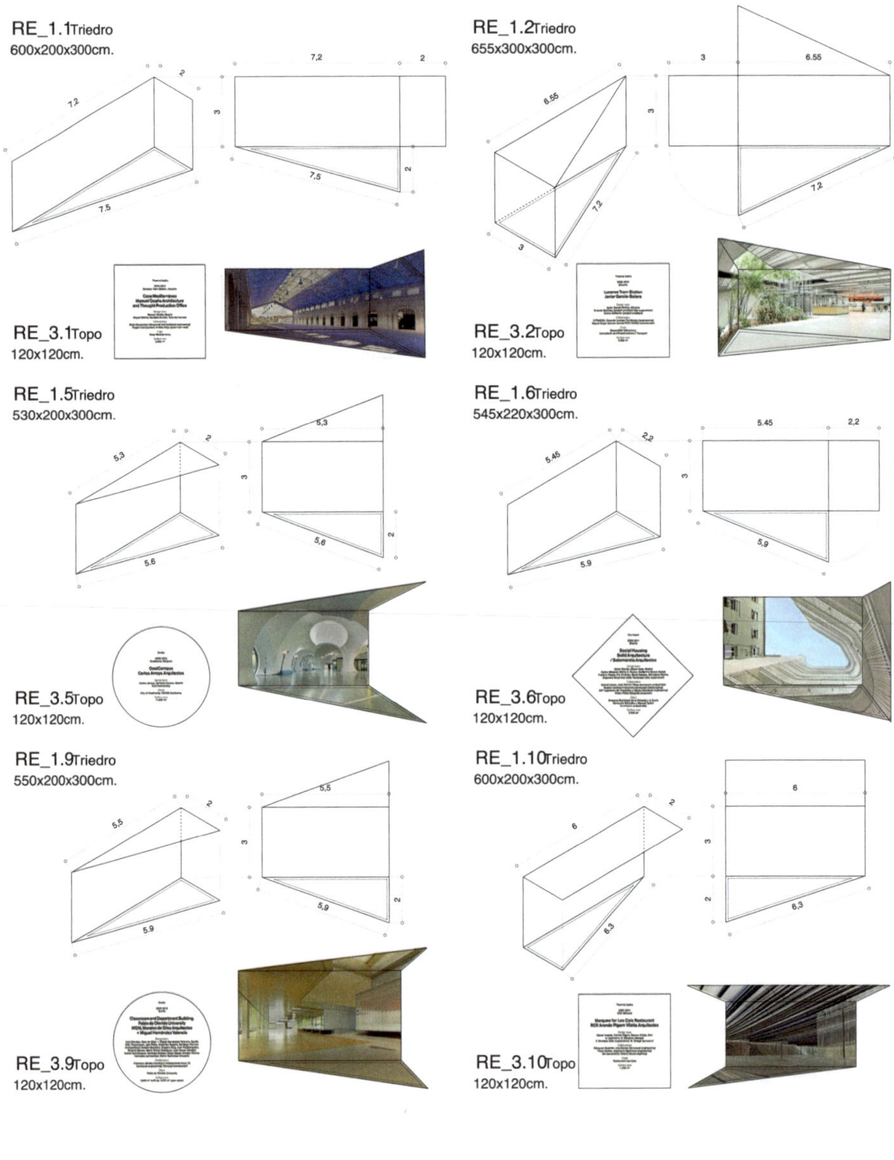

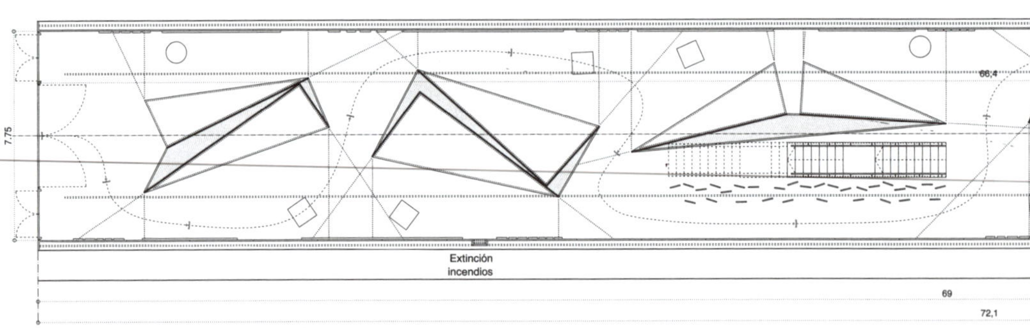

in recent years. The Spanish Pavilion in Venice's Giardini, with its blind façade made of brick, is an interior in itself and creates a labyrinth as an "interior of interiors"; a few L-shaped panels transform the central bay into twelve spaces linked by the use of three-dimensional photographs of recent interiors that introduce visitors into a doubly-interiorised experience. After the exhibition was moved to Madrid, we applied the same layout in a former metro station. To adapt the original concept to this linear space, we introduced perimeter mirrors to disrupt the linearity, and turned the complex into another labyrinthine space for people to discover places they have never been and recognise themselves there.

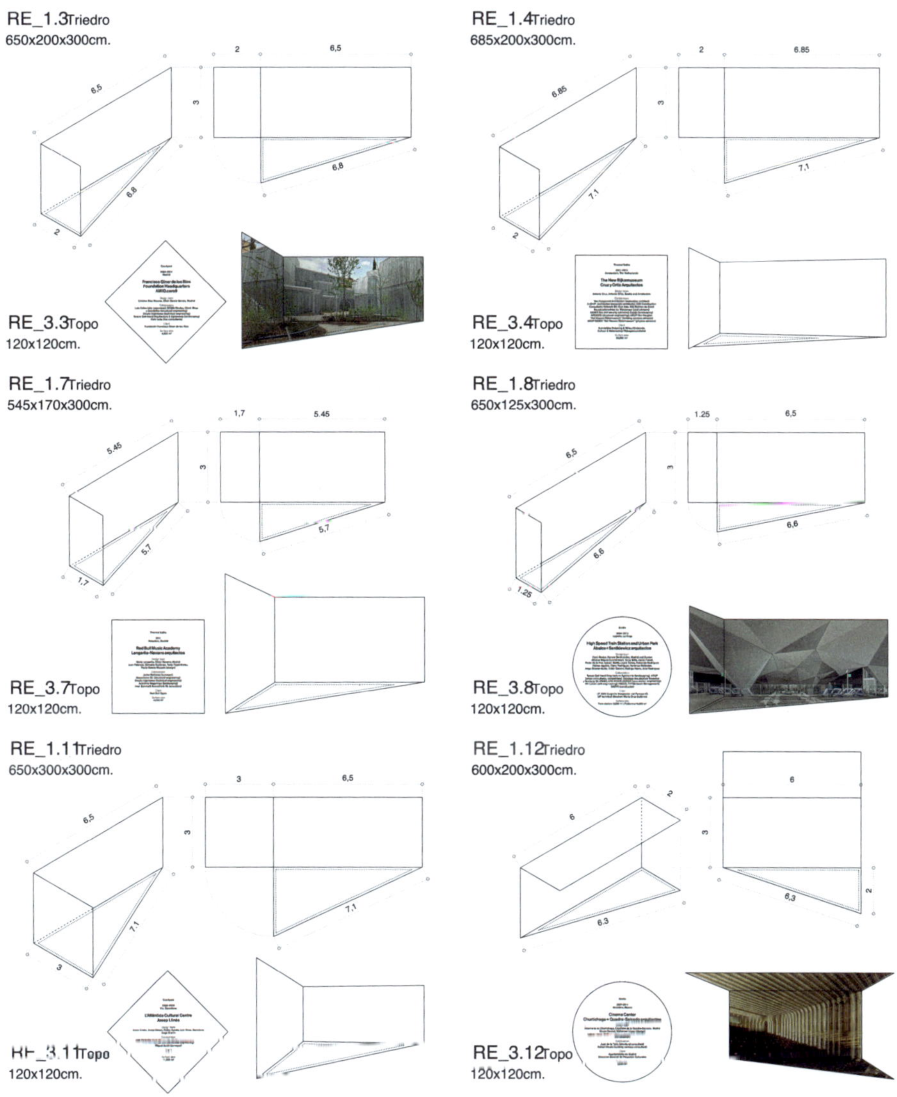

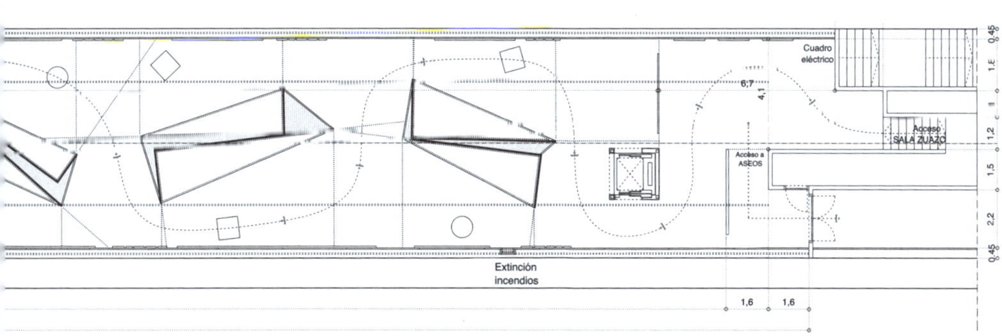

INT
ERI
O R

Gongbei Checking Complex. Zhuhai, China. 2014

Located on China's busiest border crossing, linking the country to Macau, the intervention is based on the existence of a pre-existing project that proved particularly unsuitable due to the climate in south-eastern China. AS+ took a fresh approach to this project as a sustainable alternative, which combines a bus transfer station, shopping mall, and high-rise offices in a unique mixed-use and promotional public-private complex. We conceived the design for a cladding that could respond to the local climatic conditions as well as the volume's architectural presence within its context after carefully analysing the building's exposure to sunlight and solar gain. The rotation of the building's cladding seeks the best possible orientations and protects the interior by projecting shadows, while the adaptation to a program without defined dividing lines between commercial and office spaces creates the terracing in cross-section. This decision created a prism that reduced the built area floor by floor, while the glazed area increased. In this way, the building's section adjusts its dimensions progressively in accordance with the superimposition of different programmes. The skin uses a characteristic red-coloured slate that reinforces the tectonic appearance, giving the complex a strategic urban presence for the customs office between the two areas. The complex is rounded off by the Zhuhai Contemporary Art Museum, the Customs tower, the high-speed railway station and the same mixed-use complex of Gongbei, all combining to create the landing for the long bridge that connects Hong Kong with Zhuhai and Macau.

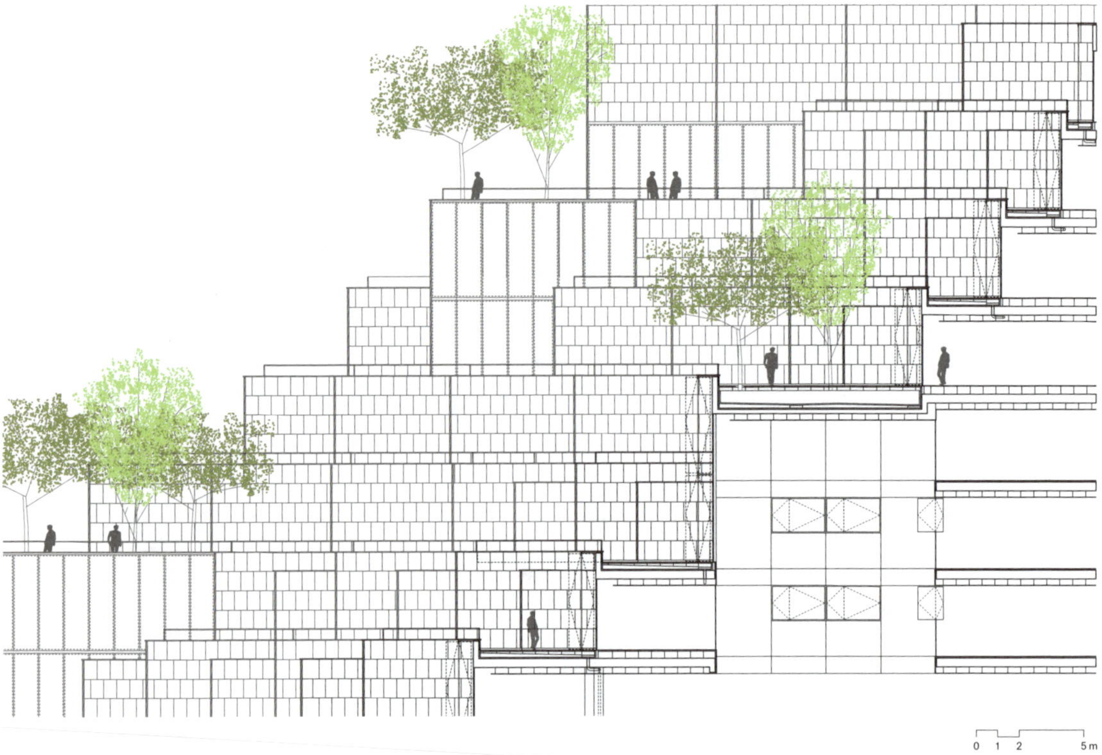

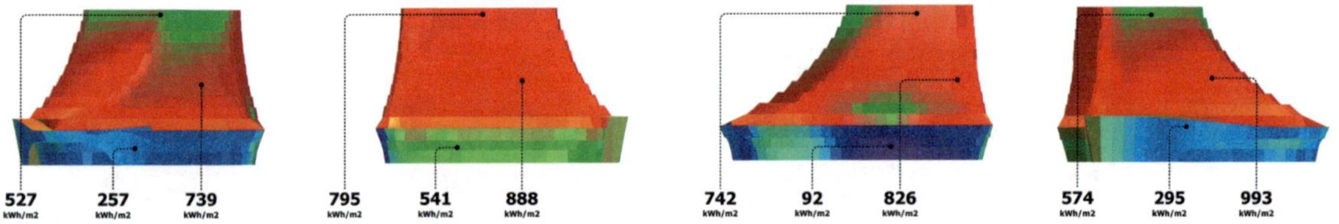

Original condition

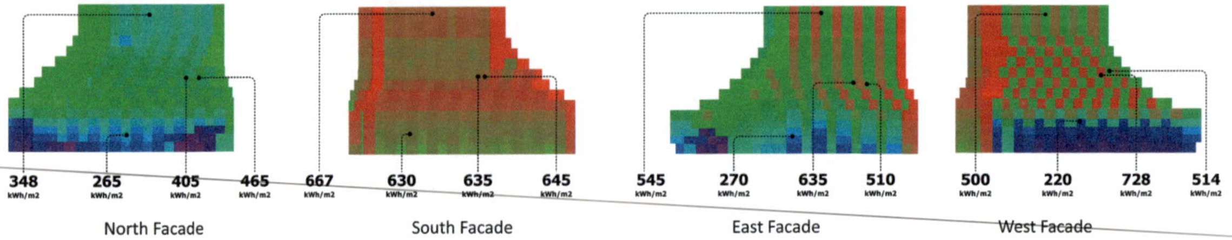

AS+ Proposal

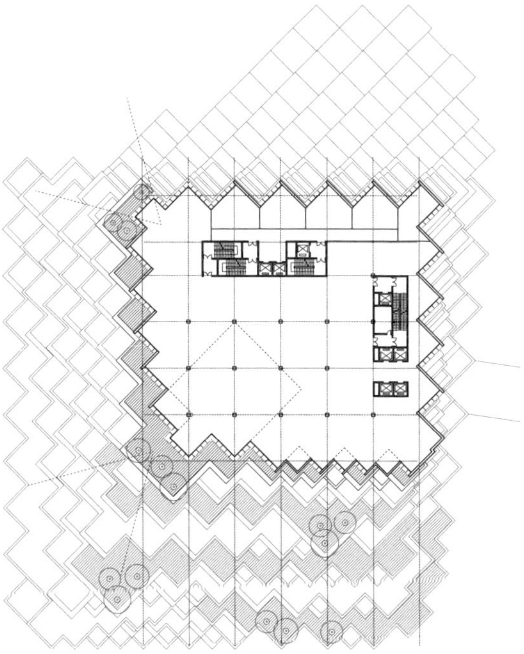

Level +37.00 m

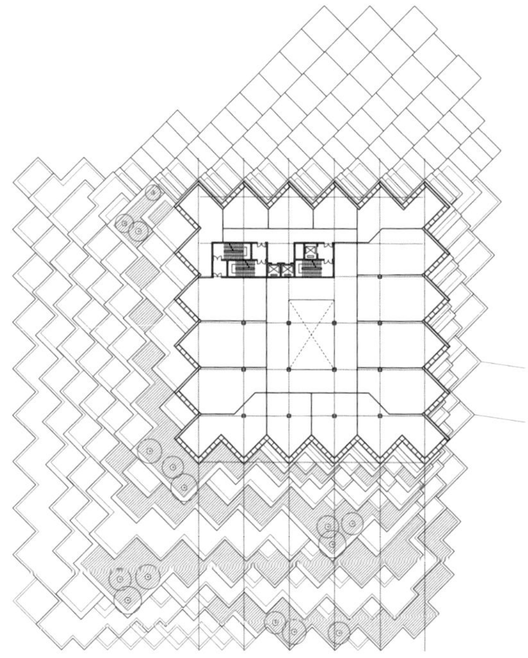

Level +45.00 m

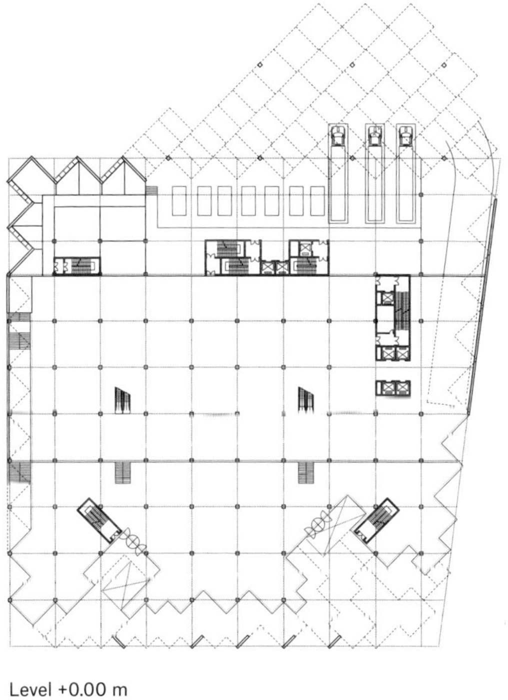

Level +0.00 m

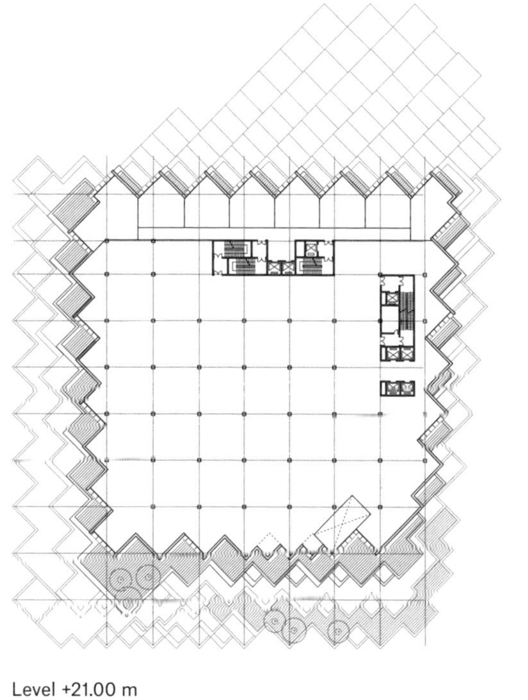

Level +21.00 m

VERSACE
PRADA

GIORGIO ARMANI
Dior

Telefónica Building. Madrid Observatory. Madrid, Spain. 2010

This project is a collaboration with students from Madrid's Higher Technical School of Architecture (ETSAM) and the CEU in Valencia. The idea was to transform Telefónica's Madrid building into a rock that can be accessed from outside and inside, from above and below, creating a new, technified garden for the 21st century. Our design proposed the complete recycling of Telefónica's building in terms of its programme and typology, condensing the public activities in the city. The objective was not only to transform the original structure—the first high-rise office space in Spain—into a large research centre specialising in the crossover between science, art and technology, but also to make radical modifications to the introvertedness of the office space by using pre-existing elements in the building to turn it into an extroverted structure that is publicly and fully accessible, inserted in a section of the city, both as a new museum typology and vertical garden, a rock to be climbed and from which to contemplate and discover the city: an observatory looking both outward and inward. At the ground level, the building empties, expanding the Gran Vía with a new plaza and metro entrance. The use of photovoltaic ceramic curtain walls, wind power generators and the metro's geothermal properties to meet the centre's energy requirements are designed to offset consumption and make the building's roof available again for public use. The programme is arranged around floors grouped together by scale, paying tribute to the book and film, *Powers of Ten* by Ray and Charles Eames: its thematic sections are the cosmos, earth, city, man, DNA and the atom.

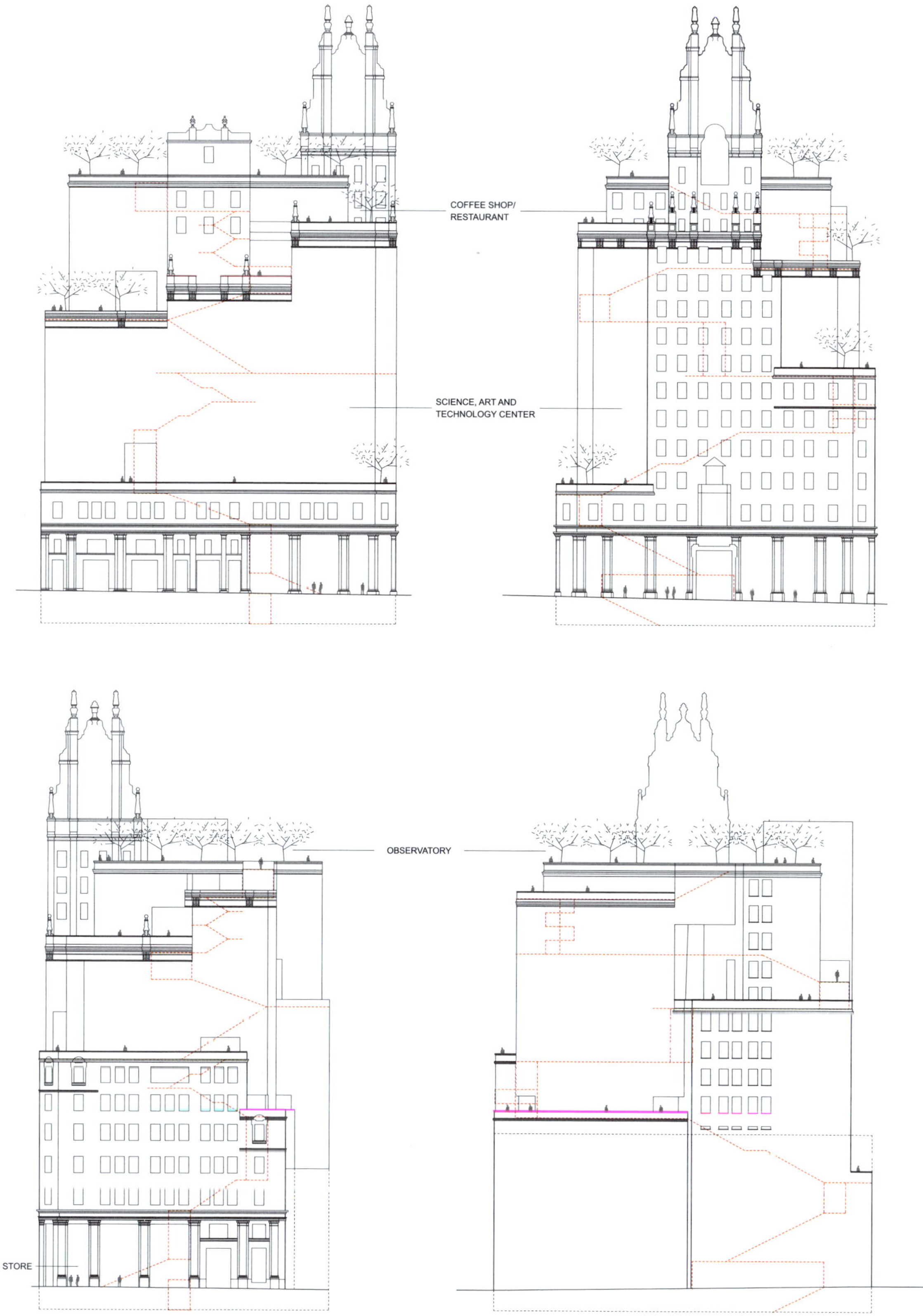
COFFEE SHOP/
RESTAURANT
SCIENCE, ART AND
TECHNOLOGY CENTER
OBSERVATORY
STORE

COSMOS
ASTRONOMY
SPACE TRAVEL
SOLAR SYSTEM
SUN
GALAXIES

EARTH
METEREOLOGY
GEOLOGY
HYDROLOGY
VOLCANOLOGY
BIOLOGY
SATELLITES
GOOGLE MAPS
TECTONIC PLATES SHIFT
EARTHQUAKES

CITY
ECOLOGY
TRANSPORT
URBANISM
LANDSCAPING
AGRICULTURE
TRANSPORTATION: AIR, LAND,
UNDERGROUND, AQUATIC
ENERGY
HEALTH
NUTRITION

HUMAN BEING
SOCIOLOGY
ANTHROPOLOGY
INFORMATION
COMMUNICATION
MECHANICS
HISTORY
INDUSTRIAL DESIGN
ROBOTICS

DNA / ATOM
NANOTECHNOLOGY
GENETICS
QUANTUM AND PARTICLE PHYSICS
NUCLEAR ENERGY
ATOMIC PHYSICS
QUARKS
PARTICLE ACCELERATOR
MICROTECHNOLOGY
MICROSCOPE

Coolidge Corner Theater (CCT) Expansion. Boston, Massachusetts, US. 2016

The CCT—with its Art Deco style and cinematographic tradition—is an iconic landmark on the country's intellectual landscape. Our idea for making the extension as unique and inspiring as possible is showing a continuity with that past, capable of stimulating a completely renewed version and therefore to make room for a contemporary architectural and cultural contribution, transforming the complex into a clear statement of optimism and faith in cinema, in the Coolidge Corner Theatre and its important public dimension.

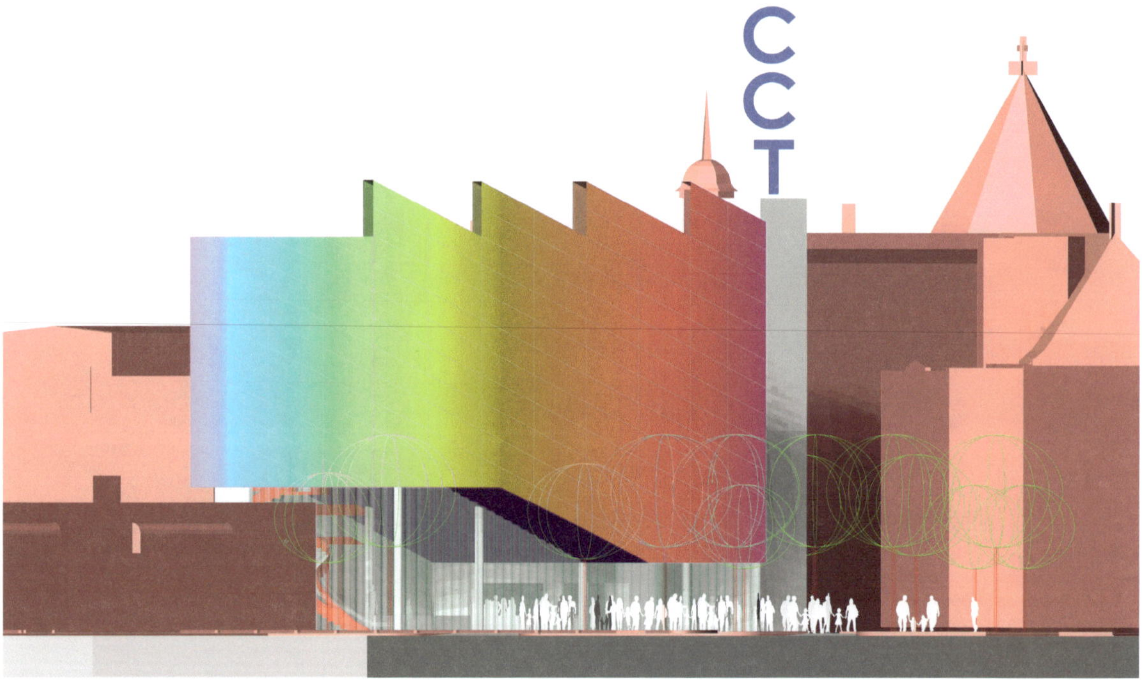

Art Deco iconographic references of the project

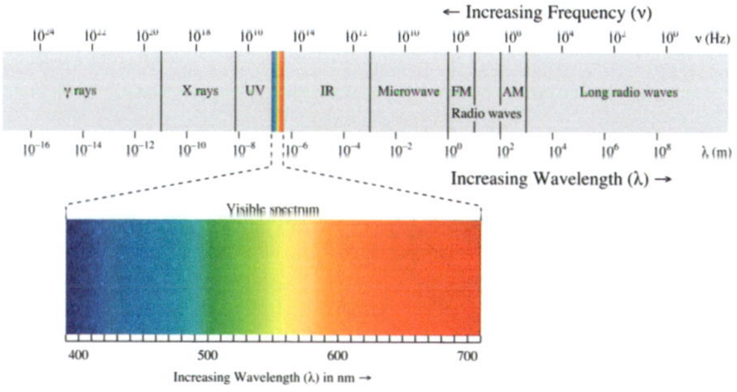

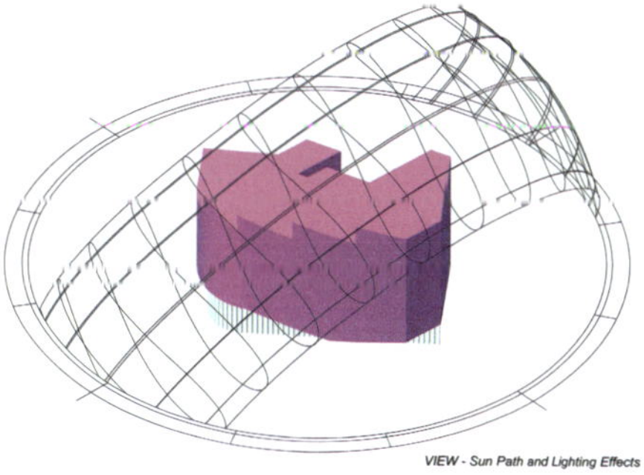

VIEW - Sun Path and Lighting Effects

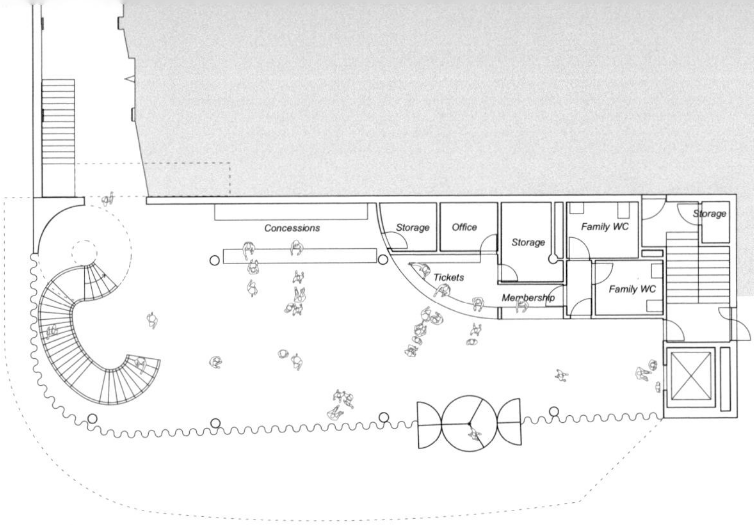

Ground floor plan

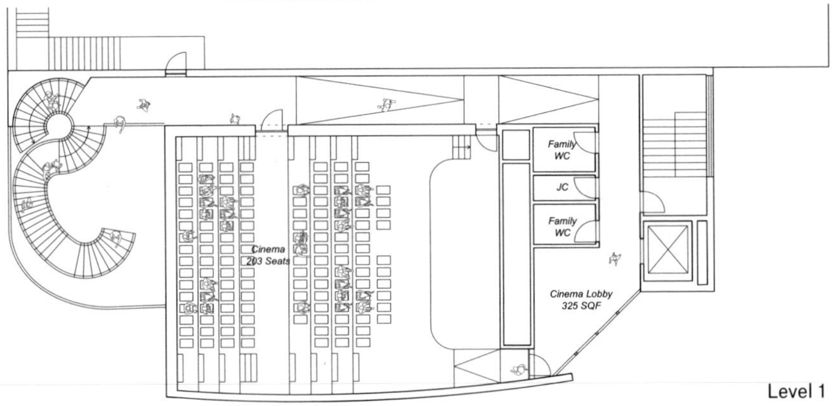

Level 1

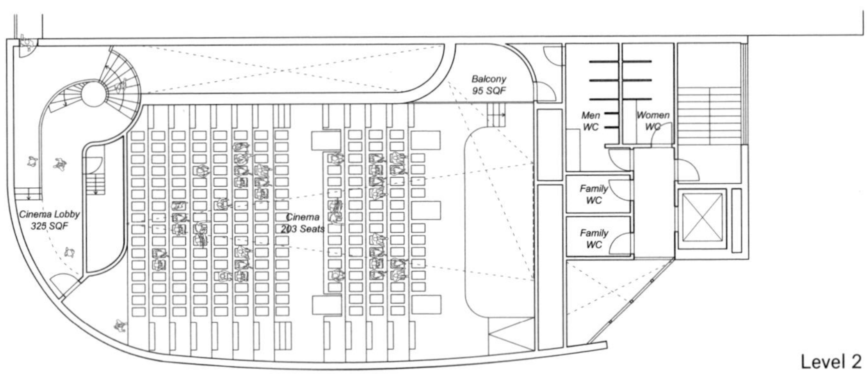

Level 2

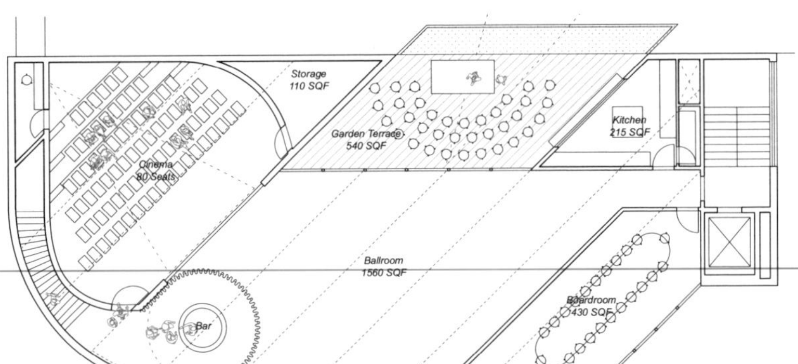

Level 3

View of the staircase that connects the different levels

New Bund Mixed-Use Block 43-01. Pudong, Shanghai, China. 2015–2018

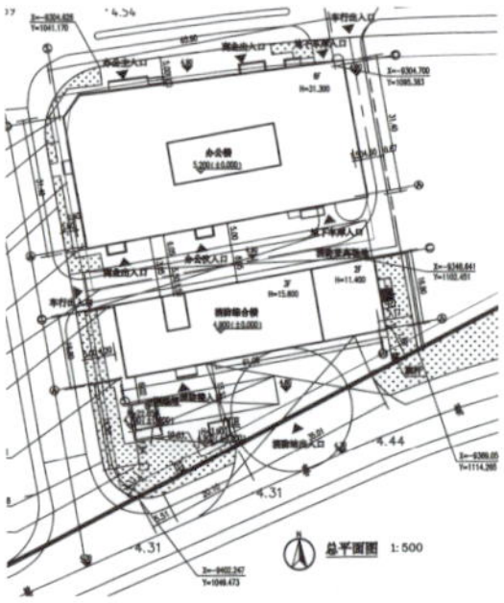

A block right at the entrance of a new Shanghai neighbourhood—perhaps an improvised, last-minute addition to the urban plan—provided the basis for incorporating programmes that the neighbourhood had been lacking: a fire station, offices, a police station, a multi-storey shopping centre, an advertising hoarding overlooking the thoroughfare... With a previous project that lacked interest, we interpreted our role as giving the complex a certain dignity, autonomy and coherence, creating a city block that evokes the scale and composition of a traditional European boulevard, appropriate for a new shopping centre of leading brands and with a recognizable appearance both day and night.

Dior

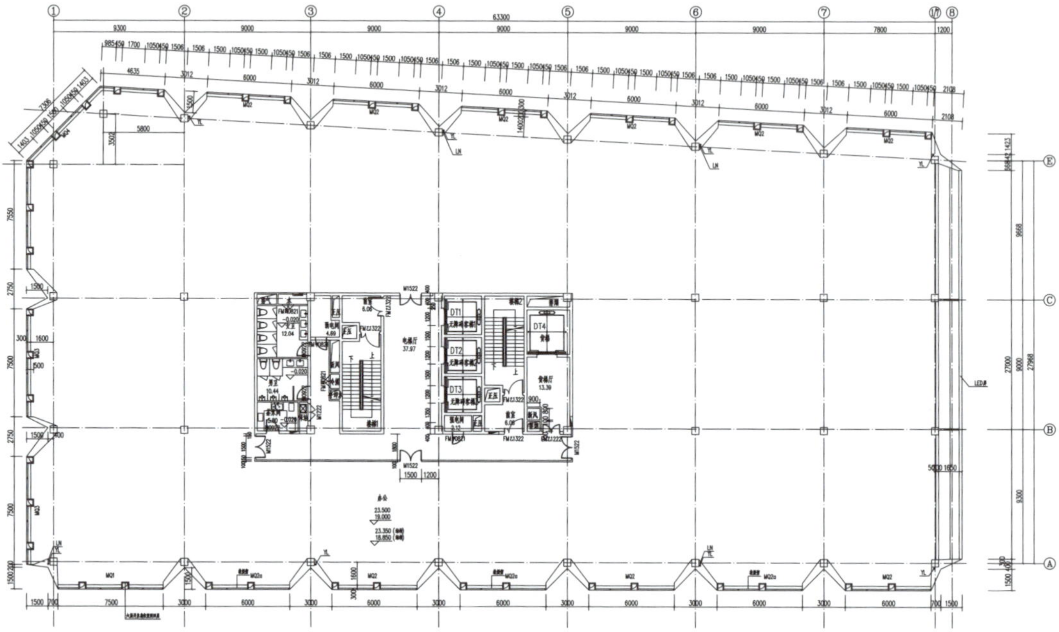

Dior
NEW LOOK

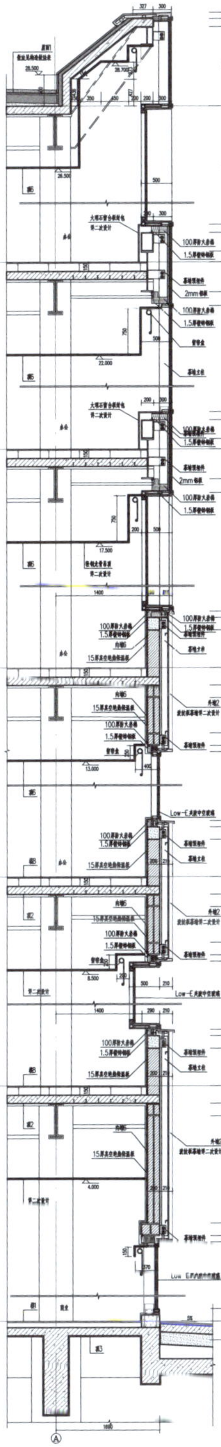

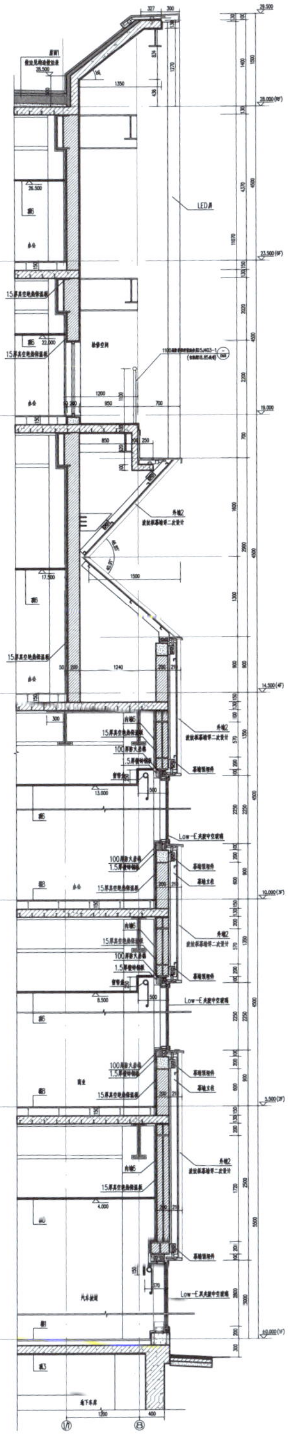

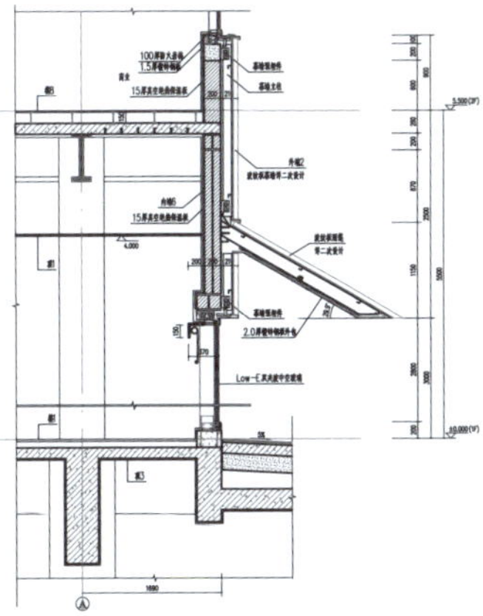

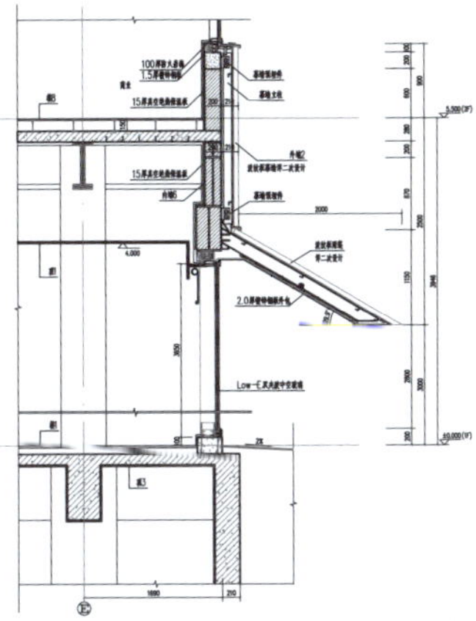

Residential Pavilion on Calle Orfila. Madrid, Spain. 2006-2009

Taking advantage of the space occupied by the former stables of Palacio Coca, this pavilion has residential units for staff working at nearby embassies, as well as shops. Respecting the building code that applies in central Madrid, we used the glazed 19th-century galleries as a thermodynamic reference point allowing us to create a contemporary building respectful of history and that uses passive temperature control systems.

7

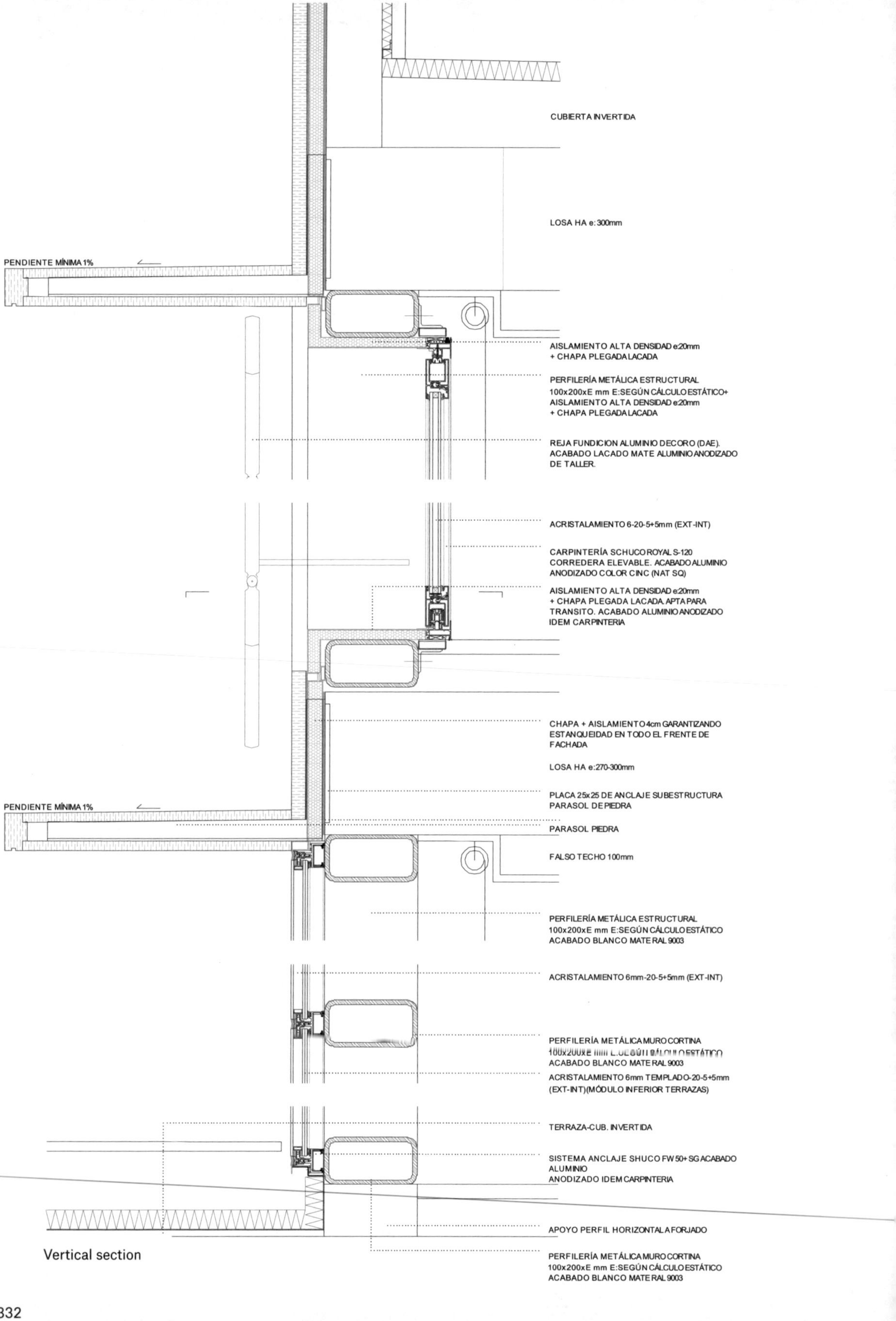

Vertical section

Credits

Longfeng Mall
French Concession, Shanghai, China. 2014–

Client: Qian Jun, Yongye International Inc. **Architecture:** Iñaki Ábalos, Renata Sentkiewicz (Abalos+Sentkiewicz AS+), Philip Yuan (Archi-Union) **Collaborators:** Alejandra Salvador, Adrián Úbeda, Chenchen Hu, Emiliano Domingo, Gabriel Muñoz, Milou Teeling, Xiaoshi Wang, Ingrid Bengtson **Structure and MEP:** Archi-Union **Interior Design:** Iñaki Ábalos, Renata Sentkiewicz (Abalos+Sentkiewicz AS+), Salmaan Craig **Landscape:** Iñaki Ábalos, Renata Sentkiewicz (Abalos+Sentkiewicz AS+) **Thermodynamics:** Salmaan Craig **Renderings:** Archi-Union **Model:** Ingrid Bengtson

Villa with Two Patios
Casares, Málaga, Spain. 2014–2018

Client: Singlehome S.A. **Architecture:** Iñaki Ábalos, Renata Sentkiewicz (Abalos+Sentkiewicz AS+) **Collaborators:** Alejandra Salvador, Adrián Úbeda, Teresa Casbas **Quantity Surveyor:** Miguel Ángel Yebra, Sergio Villena (Site Supervision), Sergio Barragán, Luis Moreno (Project Manager) **Structure:** Alejandro Bernabéu (Bernabéu Ingenieros) **Interior Design:** Ángel Verdú (BdeV Interiores) **MEP:** Manproject/CDC Ingenieros S.L. **Landscape:** Juan von Knobloch (Paisajismo Cortesín) **Construction:** Singlehome S.A. **Photography:** José Hevia

Cultural and Leisure Centre
Azuqueca de Henares, Guadalajara, Spain. 2007–2011

Client: City Council of Azuqueca de Henares, Castilla-La Mancha Community **Architecture:** Iñaki Ábalos, Renata Sentkiewicz (Abalos+Sentkiewicz AS+) **Collaborators:** Luis Alfaro, Andrés Besomi, Margaux Eyssette, Pablo de la Hoz, Margarita Martínez, Alejandro Valdivieso **Quantity Surveyor:** Ramón Paradinas **Structure:** Eduardo Barrón **Facilities:** Florencio Manteca (CENER), Rogelio Moya (Manproject) **Landscape:** Iñaki Ábalos, Renata Sentkiewicz (Abalos+Sentkiewicz AS+) **Model:** Alejandro Valdivieso **Construction:** BM3 Obras y Servicios, S.A. **Photography:** José Hevia

Four Energy Observatories
Island of La Palma, Canary Islands, Spain. 2006–2007

Client: Bienal de Canarias de Arquitectura, Arte y Paisaje, Colegio de Arquitectos de Canarias (COAC) **Deputy:** Iñaki Ábalos **Architecture:** Iñaki Ábalos, Renata Sentkiewicz, Mª Auxiliadora Gálvez, Miguel Kreisler, Lluís Ortega **Collaborators:** Carlos Bayod, Yeray Brito Hernández, Lucas Camponovo, Fabrice Corminboeuf, Carmen Jesús Fajardo Hernández, Koldo Fernández Gaztelu, Eva Fernández Navarro, Rada Fornara, Ángeles Gil González, Quirin Krumbholz, Gádor Luque Martínez, Andrés Pérez Martínez, Anna Psenicka, Antonio Rocha Quintero, Davide Scardua, Aldo Trim **Consultants:** Joaquín Mañoso, Ángel Caro **Graphic Design and Publication:** Roger Adam

Biobío Regional Theatre
Concepción, Chile. 2011

Client: CNCA, Government of Chile **Architecture:** Iñaki Ábalos, Renata Sentkiewicz (Abalos+Sentkiewicz AS+) **Collaborators:** Alejandro Morales, Francisca Cifuentes (MC2 arquitectos asociados), Andrés Durán (D+) Juan Enríquez, Rodrigo Rieiro, José Rodríguez, Deborah López (Abalos+Sentkiewicz AS+) **Acoustics:** Higini Arau, Arau Acústica

Multigenerational Centre and Start-Up Incubator
Seoul, South Korea. 2017

Client: Urban Space Improvement Bureau, Metropolitan Government of Seoul **Architecture:** Iñaki Ábalos, Renata Sentkiewicz (Abalos+Sentkiewicz AS+), María José Marcos, Sewon Roy Kim (MagicArch) **Collaborators:** Jerónimo Van Schendel, Alejandra Salvador, Eduardo López, Natalia Deus, Adriana Coca **Structure:** Xavier Aguiló (BAC ecg) **Local Normative:** Kim Min (SNP Group) **Renderings:** Eduardo López (Abalos+Sentkiewicz AS+) **Model:** Adrià Clapés, Gwal Kim (Hyperauthentic)

San Antonio Urban Regeneration
Historic Centre of Medellín, Colombia. 2015–

Client: EDU (Empresa de Desarrollo Urbano de Medellín) **Architecture:** Iñaki Ábalos, Renata Sentkiewicz (Abalos+Sentkiewicz AS+) **Collaborators:** Alexander Jacobson, Álvaro Maján, Héctor Múñoz, Eva Castiñeira, Alejandra Salvador, Sofía Lens, Claudia Vivas **Consultant:** John Octavio y EDU team **Landscape:** Teresa Galí-Izard, Jordi Nebot (Arquitectura Agronomía) **Thermodynamics:** Salmaan Craig, Alexander Jacobson

Felipe VI City Park
Logroño, La Rioja, Spain. 2008–2020

Client: LIF 2002 SA - ADIF - ADIF Alta Velocidad - Renfe Operadora - City Council of Logroño, Government of La Rioja. Santiago Miyares (Director), Mª Cruz Gutiérrez (Technical Director) **Architecture and Landscape:** Iñaki Ábalos, Renata Sentkiewicz (Abalos+Sentkiewicz AS+), Teresa Galí-Izard, Jordi Nebot (Arquitectura Agronomía) **Collaborators:** Alfonso Miguel, Jorge Álvarez-Builla, Yeray Brito, Aaron Forest, Víctor Garzón, Pablo de la Hoz, Ismael Martín, Laura Torres, Rodrigo Rieiro, José Rodríguez (Phase 1), Álvaro Maján, Eduardo López, Sofía Lens, Carlos Pascual (Phase 2) **Project Management:** Iñaki Ábalos, Rafael Alcoceba, Joaquín Espert **Site Supervision:** Eduardo Muñoz, Ana Palacios, Alberto Mecha **Construction:** Sacyr (Phase 1), UTE Vías y Construcciones-Ismael Andrés-Agua y Jardín (Phase 2) **Photography:** José Hevia

Torre Spina
Turin, Italy. 2008

Client: Franco Costruzioni Real Estate / City Council of Turin **Architecture:** Iñaki Ábalos, Renata Sentkiewicz (Abalos+Sentkiewicz AS+), León López de la Osa **Collaborators:** Alfonso Miguel, Pablo de la Hoz, Ismael Martín **Thermodynamics:** Florencio Manteca (CENER) **Renderings:** Pablo de la Hoz, Ismael Martín **Model:** Talleres Vázquez

Contemporary Art Museum
Zhuhai, China. 2013–

Client: Guangdong Huasheng Investment Group Co, Ltd. **Architecture:** Iñaki Ábalos, Renata Sentkiewicz (Abalos+Sentkiewicz AS+), Linxue Li (Atelier L+) **Collaborators (Contest):** Timothy Brennan, Chenchen Hu, Weilun Tsui (Cambridge) Mª Auxiliadora Gálvez, Juan Enríquez, Ana Fernández, Elena Vallejo, Alvaro Maján, Marina Bicca (Madrid), Yin Hongde, Li Huanhuan, Ni Runer, Liu Jieling, Wangyiqing (Shanghai) **Thermodynamics:** Bing Wang, Salmaan Craig (Harvard Center for Green Buildings and Cities) **Consultants:** TJAD Tongji University Architectural Design and Research Institute **Structure:** Hanif Kara (AKT II) **Renderings:** Jin Shang Animation **Model:** Si Fang Qi Yi Architectural Model Co, Ltd.

Battlefields

Masters' at the Laboratory of Contemporary Techniques and Landscapes, ETSAM. 2002–2003 (Research) / Colegio de Arquitectos de Cataluña (COAC), Barcelona. 2004 (Exhibition)

Client: Col·legi d'arquitectes de Catalunya **Direction:** Iñaki Ábalos **Professors:** Iñaki Ábalos, Daniel Zarza, Efrén García Grinda, Teresa Galí-Izard, Antonio Gómez Sal, José Luis Pardo, Bleda y Rosa, Nuria Enguita, Daniel Calparsoro, Ángel Borrego **Collaborators:** David Marsinyach, Javier Morales, Carlos Ríos, Eric Clearing, Luis Úrculo, Elena Cuerda Barcaiztegui, Stéphanie Chaltiel, Rubén Briongos Izquierdo, Mark Neuer (Students from the 2002–2003 academic year at the Laboratory of Contemporary Techniques and Landscapes, ETSAM)

Church in the New Bund District

Pudong, Shanghai, China. 2016–2018

Client: Shanghai New Bund International Business District Investment (Group) Co, Ltd. **Architecture:** Iñaki Ábalos, Renata Sentkiewicz (Abalos+Sentkiewicz AS+) **Collaborators:** Adrián Úbeda, Álvaro Maján, Alexander Jacobson, Eva Castiñeira, Alejandra Salvador, Hao Chen, Chenchen Hu, Teresa Casbas, Yiqun Wang **Consultant:** Pudong Design Institute **Model:** Yi Zhao Model **Photography:** Zhang Yong (ZYArch Photographer)

Yangpu Bridge Area Riverside Development Plan

Shanghai, China. 2018–

Client: Local Government of Shanghai **Architecture and Landscape:** Iñaki Ábalos, Renata Sentkiewicz (Abalos+Sentkiewicz AS+) **Collaborators:** Jerónimo Van Schendel, Andrea Vallés, Sofía Lens, Teresa Casbas, Tania González, Carlos Pascual, Vincenzo Cannata, Simin Tao, He Meiting **Heritage:** Plácido González **Art Curatorial Expertise:** Nuria Enguita **Local collaborator:** TJAD Tongji Architectural Design (Group) Co. Ltd. **Renderings and animation:** Ginsun CG

Yangpu Memory Park

Shanghai, China. 2019–

Client: Local Government of Shanghai **Architecture and landscape:** Iñaki Ábalos, Renata Sentkiewicz (Abalos+Sentkiewicz AS+) **Collaborators:** Andrea Vallés, Sofía Lens, Carlos Pascual, José de Andrés **Local collaborator:** TJAD Tongji Architectural Design (Group) Co. Ltd. **Renderings:** Ginsun CG

Intermodal Station and Urban Railway Integration

Logroño, La Rioja, Spain. 2008–2020

Client: LIF 2002 SA - ADIF - ADIF Alta Velocidad - Renfe Operadora - City Council of Logroño, Government of La Rioja. Santiago Miyares (Director), Mª Cruz Gutiérrez (Technical Director) **Architecture:** Iñaki Ábalos, Renata Sentkiewicz, Alfonso Miguel (Abalos+Sentkiewicz AS+) **Collaborators:** Jorge Álvarez-Builla, Yeray Brito, Aaron Forest, Víctor Garzón, Pablo de la Hoz, Ismael Martín, Laura Torres, Rodrigo Rieiro, José Rodríguez (Phase 1), Álvaro Maján, Eduardo López, Sofía Lens, Carlos Pascual (Phase 2) **Project Management:** Iñaki Ábalos, Rafael Alcoceba, Joaquín Espert **Site Supervision:** Eduardo Muñoz, Ana Palacios, Alberto Mecha **Technical Assistance:** Eduardo Muñoz (Phase 1), Ricardo Castejón, Miguel García Manzanos (TYPSA) (Phase 2) **Structure and MEP:** UTE Ineco-Sener (Phase 1), Ricardo Castejón, Miguel García Manzanos (TYPSA) (Phase 2) **Construction:** Sacyr (Phase 1), UTE Vías y Construcciones-Ismael Andrés-Agua y Jardín (Phase 2) **Photography:** José Hevia, Jesús Rocandio (Casa de la Imagen)

CaixaForum Museum in Atarazanas Reales

Seville, Spain. 2009

Client: Obra Social La Caixa **Architecture:** Iñaki Ábalos, Renata Sentkiewicz (Abalos+Sentkiewicz AS+) **Collaborators:** Alfonso Miguel, Margaux Eyssette, Andrés Besomi **Structure:** Xavier Aguiló (BOMA) **Acoustics:** Higini Arau (Arau Acústica) **Quantity Surveyor:** Alfonso Barrón **Thermodynamics:** Florencio Manteca (CENER) **Renderings:** Luis Cabrejas (Neograma)

Antoni Tàpies Foundation

Barcelona, Spain. 2007–2010

Client: Antoni Tàpies Foundation **Architecture:** Iñaki Ábalos, Renata Sentkiewicz (Abalos+Sentkiewicz AS+) **Collaborators:** Víctor Garzón, Haizea Aguirre, Elena Cuerda, Ismael Martín, Alfonso Miguel **Structure:** Agustí Obiol, Javier Asensio (BOMA) **Quantity Surveyor:** Eduard Casanovas (CASOBI) **Graphic Design:** Mario Eskenazi **Lighting:** Josep Mª Civit (Spaillum) **Facilities:** AB2, FLUIDSA, PREFIRE **Furniture:** Félix Fernández (Mairea) **Construction:** SAPIC

City Museum and Art Gallery

Wuhan, China. 2016–2017

Client: Huafa Investment Co. **Architecture:** Iñaki Ábalos, Renata Sentkiewicz (Abalos+Sentkiewicz AS+), Linxue Li (Atelier L+) **Collaborators:** Alejandra Salvador (Abalos+Sentkiewicz AS+) Kaifeng Zhou (Atelier L+) **Expertise:** UDg Lianchuang International **Photography:** Zhang Yong (ZYArch Photographer)

Restoration of Residential Building on Calle Barquillo

Madrid, Spain. 2009

Client: Residents' association **Architecture:** Iñaki Ábalos, Renata Sentkiewicz (Abalos+Sentkiewicz AS+) **Collaborators:** Víctor Garzón **Quantity Surveyor:** Alfonso Barrón **Construction:** CYR Proyectos y Obras **Photography:** José Hevia

Atelier Albert Oehlen

Bülher, Switzerland. 2007–2009

Client: Albert Oehlen **Architecture:** Iñaki Ábalos (Abalos+Sentkiewicz AS+), Paloma Lasso de la Vega (LeArquitectura) **Lighting:** Bernard Paule (ESTIA) **Photography:** José Hevia **Construction:** Andreas Frehner (Frehner Holzbau AG)

Co-living Aranberri

Itziar, Guipúzcoa, Spain. 2006-2014

Client: Aranberri Family **Architecture:** Iñaki Ábalos, Renata Sentkiewicz (Abalos+Sentkiewicz AS+) **Collaborators:** Alfonso Miguel, Víctor Garzón, Jorge Álvarez Builla, Rodrigo Riero, José Rodríguez **Structure:** Eduardo Barrón **MEP:** Manproject **Quantity Surveyor:** José María Roteta **Photography:** José Hevia

Seniors' Residence and Day Centre

Los Llanos de Aridane, Island of La Palma, Spain. 2020-

Client: Island Council of La Palma **Architecture and Landscape:** Iñaki Ábalos, Renata Sentkiewicz (Abalos+Sentkiewicz AS+) **Collaborators:** José de Andrés (coordinator), Carlos Pascual, Chenchen Gao, María de Sotto **Sustainability** Oriol Gavaldà (Aiguasol)

Spanish Cultural Centre
Buenos Aires, Argentina. 2011

Client: Spanish Agency for International Development Cooperation (AECID) **Architecture:** Iñaki Ábalos, Renata Sentkiewicz (Abalos+Sentkiewicz AS+) **Collaborators:** Rodrigo Rieiro, Juan Enríquez, José Rodríguez, Deborah López, Tullia Monachesi, Fernando Sánchez **Quantity Surveyor:** Alfonso Barrón **Local collaborator:** Daniel Rizzo **Facilities:** Rogelio Moya (Manproject)

Integrating the High Speed Train (TAV) Line in Atotxa Station
Donostia-San Sebastián, Guipúzcoa, Spain. 2018

Client: ETS (Euskal Trenbide Sarea) **Architecture:** Iñaki Ábalos, Renata Sentkiewicz (Abalos+Sentkiewicz AS+) **Collaborators:** Jerónimo van Schendel, Claudia Vivas, Andrea Vallés **Engineering:** Alesander Gallastegui (TYPSA) **Renderings:** Ignacio Monteserín (Poliedro)

Urban Design in Quart de Poblet
Valencia, Spain. 2018–

Client: Sociedad de Actividades Industriales Quart S.L. **Architecture:** Iñaki Ábalos, Renata Sentkiewicz (Abalos+Sentkiewicz AS+) **Collaborators:** Jerónimo Van Schendel, Andrea Vallés, Tania González **Landscape:** Teresa Galí-Izard, Jordi Nebot (Arquitectura Agronomía) **Thermodynamics:** Aleksandar Ivancic, Oriol Gavaldà (Aiguasol) **Renderings:** Ignacio Monteserín (Poliedro)

Solar Tower
Sociópolis, Valencia, Spain. 2008–2012

Client: Grupo Ática / IVVSA / Grupo Valenciano del Alquiler Protegido **Architecture:** Iñaki Ábalos, Renata Sentkiewicz (Abalos+Sentkiewicz AS+) **Collaborators:** Alfonso Miguel (Coordinator), Laura Torres, Jorge Álvarez-Builla, Víctor Garzón, Pablo de la Hoz, Ismael Martín, Luis Matanzo, Jens Richter, David Sobrino, José Rodríguez **Quantity Surveyor:** Enrique Llinares **Structure:** Antoni Ortí, José Ramón Solé (BOMA Levante) **Facilities:** Paco Mora, Jose María Barreda (ARTIN Proyectos) **Renderings:** Ismael Martín, Luis Matanzo, José Rodríguez **Model:** Jesús Medina **Construction:** Grupo Secopsa **Photography:** José Hevia

New District Citizen Square and Productivity Promotion Centre
Hangzhou Bay, China. 2017

Client: Local Government of Hangzhou Bay **Architecture:** Iñaki Ábalos, Renata Sentkiewicz (Abalos+Sentkiewicz AS+) **Collaborators:** Alejandra Salvador, Eduardo López (Abalos+Sentkiewicz AS+) **Renderings:** Ignacio Monteserín (Poliedro)

Princeton Carpark
Princeton University, New Jersey, US. 2007–2009

Client: Princeton University **Architecture:** Iñaki Ábalos, Renata Sentkiewicz (Abalos+Sentkiewicz AS+) **Collaborators:** Alfonso Miguel, Jorge Álvarez-Builla, Aaron Forest, Ismael Martín (Abalos+Sentkiewicz AS+) **Parking Consulting:** Walker Parking Consultants **Landscaping and environmental studies:** Michael van Valkenburgh Associates Consultor **Planning:** Beyer Blinder Belle, Architects & Planners, LLP. **Renderings:** Aaron Forest, Ismael Martín (Abalos+Sentkiewicz AS+)

The Flying Spine. Walkway in the Zhang Jia Bang Park
Pudong, Shanghai, China. 2016–

Client: Shanghai Pudong Properties Group Co, LTD. **Architecture:** Iñaki Ábalos, Renata Sentkiewicz (Abalos+Sentkiewicz AS+) **Collaborators:** Jerónimo Van Schendel, Alejandra Salvador, Eduardo López, Laura Florentín, Álvaro Maján, Sofía Blanco, Caio Barboza, Hao Chen, Sofía Lens, Teresa Casbas, Andrea Vallés, Chenchen Gao **Structure:** Xavier Aguiló (BAC ecg) **Renderings:** Sofía Lens, Teresa Casbas, Andrea Vallés, Chenchen Gao (Abalos+Sentkiewicz AS+) **Photography:** Zhang Yong (ZYArch Photographer)

Shanghai Grand Opera House
Shanghai, China. 2017

Client: Shanghai Lujiazui Group Co. Ltd **Architecture:** Iñaki Ábalos, Renata Sentkiewicz (Abalos+Sentkiewicz AS+) **Collaborators:** Jerónimo Van Schendel, Alejandra Salvador, Eduardo López, Natalia Deus, Laura Florentín, Héctor Muñoz, Yiqun Wang **Theatre Consultants:** Louis Janssen, Gerbrand Borgdorff, Caroline Noteboom (Theateradvies) **Structure:** Lluis Moyá, Agustí Obiol, Xavier Aguiló (BAC ecg) **Energy and Sustainability:** Matthias Schuler, Nadir Abdessemed, Raphael Lafargue (Transsolar) **Renderings and animation:** Ginsun CG **Model:** Shanghai Xiuneixiumel Make Models Co. Ltd.

PLANTA Project for Sorigué Foundation
Balaguer, Lérida, Spain. 2014–

Client: Sorigué Foundation **Architecture:** Iñaki Ábalos, Renata Sentkiewicz (Abalos+Sentkiewicz AS+) **Collaborators:** Álvaro Maján, Alejandra Salvador, Eduardo López, Teresa Casbas, Sofía Lens, José de Andrés **Documentation:** Armin Linke **Structure:** Xavier Aguiló, Gerard Clavería, Alejandro Nava (BAC ecg) **Facilities:** BAC ecg **Thermodynamics:** Aleksandar Ivancic, Oriol Gavaldà (Aiguasol) **Landscape:** Teresa Galí-Izard, Jordi Nebot (Arquitectura Agronomía) **Renderings:** Ignacio Monteserín (Show Me The Project), Eduardo López **Model:** Carlos Espinosa (Taller de Maquetas Jorge Queipo)

Shanghai Museum East
Shanghai, China. 2016

Client: Shanghai Museum **Architecture:** Iñaki Ábalos, Renata Sentkiewicz (Abalos+Sentkiewicz AS+) **Collaborators:** Sofía Blanco, Jerónimo Van Schendel, Alejandra Salvador, Álvaro Maján, Hao Chen, Caio Barboza, Eduardo López, Laura Florentín **Local collaborator:** Linxue Li (Atelier L+) **Structure:** Xavier Aguiló (BAC ecg) **Thermodynamics:** Matthias Schuller, Raphael Lafargue (Transsolar) **Lighting:** Antón Amánn (ALS Lighting Solutions) **MEP:** Julian Sutherland, José Castilla (CUNDALL Engineering) **Renderings:** Ginsun CG **Model:** Sun ChangLong

Interior. Spanish Pavilion at the XIV Mostra Internazionale di Architettura, La Biennale di Venezia
Venice, Italy. 2014/ Zuazo Gallery, Arquerías de Nuevos Ministerios, Madrid. 2015

Client: Ministry of Development / Ministry of Foreign Affairs and Cooperation. Government of Spain **Curator:** Iñaki Ábalos **Assistant Curators:** Enrique Encabo, Inmaculada E. Maluenda, Lluís Ortega **Collaborators:** Javier García Germán (Direction and coordination ETSAM) Rafael Beneytez (Coordination assistance) Vicky Achnani, Emiliano Domingo, María García, Sun Jiaqiu, Diana Mera, Saptarshi Mitra, Adriana, Pablos, Alejandra Sánchez, Snehal Sonawane, Adrián Úbeda, Zhang Yanan (Students ETSAM) **Design:** Abalos+Sentkiewicz AS+, Sio2 Arch, Manuel Ocaña **Editor:** Moisés Puente **Production:** SCP. Creación y Producción de Eventos **Publication:** Ministry of Development / Arquia Foundation **Photography:** José Hevia

Gongbei Checking Complex
Zhuhai, China, 2014

Client: Zhuhai Huafa Group **Architecture:** Iñaki Ábalos, Renata Sentkiewicz (Abalos+Sentkiewicz AS+) **Collaborators:** Chechen Hu, Álvaro Maján, Timothy Brennan, Zhenhuan Xu, José Mayoral, Alex Timmer, Emiliano Domingo, Adrián Úbeda **Energy and Climate:** Diego Ibarra (EA Buildings-Environmental Analytics) **Renderings:** Luis Cabrejas (Neograma)

Telefónica Building. Madrid Observatory
Madrid, Spain. 2010

Client: Telefónica Foundation **Architecture:** Iñaki Ábalos, Renata Sentkiewicz (Abalos+Sentkiewicz AS+) **Coordination:** Laura Torres **Collaborators:** Proyectos IV-V Curso 2008 ETSAM / Máster 2010 CEU Valencia **Model:** Mª Isabel Villar Abril, José Hernández Navarro

Coolidge Corner Theater (CCT) Expansion
Boston, Massachusetts, US. 2016

Client: Coolidge Corner Theater Foundation **Architecture:** Iñaki Ábalos, Renata Sentkiewicz, Sofía Blanco (Abalos+Sentkiewicz AS+) **Collaborators:** Caio Barboza, Álvaro Maján, Eva Castiñeira **Local collaborator:** Ned Collier (Icon Arch) **Renderings:** Sofía Blanco (Abalos+Sentkiewicz AS+) **Model:** Caio Barboza

New Bund Mixed-Use Block 43-01
Pudong, Shanghai, China. 2015–2018

Client: Shanghai Yangrui Investment Co. Ltd. **Architecture:** Iñaki Ábalos, Renata Sentkiewicz (Abalos+Sentkiewicz AS+) **Collaborators:** Álvaro Maján, Eva Castiñeira, Alexander Jacobson, Hao Chen, Jerónimo Van Schendel, Yiqun Wang **Consultants:** Shanghai Pudong Architectural Design **Enveloping:** Schmidlin-TSK AG **Photography:** Zhang Yong (ZYArch Photography)

Residential Pavilion on Calle Orfila
Madrid, Spain. 2006–2009

Client: Olabe S.L. **Architecture:** Iñaki Ábalos, Renata Sentkiewicz (Ábalos +Sentkiewicz) **Collaborators:** Víctor Garzón (Coordinator), Elena Cuerda, Juan José González, Ismael Martín, Luis Matanzo, Alfredo Muñoz **Quantity Surveyor:** Ramón Paradinas **Structure:** Alejandro Bernabéu (NB35) **Facilities:** Pedro Blanco **Construction:** CYR proyectos y obras

Our gratefulness to all who have collaborated in making AS+ dreams and ideas come true.

Photography: Jesús Rocandio (Casa de la Imagen), 2011